CLIMB A DIFFERENT LADDER

by
WALTER BELLIN

JCP

To my beloved wife Shana, who was always there encouraging and supporting me in the writing and re-writing of this book.

First published by
Jane Curry Publishing 2012
[Wentworth Concepts Pty Ltd]
PO Box 780 Edgecliff NSW 2027 Australia
www.janecurrypublishing.com.au

Copyright © Walter Bellin 2012

All rights reserved. No part of this book may be reproduced or transmitted in any form or by any means, electronic or mechanical, including photocopying, recording or by any other information storage retrieval system, without prior permission in writing from the publisher.

National Library of Australia Cataloguing-in-Publication entry

Author: Bellin, Walter.
Title: Climb a different ladder: self-awareness, mindfulness and successful leadership / Walter Bellin.
ISBN: 9780987227546 (pbk.)
Subjects: Leadership.
Management.
Dewey Number: 303.34

Cover and Internal Design: Deborah Parry
Printed in Australia by McPherson's Printing Group

TABLE OF CONTENTS

Introduction 5

Part 1 – Transformational change and the fundamentals of leadership
Chapter 1 – Leadership and transformational change 16
Chapter 2 – Authenticity 22
Chapter 3 – Essentials in the art of leadership 35

Part 2 – Who am I and where do I come from?
Chapter 4 – Developmental markers 43
Chapter 5 – Mental, emotional and behavioural treadmills ... 63

Part 3 – The Q12 Mapping System
Chapter 6 – The Q12 Mapping System 76
Chapter 7 – Relationship map 86
Chapter 8 – Action map 101
Chapter 9 – Thinking map 116

Part 4 – The dynamics of transformational change
Chapter 10 – The Q12 profiling system and levels of consciousness: Integrating the two models   132
Chapter 11 – Tina's story   137
Chapter 12 – James' story   148
Chapter 13 – Tim's story   157
Chapter 14 – Mike's story   170

Part 5 – The ladder of consciousness and higher developmental levels
Chapter 15 – A model for the development of higher consciousness   184
Chapter 16 – The emergence of the independent self   191
Chapter 17 – The emergence of the transpersonal self   203
Chapter 18 – The emergence of the unitive self   223
Chapter 19 – Levels of development and circle of influence   238

INTRODUCTION

In the art of leadership, the artist's instrument is the SELF.
The mastery of the art of leadership comes with the mastery of the SELF.
Ultimately, leadership development is the process of SELF development. [1]

THE book you are about to read has been percolating in my mind for a long time — indeed parts of it I have been thinking about, in my personal life and in my work, for at least 30 years.

There is currently a huge literature on leadership, mostly concerned with what good leaders do, or should do. This approach tends to focus on two factors: firstly, the kinds of leadership practices undertaken by good leaders; and secondly, the essential skill sets that good leaders have, or should have, in order to undertake those leadership practices effectively. Clearly this is prescriptive: learn to emulate and master the practices and skills of good leaders, and you too can develop into a good leader. I have read many high quality and useful books that have used this approach.

However, this book does not fit within the framework of that model. Rather, it focuses on developing the human qualities that create great leadership. I want my readers to gain insight into their true potential, to expand their awareness of who they could become as a person — and from this to become better leaders.

Thus, my aims are primarily about personal development and secondly about leadership development. In working with thousands of leaders over the years, I have found that the **primary path to leadership development is through personal development.** Yes, certain practices and skill sets are important, even critical for good leadership, but the bigger issue is always: what will you use these leadership skills and practices for?

The key issue for new or experienced leaders is: what kinds of outcomes do you seek through using your leadership practices and skills? What are the leader's intentions and motivations — are they narrow, self-serving or even destructive? Or are they broad, inclusive, holistic and positive? People who have mastered many leadership practices and skills can be very good at achieving either type of outcome. For example, Ghandi and Hitler both had many effective leadership practices and skills — but radically different motivations and outcomes! It is the individual leader's qualities as a person that determines their motives and outcomes. Effective leadership practices and skills are just the means to an end and do not determine the nature of the leader's motives or the outcomes they seek.

A DIFFERENT KIND OF LADDER

We grow up and live our lives surrounded by a social culture which shapes the way we perceive the world. Through our families, education, peer groups and authority figures, religion and worklife we come to believe that there are certain outcomes in life that are desirable; we may also come to value certain outcomes or achievements more than others. Some of these may be very personal and some may be financial, social or professional, for example, great wealth, social, political or economic power or status, success in a particular profession, membership of an elite group, the list goes on. And, of course, the highest achievement is to be recognised as a leader in any of these categories.

Our culture assumes that the pathway to these achievements is like a metaphorical 'ladder'. We must mount this ladder and climb it rung by rung — or if we are very lucky or ambitious, maybe several rungs at a time.

The critically important implied (but often subliminal) promise that motivates us to mount and climb that ladder is: when we do reach the top rung we will be satisfied, happy and fulfilled. However this tacit assumption is simply false and involves a profound confusion of cause and effect.

Firstly, many people who have reached the top rung and are recognised as leaders in their area of achievement are not satisfied nor happy. Secondly, for those who have reached the top rung and **are** fulfilled, the cause of their fulfilment is often not the achievement, but something else entirely.

People who are both successful leaders and have experienced that deep and long-term fulfilment, have climbed a different kind of ladder within themselves; a ladder that is quite distinct from the external one leading to their success. This is the **ladder of consciousness**. Achieving deep and long-term fulfilment is a natural result of an internal journey of personal development and awareness.

The core facilitator of all personal development and lasting fulfilment is raising our level of awareness or consciousness. This awareness includes self-awareness, which provides us with an accurate perception of ourselves, our natural strengths, current limitations, our motives, the way we think, and our emotional habits or patterns. It includes awareness of other people, their strengths and current limitations, their true motives, their ways of thinking, their emotional states and responses (this awareness is part of what is now called 'emotional intelligence'). It includes awareness of those factors that determine the dynamics of human relationships — everything from one on one relationships to group relationship dynamics. And in a more general sense, it includes awareness of human nature and the human potential and awareness of how we and others see or perceive our 'world', or 'reality' itself.

But first, what is mindfulness? Mindfulness is a state of awareness which has two predominant qualities:

- Firstly, our attention and awareness are fully in the present and we are fully, effortlessly focused on the object of our attention. We are not distracted by worries or concerns about the future and we are not mentally or emotionally anchored in the past. We are fully here, now! This does not mean that we are not planning and preparing for the future, or that we are not remembering and considering lessons from the past.
- Secondly, we are in a state that is open, accepting and non-judgemental. Whatever the object of our attention we are in an open, accepting and non-judgemental state.

These two qualities are simply the two halves of an intertwined whole. We are not in a state of mindfulness unless both are present.

What then is consciousness and how is it related to mindfulness? Consciousness is the capacity to be aware. To the degree that we are conscious, we have the capacity to be aware of various things that are internal or external to us. This awareness includes a broad spectrum of issues of which we may be more or less conscious.

It is by cultivating the state of mindfulness that we are able to raise our level of consciousness. When we are fully present in the moment, effortlessly focused and fully open without judgement, we automatically gain in both the depth and scope of our awareness. We can see ourselves, other people, life situations, problems, etc within a larger framework, which provides greater perspective. We are more likely to gain deeper insight into any issues that surround us, including insight into ourselves, how our internal psychology works, and conscious access to deeper and more empowering resources that lie dormant within us.

It is through raising our level of consciousness of such things through practising mindfulness that we are enabled to craft the kind of person we wish to become. Such awareness provides the 'workbench' upon which we can create the character traits or qualities that will define who we are, and who we wish to become. And in turn, based upon these character traits, we can develop the leadership practices and skills that will make us authentic, effective leaders.

In 1987, Kouzes and Posner developed a questionnaire with a list of twenty characteristics or qualities each with a few synonyms for clarity, and then administered it to over 75,000 people around the world. They reported that:

> *The results of these surveys have been striking in their regularity over the years. It appears that a person must pass several essential tests before others are willing to grant the title leader...* [2]

Perhaps most importantly, they noted that four characteristics have consistently received over 50% of the vote.

> *As the [2002] data clearly shows, for people to follow someone willingly, the majority of constituents must believe the leader is:*
> *Honest — voted for by 88%   Forward Looking — voted for by 71%*
> *Competent — voted for by 66%   Inspiring — voted for by 65%*
>
> *The data for 1995 and 1987 are very similar — but always these four characteristics are the top four and in the same order of ranking.* [3]

The following diagram exemplifies what I believe to be the order of importance in leadership development.

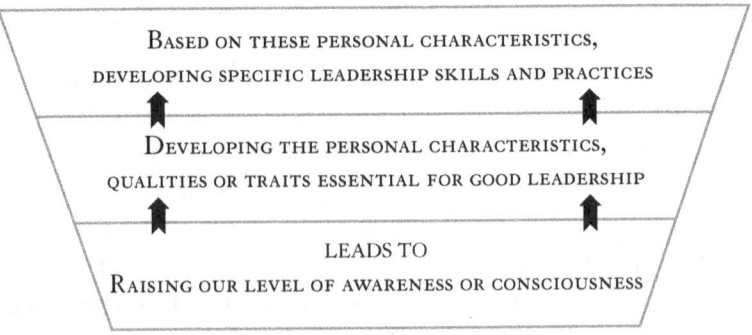

The first two (lower) levels are really about personal development. They are the precursors and basis for the ability to learn and utilise the skills and practices of good leaders. This book focuses on raising levels of consciousness, and based on this, developing certain personal qualities or characteristics that are always the foundation of good leadership. This process of consciousness raising and personal development is the pursuit of self-mastery.

LEADERSHIP AND SELF-MASTERY

This is not an academic book, rather it is meant to be a practical guide to personal and leadership development. It is largely based on my experience of running personal and leadership development programmes, over a forty-year period, with many thousands of people. And a good part of it is based on stories about myself and many of the people I have worked with. More than half of this book is made up of a number of the inspiring stories of people who have set themselves on the personal development path towards self-mastery.

The degree to which you have achieved self-mastery is the ultimate factor that determines the degree to which you can master the art of mindful leadership. Your degree of self-mastery is the most important factor in determining your ability to master all of the challenges that life throws at you — and ultimately to finding deep and lasting satisfaction in your life.

Each of you is beginning at a different level of self-mastery in each important area of your life — your work, your social life, your personal relationships with friends, partner, family and yourself. How well you are handling your professional life and workplace relationships, your personal and family relationships, will inevitably be deeply affected by how well you are handling yourself. This, in turn, will affect your level of satisfaction and fulfilment.

It is a fundamental assumption of this book that everyone has the potential capacity for leadership. Of course, some people have certain genetic predispositions that allow them to quickly learn and use leadership skills. Also, some people have had more opportunities to develop leadership skills by playing leadership roles during childhood and adolescence. This book is for anyone wishing to lead, regardless of their genetic inheritance or past experience.

Most books on leadership tend to focus on people in formal leadership positions in their work — managers or executives in corporations or civil service agencies, politicians, leaders in professions or professional organisations, leaders in civic groups, NGOs and so forth. Leadership certainly includes all of these contexts. Yet at the same time, I have seen many ordinary people, without any formal leadership position or authority, step forward to take the initiative. Often they just felt that something needed to be done and they stepped forward to engage others to achieve a result. Some of the stories in this book are about such people, and a critical element is the event that inspired them to take leadership initiative. It is my hope that these stories will inspire some of you to begin developing as leaders, even if you are not currently in any kind of formal or informal leadership position.

Leadership is an art and not a science. I do not mean that there are no scientifically validated psychological or sociological principles that apply to the leadership role. Indeed, it is quite certain that there are, and that knowledge of such principles is useful to people in leadership positions. I do believe that psychology, the social sciences, and even the evolving field of neuroscience, will continue to contribute to knowledge relevant to leadership and leadership development. What I do mean is that I have not found, in the vast literature on leadership, a complete set of scientifically validated principles that if consistently applied will always result in effective, successful leadership.

Leadership is like a creative art. However, the difference between the traditional instruments used by an artist — the brush for the painter, the musical instrument for the musician, the hammer and chisel for the sculptor — is that the leader's instrument is their own self, the whole of who they are as an individual. Put very personally, it is who you are that creates the quality of your leadership — and it is who you are becoming that creates the evolving quality of your leadership: hence the emphasis on personal development.

No matter what your current stage of development, there is always room for you to achieve greater degrees of self-mastery — and thus become a better leader. Self-mastery is a broad, holistic term that denotes an ongoing **process** of personal growth or self-development. It is not an end state, since that would imply that no more growth or self-development will occur. However, while there is no end state of self-mastery, there are definite markers along the way, specific, identifiable evolutionary stages along the path towards self-mastery.

To define these developmental markers, I use a model that identifies and describes seven possible stages in our development towards self-mastery. This is the ladder of consciousness leading to specific developmental stages. The first four stages we all automatically pass through as we progress from childhood through adolescence into early adulthood. Your experience of each of these first four stages — how successfully or completely you pass through them —

shapes your adult personality, with all of its natural strengths and limitations.

The last three stages — which can potentially be achieved as adults — are not automatic. We must take personal responsibility for achieving these developmental stages. This book will carefully define the developmental markers that identify when you have mastered each of these three adult stages. How to facilitate your own development towards these three stages is a central theme and will be illustrated by the stories of people who have made this journey.

As each of these developmental markers is reached, new possibilities, qualities and abilities awaken within us, leading to the next stage of development. We come to have the capacity to be more effective in our interaction with our daily environment and thus exhibit the potential for more effective, authentic, mindful leadership and increasing levels of satisfaction and fulfilment.

SELF-MASTERY, THE BRAIN AND THE UNCONSCIOUS MIND

'Self-mastery' is not an easy term to define. However, stating that a person has a good level of self-mastery certainly implies that they are good at managing themselves — their habits, their behaviour, the way they think, their emotional responses to people and life situations. However, what complicates the process of achieving self-mastery are not the habits and responses that are working well for us. Generally, we are very pleased with these. Rather the difficulty lies in the ones that seem to be working against us (and perhaps negatively affecting others). Two things that make it difficult to master these patterns and habits are:

- We sometimes find it difficult to know exactly why we have developed habits and patterns of thinking, emotions and behaviour that are not working well for us: the question is, why do I continue to do things I know will not have a good outcome?
- We also often find it difficult to change these habits or patterns — even when we are quite conscious of the fact that they are working against us.

The reasons for this are that many of our mental, emotional and behavioural habits or patterns are driven by our subconscious mind.

For a long time the concept of a subconscious mind was found mainly in certain fields of psychology and psychiatry — though it was also employed in a number of self-help books available to the general public. Historically, many people from the hard sciences (biology, neuroscience and the like) were sceptical. Now modern neuroscience has provided solid, biologically-based evidence for the existence of subconscious mental-emotional processes. Dr Joseph LeDoux, perhaps the world's foremost expert on the emotional brain, notes:

> *Emotional responses are, for the most part, generated unconsciously. Freud was right on the mark when he described consciousness as the tip of the mental iceberg.*[4]

To understand the working of the subconscious mind, it is very useful to know some fairly simple, basic information about the structure of our brain. In the 1960s neuroscientist Paul McLean described the brain as having three (highly interconnected) layers. The following pictograph is a visual representation of these layers:

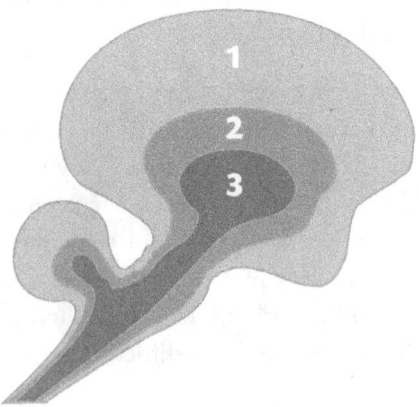

1. Primitive brain — responsible for our biological survival needs. This includes instinctive behaviour (fight-flight response) and autonomic functions (biological functions that occur or adjust themselves automatically — heart rate, blood pressure, digestion and respiration etc). Also known as the 'reptilian brain'.
2. 'Mammalian brain' — this part of the brain includes the 'limbic system' and the 'amygdala', which is about the size of an almond and is located in almost the centre of the brain at the very bottom of the limbic system. The limbic system (including the amygdala) is the emotional part of the brain. It provides us with the capacity to experience the full range of emotions and plays a critical role in storing our emotional memories.

The amygdala is often referred to as the 'emergency system' or 'panic button' part of the limbic brain. When we have experiences that feel very threatening or involve very strong emotional responses (rage, terror, humiliation or deep sadness), these emotions occur via the amygdala.

Within the limbic system there are many different subsystems involving different neural pathways for different emotions including: fear, anger, sadness, love, joy or peace. The way we experience, process and respond to these emotions involves other parts of the brain too, including various parts of the cerebral cortex.

3   The cerebral cortex — responsible for the higher mental functions (rational thought, imagination and creative thinking, intellectual, cultural and spiritual life). This part of the brain is particularly highly developed in humans.

The emotional part of the brain (limbic system) plays a key role in creating our habitual emotional patterns and responses, our thinking and behavioural habits or patterns. Yet, we are often not aware of how or why this occurs because it often functions subconsciously although it shapes our conscious experience.

As mature adults, we may have conscious intellectual beliefs that are quite at odds with the subconscious mental-emotional processes occurring within our brain's limbic system. These two parts of our brain, while neurologically highly interconnected, can under certain circumstances function quite separately. This is why we can intellectually know that doing or saying something in a specific relationship or life situation is likely to have unwanted effects and yet we find ourselves doing it anyway.

THE ROLE OF SELF-KNOWLEDGE

Whatever your stage of personal development there is always one essential requirement before you can move to the next stage: accurate, in-depth self-knowledge!

Accurate, in-depth self-knowledge requires two things:
- Firstly, that you are able to become accurately aware of how your conscious mind works and how it shapes your behaviour in daily life, including the way you relate to others. It also means being consciously and accurately aware of your natural strengths — the thinking, emotional responses and behaviour that work well for you — and your 'Achilles' heels'. These are the habits of thinking, habitual emotional responses and behavioural

habits that do not work well for you and sometimes negatively affect those around you as well.
- Secondly, that you have some insight into the deeper, **unconscious mental-emotional processes** that drive your conscious emotions, thinking and behaviour, including your natural strengths and Achilles' heels. In order to master your Achilles' heels you need to know something about the way your personal history has shaped both these conscious and unconscious processes and the behaviour that follows from them.

This book focuses on the issues of self-awareness and self-knowledge, introducing tools that will assist you in becoming more self-aware. One of these tools — the Q12 Profiling System — can play a major role in developing self-awareness.

---

1 J Kouzes and B Posner, *The Leadership Challenge*, 2nd edn (John Wiley and Sons: San Francisco, 1995) p 298.
2 J Kouzes and B Posner, *The Leadership Challenge*, 3rd edn (John Wiley and Sons: San Francisco, 2002) p 24.
3 Ibid, p 24.
4 Dr J. LeDoux, *The Emotional Brain: The Mysterious Underpinnings of Emotional Life*, (Weidenfeld and Nicolson: Great Britain, 1998) p 17.

PART 1

TRANSFORMATIONAL CHANGE AND THE FUNDAMENTALS OF LEADERSHIP

CHAPTER ONE

LEADERSHIP AND TRANSFORMATIONAL CHANGE

Transform: to change in appearance, condition, nature, or character, especially completely or extensively. [1]

PERSONAL DEVELOPMENT is the most important factor underlying leadership development. Personal development is always a process of personal change and the kind of personal change illustrated throughout this book is 'transformational change'.

What exactly is meant by the word 'transformation' in the context of personal change? How does the above definition apply to people? Complete or extensive change of what kind?

We are formed by the many experiences and influences extending from infancy through to adulthood. By the time our adult personality has emerged, we have a distinctive way of seeing the world, including how we see or experience our self and other people, and how we see 'reality'. This distinctive way of 'seeing' is a 'lens' through which we experience and respond to the world.

This metaphorical 'lens' is inherently subjective since it has evolved out of our unique history of life experiences. This subjectivity, of course, skews our perception of ourselves, other people and the world (or reality) in ways that are both useful and self-limiting. The useful 'skewing' is the basis of our natural strengths as an individual. The self-limiting 'skewing' is the base for our self-limiting mental, emotional and behavioural habits and patterns — our Achilles' heels.

Transformational change is a deep, holistic type of change intended to re-create the 'lenses' through which we see our self, others and the world. It is meant to expand and reinforce our natural strengths and raise our general level of awareness (or consciousness), while simultaneously releasing us from the self-limiting mental, emotional and behavioural patterns resulting from the old 'lens'.

As a holistic change, it affects our life as a whole. It helps to increase our general sense of what is possible for us, enables us to give and receive (non-dependent) love, and improves our general effectiveness in all that we do. It increases the accuracy, scope and depth of our self-awareness, improves our self-confidence, and increases our sense of self-esteem and self-worth.

MEDITATION AND MINDFULNESS

In the past three decades there has been an explosion of interest in meditation by scientists, resulting in over 1,000 scientific papers on its biological and psychological effects! It is perhaps the single most effective method for achieving the transformational change essential in pursuing self-mastery and mindfulness. This is because:

- Meditation has the affect of 'clearing' or releasing from our conscious and subconscious mind the negative emotional charge of those memories, left over from our life experiences, that cause many of our conscious, self-limiting thoughts, feelings and behaviour.
- Meditation also has the affect — over time — of raising our level of consciousness. This exists as a potential in all human beings, but in most of us lies dormant. Our ultimate identity is consciousness or awareness itself. Thus, by raising our level of consciousness or awareness, we increase our level of mindfulness and unfold the full scope of our potential identity, our true self.

The two long-term affects of meditation — clearing the garbage out of our subconscious mind and raising our level of consciousness — are interrelated. What holds us to our current level of limited consciousness is the mental and emotional programming that has resulted in our current way of seeing ourselves, other people and the world. Much of our current conscious ways of seeing ourselves, others and the world — our current mindset — is driven by mental/emotional processes that occur just below our conscious awareness. As long as all of this stays intact, we are stuck at our current level of consciousness, and the state of mindfulness is difficult to achieve.

TRANSFORMATIONAL CHANGE METHODOLOGIES

In the last few decades numerous personal change methodologies have been created by psychologists and others interested in facilitating personal development. In our personal and leadership development workshops and coaching practices we have used many of these and developed a number of our own. Over many years I have discovered that there are five basic requirements for any effective methodology for facilitating transformational change:

- **Ways to assist people in becoming much more deeply and accurately self-aware**: insight into their natural strengths and weaknesses or blind spots ('Achilles' heels'); greater awareness of how negative or self-limiting emotional and thinking patterns or habits generate self-limiting behaviour; and an understanding of how they have created the 'lens' through which they view themselves, other people and the world or 'reality' itself.
- **Aids to release people from the grip of their negative or self-limiting emotional, thinking and behavioural habits or patterns**: to overcome or master their Achilles' heels, thereby giving themselves a much fuller expression of their natural strengths and developing new strengths not previously thought possible, helping them to expand and recreate the psychological 'lens' that more than anything else, determines their quality of life and their degree of satisfaction or fulfilment.
- **Tools to help people establish a high level of trust and openness within themselves**: accurate, in-depth, self-knowledge and the ability to release oneself from self-limiting, mental, emotional and behavioural patterns cannot be achieved without a certain level of trust and openness, including the ability to trust oneself and be open to the change process.
- **A single, integrated conceptual structure**: to help people understand the change process they are going through in a way that is not simplistic and yet is easily understandable to people without a background in philosophy or psychology.
- **Workshop facilitators and/or coaches with in-depth insight into people and the skills to lead people through the transformational change process**: facilitators or coaches who understand in great depth, from their own experience, the transformational change process.

As with meditation, all of these methodologies lead to the raising of our level of awareness. This increases our capacity for mindfulness — the ability to be fully present and focused in the moment, in an open, accepting and non-judgemental state, whatever our current circumstances.

ORGANISATIONAL CULTURE AND CHANGE

What exactly is an organisational culture? An organisational culture has two basic elements, one public and visible and the other non-visible. The non-visible part is the collective values, beliefs, attitudes and norms shared, whether consciously or unconsciously, by most members of the organisation. The non-visible part is the 'cultural paradigm'.

The visible part consists of the patterns of behaviour, communication, relationships, and workplace practices by which the organisation's work gets done — or in the case of a dysfunctional culture, by which the work doesn't get done, or gets done poorly. Sometimes this visible part of the culture is summed up by the statement 'the way we do things around here'.

The following diagram illustrates the visible and non-visible parts of a culture.

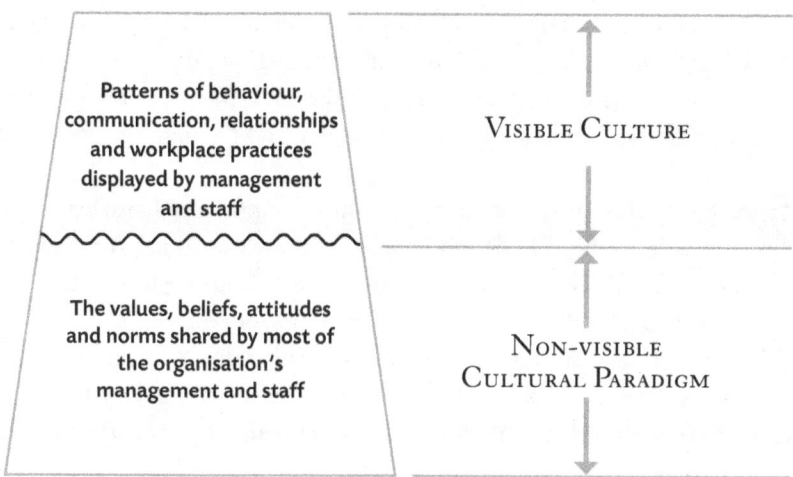

Like an iceberg, the greater part or the greater 'weight' of the culture is non-visible, yet it is the underlying basis for the nature and quality of the publicly visible part. Thus, in order to create a deep and permanent change in the visible culture, the non-visible cultural paradigm must shift or change. The result of this change process is a **cultural transformation**. Leading a cultural transformation is perhaps the most challenging type of organisational change a leader can undertake and also the most important!

It is hard to overemphasise the importance of organisational culture. The first major statistical study of the effects of organisational culture on performance was published back in 1992. John Kotter and James Heskett studied 207 large multinational companies over an 11-year period. They identified 17 of these companies, from a wide range of industries, as having superb, high performance cultures. They so massively outperformed the others that they were in a class unto themselves. For example, their profitability increased over 11 years by 756% versus 1% for the others and their share price increased by 901% versus 74% for the others.[2]

Kotter and Heskett believed that corporate culture is probably the most important single factor in determining long-term success. They found that senior management in these companies saw their role in continually building and reinforcing the desired culture as equally important to setting and pursuing their basic business strategy.

THE ROLE OF LEADERSHIP IN CULTURAL TRANSFORMATION

The quality of an organisation's leadership is the single, most important factor in creating and sustaining a healthy, empowering organisational culture. Leaders are the ultimate role models for the desirable (and undesirable) values, norms and attitudes that make up both the visible and the non-visible parts of an organisation's culture.

In most organisations, when people are hired or promoted into leadership positions, the title of the role or job is 'manager' or 'executive'. Yet they are actually expected to play two roles: a managerial role and a leadership role. While the same person plays both, the two roles are very different.

The managerial role is predominantly administrative and can be simply defined as: **creating and maintaining effective organisational systems and structures that effectively and efficiently handle a broad range of (often highly) complex variables.**

The managerial role:
- Relies upon authority within an organisational hierarchy for directing staff.
- Focuses on developing policies, processes and other control systems within which people must work.

On the other hand, the leadership role can be defined as: **gaining the alignment**

of people with the vision, objectives and strategies of the organisation to effectively produce intended change and outcomes.
- The keystone of leadership is the power of influence through communicating a vision.
- A leader pursues the organisation's vision and objectives by gaining its people's trust, respect, loyalty and enthusiasm.
- A leader inspires people to achieve intended outcomes by influencing them to personally value these outcomes and to want to achieve them.

The management role should be at the service of the leadership role. The leadership role sets the strategic direction of the organisation and builds the organisation's culture around its strategic vision, cultivating the values, attitudes and behaviours that will empower the organisation to achieve its vision. The management role is to provide the practical technologies and tools to support the outcomes defined by the leadership role. Organisational structure, systems, business processes and various technologies are the management role's practical contribution to the strategic and culture outcomes the leadership role seeks.

Thus, leadership development is about inspiring people by helping them gain insight into their true potential, and assisting them in seeking the personal development path that leads towards self-mastery.

---

1   *Macquarie Concise Dictionary*, 3rd edn (Macquarie University: Sydney, 2004).
2   J Kotter and J Heskett, *Corporate Culture and Performance* (The Free Press: New York, 1992) p 11.

CHAPTER TWO

AUTHENTICITY

AUTHENTICITY is the first and most important ingredient in the art of mindful leadership. Authenticity has a somewhat greater scope of meaning than honesty, but it includes honesty and its synonyms.

WHAT IS AUTHENTICITY?

To fully understand authenticity in the context of the art of leadership, it is important to first discuss leadership effectiveness. What is meant by **effectiveness** in the art of leadership? What defines effectiveness in people we believe to be good or great leaders?

Normally, when we think of someone as being effective, we have a specific context or type of activity in mind. We would say that they are 'very good at' or 'highly competent' in that context or at that type of activity.

Obviously, leadership is not a skill, like many other skills, that one can use by oneself. Leaders work through and with other people. A leader is someone who **facilitates the process of pursuing outcomes through and with the participation and activities of others**. The 'others' may be members of a loosely formed group, a team, an organisation, a community, a nation, or even a community of nations.

An important element of 'effective leadership' is facilitating the achievement of outcomes with the participation and activities of others. However, this alone does not define 'effectiveness' in good or great leaders. For example, Hitler, Stalin and Pol Pot were all very good at getting things done through the participation and activities of others — with hideous consequences. Arguably they were very effective tyrants, but we would hardly want to call them good or great leaders.

All of us, at some point in our life, have encountered leaders who use fear and intimidation (whether overt or implied) to achieve their ends. Equally, we have all probably encountered leaders who are highly controlling and tend to micro-manage their people. Leaders who use either intimidation or high levels of control may be successful in accomplishing tasks or goals — yet their success often brings with it a high level of collateral damage! Like the tyrants above, these leaders are very effective, but one would be hard pressed to call them good or great.

What, then, is distinctive about a different and broader type of 'effectiveness' found in good or great leaders?

Clearly, one of the differences is **how** good leaders get things done through others. For example, how do leaders treat their people while working towards their goal? Why do good leaders do what they do — what are their motives or intentions? Also, what are the scope and inclusiveness of the goals or outcomes they seek and achieve?

All of these are connected to the character of the leader: who they are as a person. This inevitably brings us to the concept of 'authenticity' and how it applies to leaders.

The term 'authenticity' carries a broad meaning and can be used in many contexts. For example, it might be said that a particular work of art, a sculpture, or a written work are authentic. In simple terms this means that it was actually created by the artist or writer who it is claimed created it. It is exactly what it claims to be.

Similarly, applied in the context of leadership, authentic leaders are real, they are exactly what they claim to be, exactly how they present themselves. This means, among other things, that what they say they believe or value is exactly what they actually believe or value; what they say are their motives or intentions are exactly what their motives and intentions are; they 'walk their talk', they do (or at least attempt to do) what they have said they will do.

Beyond this, as with a work of art, being 'real' captures only a part of the meaning of 'authenticity'. Also implied, if not stated, is something about the work of art's quality and value. Similarly, when we speak of a leader as being authentic, we are not just implying that they are real merely in the sense of actually believing or valuing what they claim to believe or value. We are also implying something about the quality of the person, their character, the quality of their values, and the quality of the actions and behaviours that flow from these.

The issue of the quality of a leader's character and values, also includes the nature and quality of their motivations, their intentions. What is the degree of inclusiveness in what they intend to achieve? Are the intended outcomes narrow and largely motivated by self-interest or broad and inclusive of the welfare of others and our environment?

For example, is the senior leadership of a particular company largely motivated only by the organisation's bottom line? Do these motivations and intentions cause them to neglect their negative impact on the natural environment, the communities they work in, and even on their own workforce and the sustainable future of the company? Certainly this has been true of the motivations and behaviour of many senior leaders and their companies over the past two decades — ultimately resulting in our recent world financial crisis and recession. We would hardly call leaders of this kind 'authentic'. Clearly there is a moral and ethical dimension that applies to the character and motives of authentic leaders.

Of course, in a private sector company, outcomes must include the bottom line. But equally, authentic leaders and their companies must take responsibility for the welfare and wellbeing of their workforce, the satisfaction of their clients or customers, the communities they affect and the environmental consequences of what they do. Pursuing these kinds of broad, inclusive outcomes is one of the hallmarks of authenticity in leadership. It is these authentic character traits that inspire people to be **willing** to follow a leader.

Thus good or great leaders must be both authentic and effective. Effective in the sense of being skilled at facilitating the process of pursuing outcomes through and with the willing participation and activities of others. Authenticity denotes something about the character of the leader as a person. It says they have good values, their motives and intentions are broad and inclusive rather than mainly narrow and self-interested, they are real and their behaviour and the outcomes they pursue are consistent with what they claim to be their values and intentions.

ARE GOOD/GREAT LEADERS BORN OR MADE?

Of course, there can be no question that the possession of certain genetically inherited traits may provide significant help or leverage in developing into a good leader. However, this is true for virtually every area of human activity or endeavour. While genetics can help, much of one's ability as a leader arises through the process of learning, development and especially practice. When it comes to the old nature/nurture controversy, I am firmly convinced that the nurture side is as important as the nature side.

However, it is also true that if someone is starting to pursue the path of leadership development as an adult, it can be more difficult than it is for someone who has had opportunities to lead in childhood or adolescence. Many who have had childhood or adolescent opportunities to lead arrive at adulthood with natural strengths that facilitate their leadership development.

However, whatever our past experience or lack of experience, the qualities or capabilities that enable people to become authentic, effective leaders exist as potentials in all of us. For the majority of us these traits and qualities lie dormant within us. It requires certain kinds of intense experiences to 'awaken' these dormant traits or qualities.

Once awakened, these qualities or capabilities need to be expanded, developed and refined into specific leadership practices and skills. This can be greatly assisted by attending leadership programmes and workshops that utilise experiential learning methods, including psychological profiling instruments like the Q12 mapping systems (see Chapter 6). However, direct experience of the problems and opportunities of leadership is also essential. But learning through direct experience can, in turn, be greatly facilitated by attending an experiential learning-based leadership programme coupled with periodic coaching sessions. By contrast, very, very little can be achieved through traditional classroom didactic learning.

The following stories demonstrate both the importance of 'awakening' experiences and the development into authentic and effective leadership. The first three stories are about people who had no formal leadership training, experience or positions and did not initially appear to have any of the traits, skills or even potential to become leaders. The last two stories are about people who had already occupied leadership positions for years but to reach the next level they needed a major 'awakening', enabling them to begin a new stage of leadership development.

HELEN'S STORY

Helen was a mother who had several children attending an inner city primary school in a poor neighbourhood in the US. The school was run down and lacked many essential resources, including textbooks. She was deeply troubled seeing her children struggle through school under these conditions.

The school board in her children's school district was massively under funded. The tax base that paid for the schools in the district was very poor, and the federal funding that supplemented the local tax base was insufficient to fund the real needs of the school.

Helen attended school board meetings, meetings of local government, and in her quiet, unassuming way tried to get a hearing about how poor conditions were in her children's school. The only answers she got were all the reasons why it was impossible to get further funding.

One evening as she came home from such a meeting, she felt a great anger build up inside her. She virtually never got angry, instead she usually experienced a quiet frustration and a sense of powerlessness. However, this night the anger awakened something in her that made her feel powerful for the first time in her life: there had to be a way to improve the school's situation.

Helen began by initiating a series of informal discussions with other parents and some teachers to explore possible ways of overcoming the school's problems. She formed a parent-teacher group which collaboratively worked out a strategy for improving the school's run down interior and providing the necessary resources. For example, they convinced owners of local businesses to provide finances for text books and extra resources; they organised working parties of parents, some teachers and some local tradesmen to go in on weekends and paint and repair the school's interior; and they convinced some of the parents and some high school students in a local high school to come in after school to tutor children who were struggling.

These improvements and increased resources lifted the moral of the parents, teachers and students to a degree that would have been unimaginable at the beginning of the year. Helen had no leadership training or experience. She was more amazed than anyone at the results, yet she felt a new confidence in herself and a sense of deep satisfaction from her achievement.

Following her example a number of other schools undertook similar programmes. Thus, Helen's leadership initiative had improved not just the teaching environment and resources available to students in her children's school, but for hundreds of other children as well.

GEORGE'S STORY

George was a very quiet and shy person who described himself as having no self-confidence and especially no social self-confidence. He had no spouse or partner and only two (as he called it) 'light' friendships.

George was an engineer working for a large engineering corporation. He was conscientious and hard working but not inclined to take the initiative.

For several years George had been listening to complaints from both customers and employees about the company's service delivery process. It was complex and bureaucratic, and a source of much frustration for employees. Customers were equally frustrated by the slowness and inefficiencies of the service delivery process.

George attended one of our personal development workshops and made a major breakthrough in his character development. After his awakening on the workshop he began to experience a new social self-confidence, something he had never before known in his life. He also found himself beginning to use his intuition and imagination.

These changes in George inspired him to come up with an innovative idea for improving the delivery of the services his company provided to its customers, and gave him the confidence to lead the process of getting it accepted by senior management.

George began by gathering together as much information as he could about the pathway and stages of service delivery within the company. He made enquiries from other departments — something that his new social self-confidence made easier than it would have been previously. Having digested this information, he spent several weeks trying to imagine alternate service delivery pathways. Then suddenly one morning while taking a shower, he had a major intuitive, innovative idea about how to solve the problem of a much better, simpler service delivery process.

After carefully outlining the idea, George approached several other employees, including two middle managers he believed would be open to the idea. He presented his idea and asked them for feedback and input on how the idea could be developed or improved so that it could be presented to senior management. Using his new social self-confidence George facilitated this whole meeting, which was a first for him.

They eventually succeeded in convincing senior management to adopt their plan and within six months there was a very noticeable improvement in customer satisfaction and employee moral. The reforms George initiated created both a better human and business environment. But most importantly from his point of view, George initiated and led the entire process of developing and getting the initiative accepted — something that would have been unimaginable to him in the past.

After the success of the initiative was secured, George was asked by his manager to enter the management stream and was promoted to a management position in recognition of his leadership.

DANIEL'S STORY

Daniel was a very successful litigation lawyer and a workaholic. He was a very cerebral person and did not easily experience or express emotions. He had a great deal of intellectual self-confidence, and he could think and argue well on his feet.

However, his intellectual style was as dominant in his personal life as in his work. He would win every argument at home, but in the process of doing so he hurt and alienated his wife and children. Eventually, his wife threatened to leave him if he didn't change. That is what brought him to our personal development workshop.

The success of our personal development workshops depends upon building up a high degree of trust and openness among workshop participants. In this atmosphere of trust and openness, people are willing to share emotions and experiences which often have a deep impact on other participants. Listening to these stories can often be the cause of the breakthrough or 'awakening' for others.

While listening to one story Daniel was deeply moved and underwent an emotional awakening, which gave him a dramatically new perspective on his life. He recognised that his family had been fragmenting over the last several years. Daniel came to see that his long working hours, his intellectual style and emotional unavailability had been major contributors to this fragmentation.

Daniel began his leadership intervention by reconnecting with his wife and enlisting her support in rebuilding the family ties. Together they worked out a plan which began with speaking to each of the children individually about the issues. The second step was for the family to meet together as a whole to come up with ideas on how they could spend more quality time together.

At first implementing the plan was difficult, as each of their habits that contributed to the family's fragmentation were deeply engrained. Daniel had to cut back his working hours significantly and hold his tongue when he was about to display his argumentative style. But Daniel was very committed and, with his enthusiasm and active involvement, they were soon a family again. Everyone was happier and more spontaneous with each other while Daniel experienced a deep satisfaction as a result of his act of leadership within his own family.

Taking the leadership role in his family and seeing its success awakened within Daniel a desire to lead at work. He went to see the managing partner and requested that he be put in charge of a practice group. The managing partner accepted this request and for the next several years Daniel focused on his leadership role at work, while ensuring that he did not neglect his family. He spent time mentoring and coaching the younger members of his practice group. He began speaking up in partnership meetings about policy issues and eventually took on the task of designing and implementing a mentoring programme for all associates in the firm who had not yet achieved partnership. He did this by first creating a 'big picture' vision for the mentoring programme, and then convinced several others to help him design and implement it in its detail.

Daniel initially met some resistance from the firm's management committee because these mentoring activities, while recognised as increasing the 'intellectual capital' of the firm, did not do much for the more tangible and immediate 'billable hours'. However, Daniel argued that in the long term this increase in the firm's intellectual capital would have the effect of allowing more people in the firm to take on higher levels of work, which would ultimately be more lucrative and therefore would eventually increase revenue: within about 10 months, this turned out to be true.

Because of his success in leading this initiative, Daniel was appointed to the management committee, where he continued developing his leadership abilities and skills. Then, when his firm merged with a large international law firm, he was asked to take on the senior leadership role for one of their offices in another country. If not for his emotional awakening and the leadership role he had played in bringing his family together, he would have never developed into the effective, authentic leader he became.

MARK'S STORY

Mark was a career naval officer who commanded a large division (approximately 8,000 naval and civilian personnel). Mark exuded power, confidence and authority. He was highly intelligent and had a remarkable ability to grasp and remember detail.

Mark had a reputation for taking initiative and getting difficult tasks done quickly and efficiently, but he also had a reputation for doing so at the expense of his people. He had an absolute absence of people skills. His communication style was often tough, blunt and could even be scathing if he thought someone was not competent or was not accomplishing what he wanted. As he put it: 'I do not suffer fools easily'.

The result was that he created a culture of fear and low moral in those around him. A culture based on fear brings a lot of negatives with it. For example: people try to hide mistakes (rather than acknowledging them and dealing with them); people try to avoid placing themselves in a position where they could be held accountable if a failure does occur (creating a culture of non-accountability); and people become overly risk adverse (and thus create a culture which discourages innovation).

During a five-day leadership workshop Mark and his senior leadership team all undertook a psychological profiling instrument. The turning point for Mark came on the fourth morning of the workshop during an exercise in which each group member had to read out the natural strengths of their own profile — and their potential Achilles' heels — to the whole group, and for the group to give feedback on how they saw and/or experienced the accuracy of this.

When Mark listened to his people telling him how they felt about his manner of speaking to them, he was absolutely astonished. All his life he had been so powerfully task and goal focused that he had no idea how he had been affecting his people. It was certainly not his conscious intention to hurt them!

In my entire career, I don't think I have seen anyone change so quickly. Almost immediately stories began to circulate throughout the organisation about how Mark had changed. The atmosphere of fear that had existed disappeared almost overnight and was gradually and cautiously replaced by one of trust and respect, and increasingly higher morale.

Mark hired me as a consultant to help plan and facilitate the process of building a new culture within his division. He also engaged me to design and facilitate a leadership development programme that would enable all the naval officers, non-commissioned officers and civilian managers within his division to help build that new culture. Mark poured enormous personal time and organisational resources into the leadership and culture building programme – programmes he would have previously considered 'soft'. Through all this, Mark 'walked the talk', increasingly becoming a more authentic and mindful leader.

Because Mark was so committed to this leadership and culture building programme, and was thus willing to put his reputation on the line doing something that might appear 'soft' in a military context, the programme succeeded remarkably quickly. A staff survey six months later showed a very significant rise in trust and morale throughout the organisation, and an equal improvement in productivity.

ELLEN'S STORY

Ellen's story also looks at awakening and change, but in addition it focuses on the childhood experiences that shaped her adult personality. These experiences created the natural strengths that brought her a long way on the leadership journey, but they also helped shape an Achilles' heel.

Ellen was a successful, intelligent, warm and attractive person, with very good people skills. Her communication style was clear, fluent and highly persuasive without being pushy. She also demonstrated good insights into peoples' character.

Although starting in recruitment, Ellen eventually became Director of Marketing for the company for which she worked. Again she was very successful in her new role and particularly enjoyed working with people who had a creative flair. The marketing staff both trusted and respected her and responded well to her leadership style. When the Managing Director of her company announced his intention to resign he suggested she be appointed to succeed him. Ellen was shocked and could simply not imagine herself taking on a role of such immense responsibility. Despite all her success she had no confidence that she could perform well in this new role.

Four issues exacerbated this lack of confidence:

- She believed the company as a whole really needed a new direction, but she lacked confidence in her knowledge of the industry as a whole to create a new strategic vision for the future of the company.
- The other seven members of the senior management team were all males and she was aware that four of them resented her. She believed this was because they begrudged her success in the marketing role and her influence with the current Managing Director. She also understood them to be old school 'macho' males who simply did not believe that a woman should be given the top job.
- The corporate culture of the organisation was very internally competitive and thus the levels of trust, respect and co-operation between individual employees, and between different parts of the organisation, were very low.
- She was unsure of, or worried about, her own motives if she accepted the job. Would this be an ego trip, or would it be because she felt she could authentically contribute to the organisation: her morals were an important aspect of her character, and doing something for the wrong motives would cross a moral boundary for her.

Ellen's breakthrough, or awakening, came on the third day of a personal development course. She suddenly became aware of the depth of impact her father and older brother had on her, and how this related to all of the four issues described above.

Her father was a clergyman who combined the attributes of being kind and loving with stern and inflexible moral attitudes. Her love for him and desire to please him caused her to take on aspects of his stern, inflexible nature that were potentially very self-limiting — factors she had been largely unconscious of as an adult.

Her father had always emphasised being moderate in one's ambitions and advocated for never taking on a task or responsibility you did not know you could fulfil effectively. Also, he impressed upon her the need to be self-reliant. It was alright — even admirable — to help others, but a person of the highest virtue should themselves be self-reliant.

In addition to her father, Ellen's older brother was highly intelligent but had a very aggressive and argumentative personality. She had always been the loser in any confrontation with him and losing was both emotionally hurtful and, even worse, sometimes humiliating. As a result, Ellen had always subconsciously feared, and tried to avoid any contact with confrontational men, such as the four 'macho' senior managers who resented her.

During the workshop, Ellen experienced a very deep emotional release from the internal emotional programming resulting from these childhood experiences. She became able to view this internal psychological legacy from an adult mindful perspective and made the decision to accept the position, if she could win it from the board.

She saw that she then faced three major challenges. The first was to develop a strategic business vision for the company and its organisational culture. This was essential if she was to achieve the other two challenges: to convince the company's Board of Directors to promote her to the position of Managing Director while also winning over the support of the four members of the senior management team who strongly opposed her promotion.

Having let go of her father's legacy of always having to be self-reliant, Ellen knew she did not have to do this alone. She enlisted the help of the three senior managers who supported her and the outgoing Managing Director as well as several specialist industry consultants and myself as a culture change consultant. Working together in a three day off-site planning session, we created a powerful and comprehensive strategic and cultural vision for the company.

Ellen had a new and deeper self-confidence after her workshop breakthrough, but she was a little nervous about presenting to the board. She felt that the first few minutes of her presentation were a little stilted and then quite suddenly something shifted inside of her. All of her concerns and anxieties suddenly disappeared and her presentation flowed with an ease, grace and power she had never before experienced. The board were mesmerised and several days later she was told she had won the appointment!

Ellen's workshop breakthrough had resulted in a transformational change — a shift in the 'lens' through which she viewed herself, others and her 'world' — she had entered the state of mindfulness. This always involves a new, deeper perspective of our sense of self. From this new perspective, whatever challenges we face seem to carry so much less weight, and whatever we need to do flows so much more easily.

Ellen made a similar presentation to the senior management team and used another strategy to win over the four senior managers who were not supportive. She knew they would be particularly put off if she pushed her own agenda aggressively. Thus, she stepped back and allowed the three senior managers who were already supportive to offer their thoughts in an open discussion with the others. Although the discussion became heated at times Ellen did not use her authority to intervene.

Using this open and accepting method worked and the managers came to an agreement on the need to implement the new vision. They agreed that the business needed a new direction and that the company's culture was in bad shape and needed to change. The levels of mutual trust and respect between different business units and between management and staff was very low; communication both vertically and horizontally was poor; morale was very low; and overall there was an adversarial rather than a co-operative relationship between different parts of the business.

Ellen, as Managing Director, led with superb skill as she undertook her programme of implementing the new business vision and transforming the organisation's culture. By the end of 18 months, the company had made a major turnaround. A customer service survey showed that clients were much happier with the company's services than before starting the change programme. Levels of trust and respect, co-operation and communication had improved immensely. Even with the added costs of expanding the business and implementing the culture change programme, profitability had increased quite significantly. But as Ellen herself said: 'It is highly unlikely that I could have led this organisational transformation if I had not first transformed myself'.

THE SHARED LEADERSHIP DEVELOPMENT PROCESS

In all five stories, the basic process of developing as leaders was exactly the same. All of them underwent an 'awakening' process that lead to a breakthrough in their personal development — a true transformational change. This raised their level of awareness, making them more conscious and mindful people who then began to develop personal characteristics and capabilities that shaped or reshaped them as leaders.

For each of them, the specific awakening was different, as were the resulting breakthroughs in overcoming self-limiting beliefs and behaviour, and developing new qualities or capabilities. Yet for all of them personal development was what enabled them to become authentic, effective leaders.

CHAPTER THREE

ESSENTIALS IN THE ART OF LEADERSHIP

GOOD or great leadership requires the leader to be both effective and authentic. Authenticity is purely a personal character trait, whereas effectiveness is the result of the leader possessing a number of character traits and capabilities. Authenticity requires an individual to have good values and character. It is essential that their motives and intentions are not narrow and self-serving but broad and inclusive. Secondly, authenticity requires honesty, truthfulness and integrity.

All leadership capabilities are based on certain character traits or qualities that are potentially present within all of us. They have been identified and described by philosophers in both eastern and western cultures for thousands of years, and during at least the last 50 years by humanistic and transpersonal psychologists. However, for the majority of us many of these lie dormant and need to be awakened. This awakening requires certain types of powerful, experiential learning processes.

It is important to reiterate that these capabilities are not simply individual skills. Each of the four capabilities consists of a cluster of character traits and abilities. These are the foundation of each of the capabilities. It is, of course, true that many specific skills are essential in both expressing and using these capabilities: for example, specific leadership skills — good communication and listening skills, good strategic and tactical thinking skills, good people skills, good coaching and mentoring skills. There are also a number of specific, critically-important technical and management skills. However, without the foundation of authenticity and the character traits and abilities that define the four capabilities, any leadership or management skills would not be guided by a consistent, integrated purpose or set of values.

THE FOUR ESSENTIAL CAPABILITIES

Capability One: The capacity to envision a new and better possible future, combined with a strong belief in that future, and the strong intention and commitment to create that future.

No matter the context, the capacity to envision a new and better future may require:

- the awakening and use of our innate human capacity for imagination and intuition. This often means using disparate pieces of information, ideas or simply facts that are already present and known, but seeing them and putting them together in new and unique ways.
- overcoming the feeling that creating a new or better future is just not possible given our personal limitations, or the intrinsic difficulties or major problems that may obstruct the achievement of our vision.
- a potential shift in our values system. The new (or renewed) values provide the motive to see, believe in and pursue a vision for a better future.
- awakening to a new, expanded sense of 'reality' — a new and different way of seeing the world, and/or a new of different way of seeing ourselves — any of which can open up a new realm of possibilities for us.

This power of imagination must be backed up by a strong belief in that possibility and an intention and commitment to actually create the new and better future. This requires purpose, a strong sense of commitment and tenacity.

Capability Two: The capacity to engage with and inspire others to embrace and share that envisioned possibility, and find the strategy and solutions for realising that vision.

Engaging with, and inspiring others, inevitably requires a huge amount of communication. For this communication to be effective:

- the leader must be an authentic embodiment of his/her vision. They must have a deep faith in the positive value of the new future they envisage.

    While communicating we convey or receive meaning and authenticity by the combination of verbal and non-verbal cues. These are contained in our tone and body language (especially facial movements).

It is our brain's right hemispheric function which subconsciously but simultaneously picks up these non-verbal cues, while our conscious mind is listening to the words. According to extensive studies by psychologist Albert Merabian, only 7% of a message's impact is conveyed by words while 93% is through non-verbal cues.

When we are speaking, the right brain of our listeners is subconsciously picking up and assessing the congruence of these non-verbal cues with the words they consciously hear. If they are congruent, there is a greater likelihood that the listener will accept and be positively influenced by the message. Conversely, if they are incongruent, the listener will experience a kind of internal 'dissonance' and be more likely to reject the message and (perhaps) become sceptical or cynical about the speaker.

- most of the communication must be two-way. There is, of course, a place for an inspirational monologue — but the ability to engage people and win them over through inspirational monologue is only a starting point. Engaging with others requires a dialogue. In the end it is this active engagement with others in two-way or even multi-way communication that is essential in engaging and inspiring others.

The second set of abilities essential for this second capability involves finding strategies, tactics and solutions for realising the vision by working through and with others. This is where the character trait of humility becomes important. No matter how smart you are, you need the humility to know that you could not possibly come up with the most effective strategies, tactics and solutions on your own. You need the ideas, perspectives and feedback from those you have inspired to share your vision, and also from the views of others who do not share your vision. With the first group — those who share your vision — you must act as a facilitator to draw out ideas and strategies. The strategies must result from a collaborative, collective effort.

For the second group — those who do not share your vision — you need their input as well. This could include people who actually disagree with you, but equally it could include people who do not disagree with you but are just not part of your project. These people will have a different perspective and perhaps a different knowledge base. They are likely to see potential barriers, problems and/or information and opportunities that you, or those in your group, don't.

Capability Three: The ability to facilitate the formation and bonding of a team, organisation or network whose purpose is to actually create that future. This team, organisation or network must be built around a culture that is:
- driven by a strong commitment to the common purpose of achieving the envisioned possible future
- committed to a set of common values specific to that team or group, but which always includes mutual trust and respect.

There are several different scenarios we can consider. The first occurs when a leader is starting a team or organisation from scratch. The upside of this is the freedom the leader has to create the team or the organisation and its culture from the beginning — installing the desired vision and values from day one, without having to transform a pre-existing culture. The downside is, of course, the difficulty one often encounters in creating an organisation from day one (eg lack of resources, people not being used to working with each other, etc).

The second possible scenario involves a situation in which there is a network that may or may not be legally incorporated and which does have paid staff, but also uses a huge amount of unpaid volunteers. Many charities, non-government organisations and political campaigns use this type of organisational network. The Obama campaign in the 2008 presidential race was a well-run classic network of this kind.

The final scenario involves becoming a leader in a previously existing organisation, of any size, in which the big challenge is major organisational change: changes in products or services, changes in business processes and systems and changes in organisational structure. Changes in business processes and systems are often part of the process of 'restructuring' which involves mainly management skills and is not, in and of itself, part of the leadership role. The leadership role in this scenario is to communicate *why* such changes are necessary if the organisation is to realise its envisioned future. The management role is to *design* the system and structural changes.

However, by far the most important part of the change process is transforming a team's, organisation's or network's culture into one that embodies the purpose and the values that will empower its people to bring that future into reality. Creating the right culture is a major leadership responsibility.

WHAT IS AN ORGANISATION?

Teams are the basic building block of newly formed or pre-existing organisations. A team or organisation is more than just a group of people who share a common purpose. Though built around a common vision or purpose, a team or organisation consists of an internal network of relationships and shared responsibilities and tasks. The team's shared responsibilities and tasks are designed to facilitate achieving specific outcomes that, over time, will contribute to the realisation of the envisioned possible future.

It is the usual practice to divide up the team or organisation's collective responsibilities into individual tasks and responsibilities, with specific individuals accountable for different tasks or responsibilities. These tasks and responsibilities are highly interdependent with the tasks or responsibilities of others. Thus, if a team is to operate effectively, there must be high levels of co-operation and co-ordination, and, at best, collaboration. For this to occur, the network of team/organisational relationships must be based on a high level of mutual trust and respect.

To achieve this:

- **A leader must treat others with trust and respect** — showing, through their attitudes and actions, that they have the capacity and preference for trusting others. To be trusted, a team or organisational member must, in turn, demonstrate their professional competency, trustworthiness and other positive personal traits (eg conscientiousness, co-operativeness and good will).

    This is also dependent upon to the leader's good judgement, which includes both having accurate insight into the personal traits or qualities of team members and a good assessment of their professional competency. This kind of judgement will determine how effective the leader is in hiring, developing and promoting people who can be trusted in all of these ways.

    The most common alternative to trusting people is for the leader to place a great deal of emphasis on control, either directly dominating or micromanaging individuals and/or setting up heavy bureaucratic machinery. Either of these invariably lowers team members' morale and thus team efficiency, effectiveness and productivity.

- **A leader must show, through their attitudes and actions, that they have a genuine concern for the welfare and wellbeing of the people in their team or organisation** — while team members each have a task or goal that they are responsible for, they must also be assured that the leader treats each

person as an end in themselves, not just a vehicle for achieving an end.
- **A leader must show that they are honest and fair in their communications and interactions with team members, and that they will keep their word**
— people need to know that they can depend on their leader's honesty and fairness.

These traits and abilities are essential for earning trust and respect. They set the tone for the team or organisational culture, determining the quality of co-operation and collaboration that is likely to occur.

Capability Four: The ability to manage oneself effectively, including behaviour, thought and emotions, based on accurate and in-depth self-knowledge.

Most books on leadership that address the issue of self-management place a great deal of emphasis on managing one's behaviour effectively. This includes managing potentially destructive behaviour based on negative emotions, negative thinking or the need to control. The assumption is that often we can't control our emotions or our thoughts but we can learn to control the behaviour that results from them.

It is true that our emotional and thinking habits and patterns often occur automatically. For example, these habits and patterns are often triggered by specific situations. When we are around certain people or in certain types of situations, habitual patterns of negative or self-limiting thinking and emotions do just occur spontaneously. Even if we can control and manage the behaviour that might result, we are often unable to control our thoughts or emotions.

Our approach in this book is different. We will explore a deeper form of self-management which involves gaining mastery over our thoughts and emotions, not just our behaviour. This does not involve any form of suppression or (even worse) repression of our thoughts or feelings. Suppression or repression only bottles up mental and emotional energy, eventually creating psychological or physical health problems.

When we can learn to observe ourselves objectively and non-judgementally in situations that usually bring up strong negative thoughts or emotions, these thoughts or emotions diminish in intensity and gradually disappear. The objective, non-judgemental perception of ourselves occurs in the state of mindfulness — which is a natural expression of higher states of consciousness. Achieving this mindful state is a key to mastery over our thoughts and emotions.

The Q12 Profiling System can play a critical role in helping to achieve this mindful way of perceiving yourself and the life situations you are in. It can provide deep and accurate insight into your character structure as it is now, and indeed your current sense of identity. It can help you identify both your natural strengths and possible 'Achilles' heels'. It can provide insights into the kinds of formative experiences that created your character structure and sense of identity. And finally, it will provide the opportunity to create a practical, step-by-step plan to gaining the increased self-mastery that will allow you to manage yourself truly effectively – as a person and as an actual or potential leader.

However, before turning to the Q12 Profiling System, we need to explore the processes by which our psychology is shaped during the period from childhood through adolescence into adulthood. This will provide potential insight into why we possess certain natural strengths and also why we sometimes respond mentally, emotionally and behaviourally in ways that work against us, and perhaps negatively affect others.

PART 2

WHO AM I AND WHERE DO I COME FROM?

THE SHAPING OF OUR THINKING, EMOTIONAL AND BEHAVIOURAL PATTERNS THAT WORK BOTH FOR AND AGAINST US

CHAPTER FOUR

DEVELOPMENTAL MARKERS

THE SOCIALISED SELF

Everyone has a personality. We often think that personality defines identity, either in ourselves or in others. We may or may not like aspects of our personality but nonetheless we often consider that it defines who we are.

However, the word 'personality' tends to focus on the external, recognisable features of an individual — including how they look, their facial features and typical facial expressions, their voice qualities, ways of speaking and their typical behavioural patterns. In other words 'personality' tends to focus on only what we typically see and hear when we encounter the individual. There is much more that defines us as individuals than these externally recognisable features. There are aspects of ourselves that we share with few if any others, plus a huge domain of mental-emotional processes, attitudes and assumptions of which we have no conscious awareness.

Identifying our self as our personality is thus an oversimplification and misleading in important ways. Therefore I will be using the term 'socialised self' to designate the fullness of who we are when we emerge from adolescence into early adulthood.

Our 'socialised self' is the whole of what we have become; it is the result of a process of social-emotional programming in response to a myriad of people and circumstances throughout our lives. While each of us genetically inherits different basic temperamental traits, aptitudes, physical features and intellectual capacity, the way we learn to experience these internally and express them externally in our behaviour is the product of this social-emotional programming.

Our socialised self is a set of emotionally-based belief systems including:

- **Our beliefs about ourselves** — Who or what we are (our 'identity'); what we can/can't do; what we value/don't value; what we should/shouldn't feel, believe or do.
- **Our beliefs about other people** — Family, spouse or partner, friends, enemies, co-workers and various authority figures.
- **Our beliefs about our world** — The larger reality in which we live our lives, including what is real and unreal, how the world and social order is and how it should be. Though we may not use the term, this is our 'philosophy of life'.

The socialised self also includes observable behaviour which has its source in our belief systems. We perceive, understand and respond to our environment through the filter of these belief systems. These belief systems are the 'lens' discussed earlier. Our habitual behavioural responses happen because this 'lens' causes us to perceive ourselves, others and our world in a certain way.

Because our inner subjective world drives our habitual external behavioural responses, a permanent change in our behaviour must always be anchored in a change in this 'lens'. So, how did we become the people we are today?

THE LADDER OF CONSCIOUSNESS: A SEVEN-STAGE DEVELOPMENTAL MODEL

While there is no final 'end state' of self-mastery, there are definite stages and developmental markers along the way. To define these developmental markers, I use an evolutionary model that identifies and describes seven stages in our development towards self-mastery. The first four stages we all pass through from birth through adolescence into adulthood. At each of the first four stages of development, there is the potential for achieving a greater degree of self-mastery. For example, a 10-year-old child has a greater potential for self-mastery than a 5-year-old. These first four stages are what shape our adult socialised self, with all of our natural strengths and possible limitations.

Our passage through the first four stages is automatic. This is partially due to genetic factors and partially due to the influence of the social culture in which we grow up (family, schools, authority figures, playground, peer groups and religion).

DEVELOPMENTAL MARKERS

UNITIVE SELF	Stage 7
TRANSPERSONAL SELF	Stage 6
INDEPENDENT SELF	Stage 5
ADULT SOCIALISED SELF / **ADOLESCENT SELF** — 12/13 years through adolescence to early adulthood. Ends at Adult Socialised Self Stage	Stage 4
LATE CHILDHOOD SELF — Approx 8 years through approx 12 years	Stage 3
EARLY CHILDHOOD SELF — Approx 21 months through approx 7 years	Stage 2
PRE VERBAL 'BODY SELF' — Approx 5/6 months in womb through approx 21 months	Stage 1

While we all automatically pass through the first four stages, our passage through may be more or less complete or successful. It is these experiences that shape our mental, emotional and behavioural qualities and traits as we enter adulthood. We may or may not like these habits or traits, but the good news is that we can change any of these if we want to.

Our evolution through the final three stages occurs during adulthood and is not automatic. As adults, we must take personal responsibility for facilitating our passage through stages five, six and seven. These will be referred to as the 'higher' levels of development (or consciousness) since the majority of people never complete these stages. What provides the greater potential for self-mastery at each stage are genetically pre-programmed potentials within us that must be 'awakened'.

As each new level emerges, it brings with it three basic elements of consciousness:

1. A new type of **awareness** emerges, and with that awareness, new kinds of abilities, such as new ways of thinking and new ways of interacting with our environment.

2. New **motivational factors** emerge that drive our behaviour; new needs, desires, values, goals that were not fully present in the earlier stages. These motivational factors open up new potentials and possibilities for development.
3. The new awareness, abilities, and motivational factors create a newly emerging sense of **identity**.

It is important to understand that each new level of awareness/ability is genetically pre-programmed into us as a basic potential. Each new level only needs to be awakened by the right experiences. Once awakened, we need to use the new level of awareness/ability to develop, and ultimately master, the new potentials inherent in that level.

The goal and purpose of each level is to master the basic positive potentials and possibilities inherent at that level. Obviously this does not mean doing everything that you could do at that level. There are an infinite number of things that could be done and we are finite beings. What it does mean is that through practice, we can master the use of the awareness/abilities specific to that level.

A simple analogy is that we genetically inherit the ability to learn and use language. However, once that ability is awakened in infancy, we need much practice over many years to achieve an adult's mastery of language.

OUR FIVE FUNDAMENTAL NEEDS

There are five primary human needs that drive the first four levels of development. The first four are those identified by Abraham Maslov in his hierarchy of needs:

- (physical) **survival** needs —good nutrition, warmth, shelter, medical care when needed
- **security** needs —safety and security in the home, school and social environment
- **belongingness/relationship** needs — the need to be liked, loved and accepted by other individuals and groups
- **self-esteem needs** — the need to feel valued by other individuals and groups because of our traits, skills and accomplishments

In addition to the above four needs, I would add one more that underpins the others: the need for **unconditional love**.

This is especially important during the first seven years. With a stable, solid foundation of unconditional love a child learns to love and accept themselves. And it is this self-love that is the basis of all healthy relationships.

If this need is not adequately or appropriately met its absence can cause one of the most painful forms of emotional dependency: a yearning for some other human being to fill an empty hole inside of us. This yearning manifests in all the forms of love dependency found in our society and the term most commonly used to describe it is 'co-dependent'. When we love someone in that way, we are completely dependent on that person for our sense of wellbeing.

We learn self-love by experiencing unconditional love as a child. We internalise this love and it transforms into self-love. When we feel lovable people are attracted to us, which further reinforces the feeling. Conversely, if we do not learn to love ourselves, we come to feel unlovable. In numerous ways other people pick this up, often quite unconsciously. As a result, they are instinctively not attracted to us and this further reinforces the feeling that we are not lovable.

THE SOCIALISATION PROCESS

In addition to meeting these five basic needs, the socialisation process plays an equally important role during the first four stages in shaping our socialised self. Rudiments of this process occur even before we begin to use language, as parents or caregivers encourage and discourage certain types of behaviour. However, language is the major tool through which socialisation occurs. Anthropologists call this process 'enculturation'. Socialisation (or enculturation) is a form of psychological and emotional conditioning or programming.

This process is influenced by numerous people, groups and institutions within our social or cultural environment:
- immediate family, especially parents and grandparents and other family members or caregivers
- other adult authority figures, eg teachers, coaches, religious leaders etc
- our peer group

Methods of input include direct attempts to influence our thinking, attitudes and behaviour through verbal persuasion, rewards and verbal promise of rewards, positive or negative feedback, and punishment or verbal threats of punishment. Notice how much of this is accomplished by the use of language.

Indirect influences come from observing how our parents and other authority figures actually behave, and from watching the behaviour of our peer group. These types of indirect influences are often at least as important to our socialisation process as the direct ones. Indeed our observation of what people actually do will often affect us more than what they say, although language is still central.

IDENTITY AND SUBJECT-OBJECT RELATIONS

The stages of development are discussed by using a 'subject-object relationship' model. When we achieve each new stage of development, we view our previous selves as 'object'. Our new identity or self-concept views our old self as something 'else'. At the new stage we are the 'subject', the old self the 'object'.

Put simply, think of a 10-year-old saying 'I'm not a little kid anymore' – as if to distinguish themselves from who they were as a younger child. They can remember who they were at that time but the younger self has, in a metaphorical sense, become an 'object' in the new self's psychological landscape.

STAGE I: THE BODY SELF STAGE

The body self stage is pre-verbal and lasts from about the 5th or 6th month in the womb until approximately 21 months.

This stage of development begins with the emergence of consciousness itself. From a biological perspective consciousness is thought to begin within the 18–22 week period of foetal development.[1] This initial consciousness gives the foetus the ability to experience sensory input and feelings, yet it has no ability to distinguish itself from the sensory inputs and feelings or its environment. The foetus (and later the infant) experiences itself as the ongoing flow of sensory input and feeling, which results from its environment.

For example, with regard to feelings, as adults equipped with a view of the world created by language, we would describe it this way:

Subject	Verb	Object
I	Experience	A Feeling

This implies that there is an 'I' who is having a feeling but it is distinct from the feeling. For the foetus and infant the feelings are me. I am these feelings and the sensory input from the environment. At this beginning phase of the body self stage there is no ability to make the subject/object distinction.

This beginning phase can have a powerful influence in the developing child's later psychology.

We know that the unborn child is an aware, reacting human being who from the sixth month on (and perhaps even earlier) leads an active emotional life.....a corollary to this study is that what the child feels and perceives begins shaping his [psychology]. Whether he sees himself and, hence acts as a happy or sad, aggressive or meek, secure or anxiety ridden person depends, in part, on the messages he gets about himself in the womb. [2]

The foetus/infant's basic needs are:
- **Physical needs in the womb** — good nutrition and an absence of harmful substances (alcohol, drugs)
- **Psychological needs in the womb** — a basically happy and contented mother who loves and wants the child, with an absence of any chronically negative emotional states
- **Birth experience** — as much as possible, a non-traumatic, natural birth experience, where the infant receives a warm, loving welcome into the world
- **Physical needs in the first 3–4 months** — the infant is kept warm and comfortable with good nutrition
- **Psychological needs in the first 3–4 months** — a warm, loving welcoming human environment with much loving physical contact

For the remainder of the body self stage, the infant/toddler learns to make the subject/object distinction. At around 3–4 months, the infant begins to experience the environment as separate and distinct from itself, and to intentionally (not just instinctively) interact with its environment. For example, during the first 3–4 months, if you wave a ball back and forth in front of a child, it will follow the movement with its eyes and hands, but it will not try to reach out and grasp the ball. What the infant sees is not experienced as separate and distinct from itself but rather experienced as a single continuum.

At approximately 4 months, the child's response to the waving of the ball changes. It will begin to make grasping movements, trying to reach out for the ball. The object is beginning to be experienced as separate from the child. This indicates that an expansion of consciousness has occurred, which allows the child to make distinction between 'self' and 'other'. This new consciousness enables the development of our ability to consciously and intentionally interact with our environment. The child's sense of self is tied up completely with its body including all of its immediate, instinctive impulses and needs.

The survival and security needs, and the need for unconditional love are the predominant needs during the body self stage. The survival needs are quite straightforward — good nutrition, shelter and good healthcare when needed. The need for unconditional love is equally straightforward. However, the security needs are tied to very specific needs and impulses that drive the infant and toddler's behaviour:

- **The child's immediate, impulsive wants, needs and desires.** The pleasure-pain principle predominates during this stage. The child seeks to do and experience things that are pleasurable and avoid doing or experiencing things that aren't. If most of the child's experiences are pleasurable, this provides the groundwork for a later view of the world as a source of pleasure and fulfils the need for security. If the balance is tipped towards mainly unpleasant experiences, the foundation is laid for a later view of the world as a painful and unpleasant place which violates the need for security.
- **The child needs to have a rich, interesting environment with a variety of people and things to explore, get into and take apart.** As the child begins to crawl, walk, pick up and handle things, they are laying the psychological groundwork for their later relationship to other people and to their environment generally. It is very important that this need is not consistently frustrated since this stage can lay the emotional ground work for very positive or negative feelings about themselves or the world in general. Again, these experiences either fulfil or violate the child's need for security.
- **At least one of the caregivers with whom the baby is familiar is always around.** During the body self stage, as the child learns to crawl and walk, they do not want to be held or constrained much of the time. They want to be free to explore and interact with their environment. However, if they hurt themselves or become frightened they want to immediately go to one of the primary caregivers to be comforted. This is profoundly important in developing a sense of security as a foundation for later stages in life.

During the body self stage, a very basic foundation is laid for our later self.

STAGE II: THE EARLY CHILDHOOD STAGE

From approximately 21 months through approximately 7 years.

Over this period there is a gradually emerging awareness that there is a 'me' which is not my body and its immediate, instinctive impulses. This new 'me' — being distinct from my body and its impulses — can potentially provide the beginning of an ability to gain some control over my body's immediate, instinctive impulses. Gaining the beginning of this control is at the heart of the socialisation process during the early childhood stage.

Much of our behaviour in early childhood arises from the instinctive, biologically-based impulses to gratify our own wants, needs and desires. If acted on as adults, many of these impulses would result in behaviour that would violate the social sanctions of any civilised society. These impulses are in their nature self-centred and they have deep biological roots. They include aggressive impulses, but also sexual or pleasure-seeking impulses, curiosity and the desire to play.

One major purpose of the socialisation process, during the early childhood stage, is to assist the child in gradually gaining some control over these impulses, and learning to express them in creative and socially appropriate ways.

This occurs through a set of injunctions: what we should and shouldn't do, say, think (believe) and feel (attitudes). These injunctions initially come from parents, caregivers and other authority figures. During most of the early childhood stage the source of authority is external.

The process begins at around 18 months to 2 years, with a number of do's and don'ts about behaviour. The purpose of the do's, of course, is to encourage certain behaviours. This is accomplished by rewarding desired behaviour with positive physical responses (hugging), positive verbal feedback or through gifts.

The purpose of the don'ts has at its core the setting of limits. Certain behaviours are beyond those limits and thus unacceptable. For the setting of limits to work there must be sanctions or consequences for violating the limits which must be consistently applied. The way in which these limits are explained to the child, the types of sanctions used and the way they are applied, are of enormous importance in laying the foundations for a healthy self-concept.

The methods used by various social cultures and individual families differ immensely. They range on a continuum from extremely harsh and authoritarian through to over-indulgent. However, to achieve a healthy self-concept in the child, this socialisation process must occur in a balanced way, loving, sensitive but being firm when necessary — rather than using either harsh authoritarian methods or being over-indulgent. If this balance is achieved, it is very likely that the child's spirit will remain fully intact: the powerful, life-giving, biologically-based impulses will begin to find positive, appropriate and creative ways to be expressed.

The internalised injunctions provided by parents and other authority figures must not be so limiting as to allow no outlet for these impulses. The rules and norms in the socialisation process must provide socially appropriate ways for the expression of these impulses. Part of this involves training the child to know the time, place and circumstances where these impulses can be expressed while also training the child about how to give expression to these impulses.

By the age of about 7, these socialising injunctions tend to become internalised within the child's psyche. The child may or may not like these injunctions, but whether she/he likes them or not, many of the behavioural patterns will develop as consistent with, or in reaction against, these injunctions. This process involves the classic resistance/absorption principle that can affect much of human psychology through childhood and adolescence.

The resistance/absorption principle is very simple: the child may directly absorb the socialising injunctions and their thinking, emotions and behaviour will clearly demonstrate this. Or, the child may resist the injunctions, and their emotions, thoughts or behaviour will demonstrate this in some form of resistance or rebellion.

As the child's socialisation progresses, he/she gradually becomes aware of the socially defined concept of belonging. He/she begins to experience and understand what it means to be liked and accepted or disliked/rejected by an individual or group. By the age of 7 the basic social concept of inclusion and exclusion is understood. If the child has had mostly good experiences with being liked and accepted, they develop a basic security and confidence in their ability to establish relationships and to be accepted by whatever groups they wish to join. There is security and confidence that their 'belongingness needs' will be met. This lays a strong positive foundation for the development of social skills and the ability to form relationships, join groups and be accepted.

On the other hand, if the child experiences a lot of rejection, a fear of rejection and exclusion will result. This fear will invariably be accompanied by a feeling that there is something wrong or lacking in them accompanied by feelings of insecurity and low self-confidence.

These feelings — positive or negative — will begin to be part of the child's self-concept, the emotionally-based beliefs about who or what he or she is. They may also engender emotionally-based positive or negative beliefs about other people and the world such as:

- people are (or aren't) open and friendly
- the world is (or is not) an open, accepting and friendly place.

Once such beliefs are in place, they will cause individuals to behave in ways that result in similar positive or negative outcomes, thus further reinforcing these beliefs.

Finally, in the early childhood stage, there is a strong tendency to 'subjectify' the environment. Children do this through the ability to engage in 'magical thinking' and the inability to understand the environment objectively (confusion of cause and effect, etc). Pretending is very real, they are the people or creatures they image themselves to be.

By the age of about 7 this all begins to change. As the child enters the late childhood stage, they become more interested in things as they are. They still fantasise, but the fantasy will more often be about things that actually could be. For example, a 9 or 10-year-old might fantasise about being a doctor one day, but they don't experience themselves as actually being what they are fantasising about as in the magical thinking of the 5-year-old.

As they grow the child gradually develops the beginning of a verbal, mental self-concept consisting of emotionally-based belief systems about him/herself.

This new self-concept of emotionally-programmed belief systems is formed by about 7 years. Because the beliefs have such a strong emotional base, they are not like purely intellectual beliefs that an adult might have. They are an integrated combination of feelings and beliefs and thus we will coin a special term for them: we will call them 'feeliefs'.

The contents of the self-structure — made of these 'feeliefs' — consist of, and result from, the child's experiences:

- **The outcome of the need for unconditional love.** Does the child basically feel loved, lovable within itself, or quite the opposite?
- **How well the newly emerging socially defined belongingness/relationship needs are met.** What are the child's 'feeliefs' about whether he/she is liked (likeable), accepted (acceptable) in individual relationships or in groups?
- **The impulsive self and the internalised injunctions (the socialised self) in dynamic tension with each other.** Sometimes the impulsive self wins out, but sometimes the socialised self wins and the impulse is controlled or channelled into an appropriate, perhaps creative response.

STAGE III: THE LATE CHILDHOOD SELF

From approximately 7–8 years through to approximately 12 years.

There are four awarenesses/abilities that emerge during this period:

1. An increasing awareness of their social and school environment's complex rules, norms, attitudes, concerning relationships, membership and 'belonging' (inclusion/exclusion)
2. An emerging awareness of their social and school environment's judgements about the relative value and merit of people's abilities, skills and achievements
3. An increasing awareness that they are not their impulses and that they therefore have an increasing capacity for impulse control
4. An emerging desire and capacity for self-sufficiency and independence

RELATIONSHIP/BELONGINGNESS AND SELF-ESTEEM NEEDS

The socially defined self-esteem needs are: the need to be held in esteem by other individuals and groups because of our skills and accomplishments.

During the late childhood stage, much of the developmental process occurs through becoming aware of, and learning to operate in, an environment of rules and roles. For example, during this stage the child increasingly begins to play more structured, formal roles. As a student they study different subjects and begin to see themselves as falling on a continuum from very good to very poor at each subject. Similarly on the playground: games and sports are much more structured than those played in early childhood. Just as with school subjects, the child learns that he/she falls on a similar continuum.

It is these sorts of judgements — whether verbally expressed or not — that the child begins absorbing in the 8–12 year old period and these absorbed judgements bring with them feelings of high to low self-esteem.

At the same time, the socially defined relationship/belongingness needs become increasingly more important: the need to be loved, liked and accepted by other individuals and groups. This need is what motivates children to attempt to create desired relationships (friendships) and to join in, and be part of, a desired peer group. If they are successful they should internalise that experience and thus feel loved, liked, accepted and included. Learning good social skills at this point is at least as important as the academic content they learn at school, or the sporting or extra-curricular activities and skills they learn.

One of the complexities of this late childhood stage is that the socially defined relationship/belongingness needs become entangled with the self-esteem needs. The child increasingly plays peer group roles that begin to be rated in the same way that school or playground and sports performance are rated. Internal peer group hierarchies begin to emerge during this period, although they become much more serious during adolescence.

SELF-SUFFICIENCY AND INDEPENDENCE

Self-sufficiency and independence are critical parts of children's self-esteem needs in late childhood, and manifest in many ways. For example, they often want a minimal amount of adult interference in what they do. By the same token, the desire for independence can equally manifest in the opposite way. If the child wants something that does require help, and they are able to talk their parents into it, this is a demonstration of their control and therefore their independence.

Parents have a difficult parenting path to walk in dealing with this desire for independence in late childhood. Children of this age sometimes want a degree of independence simply not possible or realistic. It is also very easy to embarrass or even humiliate a child in this age range by insensitive ways of dealing with their attempts to express their self-sufficiency and independence.

THE CONTINUING SOCIALISATION PROCESS

As the child makes the transition from early to late childhood, the capacity to absorb and understand the reasons behind ideas like fairness, sharing and taking turns increases. As the rules become more complex in school, games, sports and at home, the roles also become more important and more complex. It therefore becomes more important that the child understands the 'why' behind the rules and roles.

The optimal method for doing this involves verbal appeals to the child's own experience and utilises statements or questions such as: 'How would you feel if someone else hit you, had all the turns, was not fair?'.

Without these verbal interactions that explain the 'why', the injunctions can seem arbitrary and rigid. Empathy is developed by appealing to the child's own feelings. Understanding and empathy are far more powerful forces than behavioural rules in ensuring a child treats others well and fairly. Above all, when understanding and empathy are the motivating factors, fear does not play a central role in the child's socialisation.

Children also learn the basics of socially appropriate behaviour and communication; 'socially appropriate' means 'within the behavioural norms of a given society'. Part of this is just learning not to embarrass yourself or others by doing or saying things that, in a particular social context, would make you or others look foolish. Part of this is knowing how not to needlessly do or say things that upset people. Part of this is simply learning social skills that facilitate positive relationships and interactions with others.

Finally, there are certain core values that any healthy society will need to

begin instilling within children during the transformation from the early to late childhood period. These are basic principles such as:
- do unto others as you would have them do unto you
- treat each other with care and respect
- share common resources
- take responsibility for what you do and say
- act with honesty and integrity

The verbal interactions around these issues should take the form, 'What does it feel like for you to be on the receiving end of behaviour that either adheres to or violates these principles or values?' The purpose of these non-authoritarian types of communication is to assist the child in internalising sociably essential core values. This internalisation process is a form of positive emotional conditioning. It results in the development of empathy and a conscience.

Non-authoritarian methods seek to appeal to the self-evident validity of these core values. They do not emphasise these values as coming from a rigid external authority, or rely upon harsh punishments for behaviour that violates these values. If all of this works out, by about age 7 or 8 these will have begun to be internalised and the process of the internalisation will continue throughout late childhood and adolescence.

However, it is important to understand that it is not until the child enters adolescence that the full capacity for empathetic based relationships — founded on full interpersonal mutuality — can develop. Without a healthy foundation being laid in the late childhood stage, it will be much more difficult to achieve the full flowering of this during adolescence.

By the time the child has reached the age of 12, and begins the transition into adolescence, their late childhood identity will have become a complex, interconnected mixture of emotionally-based beliefs:
- They will have a set of emotionally-based beliefs based on their success or failure in meeting the (intertwined) relationship/belongingness and self-esteem needs. This part of the child's self-concept can be made up of emotionally-based beliefs that can run from very negative to very positive about his or herself. Also, these judgements can be very negative in one area of life and very positive in another (good at maths; bad at English; good at school; poor at sports; and the like).
- How well they have managed the issue of self-sufficiency and independence. Depending on whether their parents have handled this well or poorly, and on how the child has reacted to this, there are several

possibilities: the child may have submitted to and absorbed a feeling of dependency that makes him/her feel weak or submissive (and perhaps covertly resentful); the child may have become rebellious or overly obsessed with self-sufficiency; or the child will have a balanced, healthy feeling of self-sufficiency appropriate to their age.
- The late childhood response to the socialisation process during this stage will also become part of the child's self-concept. Again, the net result will have a lot to do with the quality of parenting and the child's experience with, and reaction to, other authority figures and to their peer group. At its very best, the child will have internalised, with understanding and empathy, the basics of the values and norms that result in the ability to co-operate and get along with others, without having their spirit broken or individuality submerged.

MODE OF THINKING: CONCRETE OPERATIONAL

In the early childhood period, the mode of thinking was magical, and the child subjectified the physical environment. In late childhood, the mode of thinking about the physical world becomes 'concrete operational', a term I believe was first coined by the developmental psychologist Piaget. Children at this stage like to think about things as they actually are, and no longer tend to view the world through the lens of magical thinking. They can still do imaginative, magical thinking, but they understand that it is a form of pretending and is not a physical world 'reality'.

STAGE IV: ADOLESCENT SELF

From approximately 12 years through adolescence into early adulthood, ending at adult socialised self stage.

During this period the adolescent potentially gains a greater, more sophisticated awareness of the social environment's bases for the socially defined relationship/belongingness and self-esteem needs. This includes:
- A much more sophisticated awareness of the complex rules, norms, attitudes and expectations concerning personal and professional relationships and membership or 'belonging'. In adolescence there is a newly awakened capacity for true interpersonal mutuality, for a true shared reality in relationship to individuals and groups
- A much more sophisticated awareness of the social/economic/professional environment's judgements about the relative value and importance of

people's abilities and achievements; and the relative value and status of people's work or profession, economic and social status

During the adolescent self stage, Maslov's relationship/belongingness and self-esteem needs become even more important motivating factors than during late childhood. These include:
- A desire to create and maintain good personal and (later) good professional relationships with the 'right' people and to belong to the 'right' groups, and the fear of rejection by the 'right' individuals or groups
- The desire or drive to develop and pursue personal and (later) professional traits, skills and successes that earn the adolescent and early adult esteem in the eyes of the 'right' individuals or groups, and the fear of failure and thus earning other's negative judgements

During adolescence peer group hierarchies become even more pronounced. There are even more factors that determine our place in that hierarchy: the family's socio-economic class; choice of school; performance in school, sports or other extra curricular activities; the level of social skill; physical attractiveness; and attractiveness of personality.

The desire to be respected, admired and in the 'right' relationships and the 'right' peer groups is a very strong motivator. Adolescents become very self-conscious and often try to consciously project an image of themselves as they would like to be. They may also begin hiding aspects of themselves that they feel would diminish them in the eyes of others.

In psychological terminology we call this the **projected persona** and the **hidden persona**. The projected persona consists of: traits or qualities that we want others to think we have and what we want others to think we want, believe, value or feel because:
- we believe that is what they expect, want or need of us; and/or
- we believe that this will make them think better of us

Essentially, the projected persona is: 'how we want others to see us'.

The hidden persona is what we don't want others to know about ourselves, including: what we actually believe we are but don't like about ourselves – and important desires, beliefs, values or feelings we have which we believe:
- are contrary to what others expect, want or need of us; and/or
- would diminish us in the eyes of others if they knew this about us

Essentially, the hidden persona is: 'how we don't want others to see us'.

It is common for individuals to begin experimenting with different projected personas during adolescence — confident, talented, bright, witty, 'in the know', tough, aloof, independent. Eventually, as they enter late adolescence and early adulthood, their projected and hidden personas stabilise and become part of the structure of their adult socialised self identity.

All of this is made more complex in adolescence by desires that emerge as strong motivators within the intertwined relationship/belongingness and self-esteem needs:
- The desire to be a kind of independent, individualised heroic figure (even though the adolescent still wants to fit in) and for adolescents who are rebels, the desire to be an independent, individualised anti-hero
- The newly emerging desire for romantic love, including sexual desire

Every adolescent dreams about being the heroic figure who stands above the crowd. The traits or qualities always included in this dream are: being unique and individualistic (yet still 'fitting in') and highly independent.

For some adolescents this is only a dream, since they are convinced that they could never in reality be that kind of heroic figure. In these cases the dream becomes the basis of a negative or self-limiting judgement about themselves and this remains in their hidden persona, lowering their internal self-esteem.

For others, the dream becomes something to strive for, especially if they show outstanding traits or skills (in sport, school, social skills or other extra-curricular activities). Thus they can earn the approval and esteem of peer groups, parents or other authority figures or heroic figures.

The emotional impact of gaining all this approval and esteem from others can lead to a form of addiction which, in turn, leads to getting on a series of success treadmills (discussed in Chapter 5).

ABSTRACT THINKING, RELATIONSHIPS AND THE SOCIALISATION PROCESS

As children enter and move through adolescence, a new type of thinking emerges that we call 'abstract thinking'. This allows the adolescent to study and understand abstract subjects at school. More importantly, from the perspective of the socialisation process, this kind of thinking allows us to enter another person's psychic reality and to create from that a shared psychic reality.

Part of abstract thinking is a capacity to think and talk about things that actually exist, but are not directly available to the senses as concrete objects. One domain of stuff that actually exists but cannot be directly, externally observed is our inner psychic life. This is the world of our thoughts and feelings. As an adolescent, we become more self-consciously aware of our inner world of thoughts and feelings: under optimal conditions, we can learn to talk about them to someone else.

The other element of abstract thinking is the ability to fully imagine how someone else might be feeling. In a sense, we can share their reality through our imagination, generalising from our inner experience to what theirs might be, thus creating the possibility of true interpersonal mutuality.

The ability to have this shared interpersonal reality produces the potential for a huge evolutionary leap in the socialisation process. It can become a strong basis for empathy, which leads to the golden rule — 'do unto others as you wish them to do to you'. Treating others well and fairly, showing kindness and understanding to others can all now be based on imagining and empathising with other people's inner reality. (Adolescents can also be very cruel, but this is sometimes because they want to fit into a particular group.)

This new interpersonal shared reality can produce relationships of a very different kind from even very good friendships at the late childhood stage. The relationships can become so close that it's as if each is part of the other person's identity, part of the structure of their self. (However, I should point out that this closeness is not intimacy, which can only really occur between two people who have achieved a high level of independence, as we will discuss later.)

When an adolescent falls in love, and the love is returned, it is ecstatic but also often frightening. The fear can come simply from loss of the emotional boundary between the individuals. But equally, two adolescents in love can be so emotionally dependent on each other that it is as if the other person is their whole world. Thus, the pain of potentially losing each other feels unendurable.

Then there is the pain of unrequited love. For adolescents, unrequited love brings with it two issues. Firstly, the pain of being incomplete and the deep, but frustrated, yearning for another's love. Secondly, the need to hide these feelings — to keep them in the hidden persona — at the risk of being humiliated if they are exposed.

Finally, there is the tension between two interdependent needs/desires: the desire to have a friend with whom there is romantic love and the desire to be (or appear to be) independent and self-sufficient. This is further complicated by the fact that one of the things that adolescents believe will attract the most desirable person to love them is their independence and self-sufficiency.

As the adolescent enters early adulthood, one of these — the desire to merge with another or the desire for independence and self-sufficiency — usually becomes more dominant.

THE SOCIALISED SELF

The self-concept that finally emerges from adolescence will be made up of emotionally-based belief systems that are built on the perceived successes or failures in meeting relationship/belongingness and self-esteem needs. The mental-emotional responses to these successes and failures make up our 'mental-emotional programming or conditioning'. We can respond by directly absorbing the self-concept resulting from earlier formative experiences or by reacting against the experiences.

If we directly absorb it, the new self-concept will result in a more sophisticated form of the same basic self-concept we had at the end of the previous stage. If we react against the formative experiences (and thus the self-concept) of the previous stage, our new self-concept will seem different from the previous stage. Yet in fact it will still be driven by the same unmet needs as the previous stage, but now in a disguised form.

For example, a child whose relationship/belongingness needs were not met with the main peer group they wanted to be a part of at the late childhood stage, may begin in adolescence to project an image of themselves as an independent loner who only hangs out with rebels and outsiders. This behaviour is still driven by the hurtful emotions left over from the unmet need in late childhood. However, those feelings are now disguised by the projected persona of the rebel outsider.

As an adult we carry the legacy of all four developmental stages. Some of the experiences that are part of that legacy we are not consciously aware of. This could simply be because we have not explored our past, because we are in denial, or have perhaps even repressed the memories of these early formative experiences.

Regardless, the resulting adult socialised self is metaphorically shaped like an onion. That is, it has layers, with the core of it being our sense of identity, and its outer most layer our visible personality and behavioural habits or patterns.

Five Layers of the Socialised Self

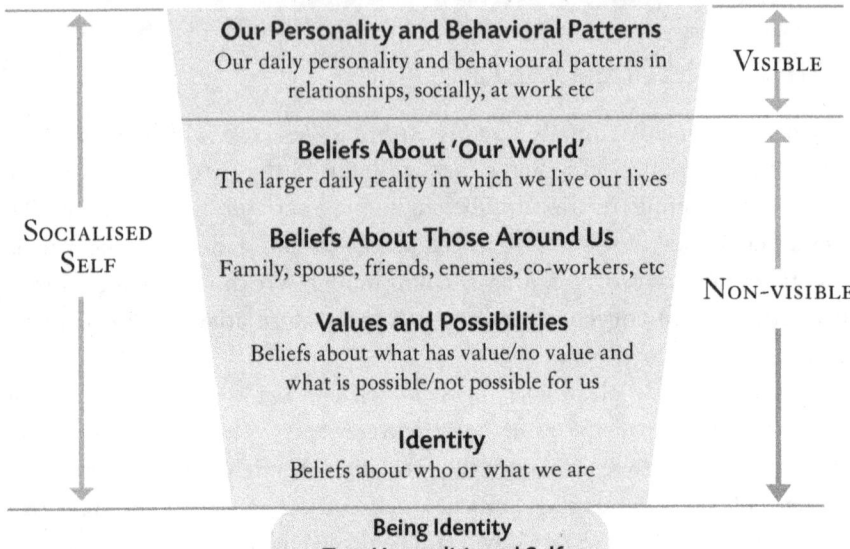

You will notice in the diagram, below the socialised self, there is something called our 'Being Identity'. This self is a source of unlimited potential that lies within all of us, untouched by the emotional programming or conditioning of our process of socialisation.

This deeper Being self (discussed in more detail in Chapter 5) can be experienced and used as a resource, and one of the time-honoured methods of doing this is through meditation.

By the time we have reached early adulthood, our socialised self has been fully formed. This does not mean that it never changes in adulthood. Indeed the process of adaptation may continue throughout our lifetime. However, the deepest emotional roots for our adult socialised self are anchored in our early experiences. They shape our view of ourselves, others and our world, and they tend to remain intact, unless we consciously, intentionally work on ourselves to change them.

---

1   T Lipson, *From Conception to Birth: Our Most Important Journey* (Millennium Books: Newtown, 1994), pp 66–67.
2   T Verney and J Kelly, *The Secret Life of the Unborn Child* (Sphere Books Ltd: Great Britain, 1982), pp x and xi.

CHAPTER FIVE

MENTAL, EMOTIONAL AND BEHAVIOURAL TREADMILLS

MASLOV called his four needs — survival, security, relationship/belongingness and self-esteem — 'D-cognition' values. The 'D' was used to indicate that these were 'deficiencies' or 'deficits' that need to be completed. Once completed, these would become the foundation for higher order values which he called 'B-cognition' values (the letter B stood for 'Being' values). 'Being' values are typically those associated with the higher levels of consciousness — aliveness, wholeness, justice, and so forth.[1]

What exactly is it like when these first four needs are truly fulfilled or 'complete' (or 'incomplete') for an adult?

The first indicator that each of the first four needs are 'completed' for you as an adult is always a feeling of deep inner security and confidence about that need, including the security and confidence that you will be able to continue meeting that need for yourself even in difficult circumstances.

The second indicator of any one of the first four needs being 'completed' is that this need is no longer a strong motivator for you. You will feel 'relaxed' rather than driven around that area of need. There is a feeling that there is nothing left to prove to yourself or others.

If on the contrary if you are 'incomplete' with respect to a given need, you will lack the secure feeling that the need has been met, or that you will be able to meet it in the future. That need will continue to be a strong motivating desire in your life, whether or not you feel hopeful or hopeless about it ever being fully met.

NEED	INDICATORS OF COMPLETENESS	INDICATORS OF INCOMPLETENESS
Survival and Security	• good quality food, healthcare and shelter • a reasonable degree of financial success and security • good physical and mental health • a reasonable degree of life stability Most importantly, completeness would also include feeling secure that you will be able to continue meeting those needs in the future, even if you go through some difficult times.	A continuing fear of: • financial failure • physical or mental health breakdown • extreme personal/professional trauma As a result, you would have a strong need to keep seeking financial, professional and emotional security.
Relationship/ Belongingness	• feeling that you are lovable and likeable • feeling of belonging You should feel confident in your ability to create and maintain good personal and professional relationships, and be part of any group you wish to join.	• lack of social self-confidence • fear of rejection This could cause you to endlessly pursue new relationships or groups to belong to — or become withdrawn and a loner.
Self-esteem	• confident, secure, internal feeling of high self-worth • achievement of personal and professional successes You should feel a relaxed confidence in the ability to create new successes and achievements by utilising your personal and professional traits and skills.	• fear of failure • fear of 'not being good enough' in the eyes of yourself or others This could include feeling that you need to keep proving yourself over and over again — or withdrawal into a feeling of being hopelessly low in self-worth and self-esteem.

Where each of the needs is 'complete', at the adult socialised self stage, trying to fulfil that need ceases to be a motivator. Your relaxed confidence in your personal, professional and social traits and skills means that, in the normal course of your daily activity, you should be able to continue meeting those needs. You would then have a strong foundation for pursuing higher order values — Maslov's 'B cognitive values'.

On the other hand if you are 'incomplete' with regard to one or more of Maslov's first four values, they will still remain strong drivers of your emotions, thoughts and behaviour. In this case you may or may not be conscious of exactly what is motivating you. However, whether conscious or unconscious, the motivating values are 'deficit driven'; they represent deficiencies that need to be fulfilled or completed.

TREADMILLS AND DEFICIT MOTIVATION

Treadmills are defined as:

Persistent, repeated patterns of thinking, emotional response and behaviour, based on conscious or unconscious deficit motivation, leading to failure or success — but even when successful, ending without deep satisfaction or fulfilment. Thus, there are both failure and success treadmills.

Deficit motivation, and the resulting treadmills, can be the consequence of three types of experiences:
- A need not being met at a particular stage of development — thus leaving a psychological 'hole' that you try to fill by continually enacting the same mental, emotional and behavioural patterns
- A deep feeling of not wanting to disappoint or let down parents (other loved ones or authority figures) by continuing to live up to what you believe are their expectations of you
- Certain belief systems programmed into us by our social/cultural environment, particularly the belief that when we have achieved or acquired enough of what is held to be of value in our society, we will be happy or satisfied. In this case those things we seek are expressions of Maslov's first four needs. Therefore, you keep on undertaking activities and pursuing goals that are meant to fulfil your survival, security, relationship/belongingness and self-esteem needs even after these needs have been fulfilled and completed

All three types of deficit motivation and treadmills can be operating at the same time.

However, deficit motivation is often an unconscious driver. That is, we may have a conscious reason for feeling, thinking or behaving as we do, which may actually be true at a surface level. Yet there are actually deeper deficit drivers for our thoughts, feeling and actions of which we are not conscious.

JOHN'S STORY

John was a 35-year-old single male: a successful professional with a good income. He was an intelligent, attractive man with a great sense of humour. Women were easily attracted to him, and he had been in 6 relationships over the past 8 years.

Each relationship lasted for 6 to 8 months until just about the time when the women wanted some kind of commitment. Each time the relationship got to this stage, he said something would 'shut down' in him. He would simply stop having the feelings for the woman that had made the relationship so rich up until this point. Then he would always gently but definitively end the relationship. His reason was always true on a conscious level. He said he no longer felt love and was just being honest and doing the right thing by breaking off the relationship. However, the real reason behind this relationship treadmill was a deep fear and insecurity about being in a long-term, committed relationship.

During a personal development exercise, John discovered where that fear came from: when John was four years old, his mother left his father for another man. As far as John knew, there were no signs or indications that she was going to leave until it suddenly occurred without any warning.

This shocking break-up had a devastating affect on John and his family. Though his father had generous visitation rights, the loss of his family was catastrophic blow and he never really recovered from this and never attempted another relationship.

John was personally devastated by his father's hurt and at the age of four he did not have the resources to deal with it. Thus, his response was to repress the hurt. As an adult he could remember that he felt bad for his father, but having repressed it, he did not actually feel any of the pain.

This was a severe violation of John's security and relationship/belongingness needs. Thus, John had a fear-based deficit need to never expose himself to the possibility of that kind of hurt. This was the deficit drive behind his relationship treadmill. Each time a relationship reached the point where a long-term commitment was considered, his feelings would shut down (an automatic, self-protective somatic affect) and he would break off the relationship. This kept him safe from any possible hurt that might occur if a long-term partner suddenly left him.

Thus, while the conscious reason given for breaking off each relationship was perfectly true at a surface level, the deeper, unconscious deficit motivation was the security need to avoid the possibility of deep hurt.

Having identified his deficit motivation John was eventually able to free himself from the stored childhood emotions that drove the treadmill. He was then able to commit to a long-term relationship.

In John's case, his deficit driven treadmill caused what he saw as a failure — failure to maintain a long-term relationship. Thus, we refer to this as a failure treadmill.

SUCCESS TREADMILLS

The success treadmills are the cognitive, emotional and behavioural patterns that result from our natural strengths. These natural strengths are what produce our personal and professional successes. However, what distinguishes success treadmills from other types of success is that — as the word treadmill implies — all the successful activity isn't taking us anywhere. Our successes don't lead to any deep or lasting satisfaction or fulfilment.

Success treadmills, like failure treadmills, may have their origins in a need not being appropriately met during one or more of our first four developmental stages. When we cannot get these needs met at the appropriate time and in the appropriate way two results usually follow:
- We experience feelings of distress (fear, anger, hurt, etc) and feelings of powerlessness
- We develop a negative self-image in the area of life where failure has occurred

These negative feelings or beliefs can have many forms — lack of confidence, self-doubt, feeling that there is something wrong with us, or that there is something lacking in us. In order to resist these distressful feelings of powerlessness and negative self-image, we may develop compensation responses. These compensation responses can occur in two ways:
- we develop new traits or skills in other areas of life where we can get successful results
  and/or
- at a later stage in life, when we have more internal or external resources, we may intensively develop traits or skills in the area of life where the original failure occurred

COLIN'S STORY

Colin was a very successful co-founder of a software company. He had a genius for software programming and his role was as the leader of the software programming team. He was a shy and withdrawn person, and found it difficult to form close relationships of any kind.

Colin was a single child in a family where the parents were both unemotional. His mother was shy and withdrawn and his father was at work most of the time. Thus, Colin grew up without the emotional contact that is the basis for learning social skills that are needed to build friendships and to become involved in group activities.

During his early and late childhood he never felt he 'belonged' anywhere and he had no close friends. Then he discovered he had a natural talent with computers. He won a university scholarship to study computer science before working as a software engineer for about five years and finally co-founding his own company.

Colin was a classic case of the failure to have a need met in one area of life — the belongingness/relationship need — leading to the compensation response of discovering and developing his traits and skills in another area of life, for which he had a natural talent, leading to great success. All of this new, intense and successful activity feels good in and of itself, and leads to a surface level self-esteem.

This successful activity was a compensation response which served the psychological purpose of resisting and covering up the feelings of sadness and loneliness he had felt in his childhood. However, this kept those childhood feelings alive, locked in his subconscious, still needing to be met in their original form. The subconscious pressure of this need caused him to become a workaholic. Thus, despite his success, he felt increasingly less fulfilled and unhappy. He was on a classic success treadmill.

Fortunately for Colin, on a personal development workshop he was able to make contact with and release the childhood sadness and loneliness that had been covered up by the intense mental activity of his success treadmill. After this awakening, he started to make some very important changes in his life, placing much more emphasis on relationships rather than his computer. He began to get to know individuals in his team as people (their personal interests, family life, etc), which was an entirely new experience for him. He actually became more successful, but now with the addition of his new found friendships, began to enjoy and find a deep satisfaction in those successes.

MY STORY

During my childhood and adolescence I became a rebel in response to my father's severe authoritarian parenting. Part of this rebellion was not studying or paying attention in school. As a result, I got very poor grades and developed the belief that I wasn't very smart.

When I eventually turned my life around and entered university I performed really well. However, I found that I was always very hard on myself in terms of my expectations. I felt that anything less than an 'A' was a failure. The problem was, that in spite of the fact that I got mostly A's, I still lacked any real intellectual self-confidence.

Regardless of my high level of performance, nothing ever proved to me that I was really smart. I was definitely on an intellectual success treadmill.

The deficit motivation behind this was the feeling, emotionally programmed into me in my school years, that I wasn't very smart. This was a humiliating feeling and a violation of my self-esteem needs. The feeling was deeply programmed into my subconscious mind and no amount of intellectual success could remove it. Thus, none of my successes brought any deep or lasting satisfaction or fulfilment.

This deficit motivation driven success treadmill did not end until I learned how to meditate. Eventually, after about 18 months of meditating about half an hour each day, I noticed that I had lost the underlying feeling that was driving my success treadmill. I began to feel a natural, relaxed, intellectual self-confidence, which added to a general sense of well-being. While I still had all the intellectual skills I had learned while on the treadmill, I was no longer driven by it.

POSITIVE EXPERIENCES AND DEFICIT DRIVEN SUCCESS TREADMILLS

While some people's success treadmills are shaped in response to negative and traumatic childhoods, many people with deficit driven success treadmills in fact had positive childhoods. There are usually two possible explanations for the deficit drive behind the treadmill:

- It can be due to the way a child came to **perceive** certain events rather than the events themselves
- It can result from a feeling of not wanting to let down or disappoint the **perceived expectations of others** — especially where they have treated us with love, respect and provided us with opportunity.

SARAH'S STORY

Sarah was an attractive middle aged woman who had a lifetime of major achievements. She was always at the top of her class. She also excelled at sport and almost everything she undertook. After university she entered corporate life, where she moved up the ladder rapidly. She was also liked and respected by her peers and her boss.

Yet Sarah felt a strong feeling of discontent, at times bordering on depression, and she could not understand why. She also felt she was not the kind of person whom someone could love. She had had two serious relationships as an adult but each time her partner had left her. She had never married. She knew she was physically attractive, but she felt there was something lacking within her that made her unlovable.

The source of Sarah's problems was a certain type of experience in her childhood. When we are children perhaps our greatest single need is to be unconditionally loved. However, children sometimes notice that parents can show more affection and appreciation for them when they are achieving.

It is quite common, over time, that the connection between greater affection or attention and successful performance is interpreted by the child as greater love. Thus, they begin to perceive the love as contingent on performance and achievement. Although they may be unconditionally loved (Sarah was), children can develop a sense that they are not. This can drive them to strive harder and harder for greater accomplishment.

However, the appreciation and attention resulting from the achievement cannot by its very nature meet the need to be unconditionally loved. The internal psychological hole remains, resulting in an increasingly compulsive striving for success. The individual is caught in a vicious cycle. They are on a success treadmill with lots of activity and success but no deep feelings of satisfaction and fulfilment resulting from the success.

Sarah's parents showed her a lot of affectionate acknowledgment at each of her successes and were also very encouraging, supportive and helpful. They were always ready to help with homework, to drive her to games and watch her train. In her mind they could not have been more supportive.

The result of this was that she developed strong feelings of not wanting to ever let them down. In her child's mind, all the encouragement and support signalled that her parents had high expectations of her. She felt she had to continue to improve and perform in order to not fail in meeting those perceived expectations. This was a second deficit drive to strive for greater and greater accomplishment.

Sarah was a compulsive achiever and workaholic. Yet, no matter how much she achieved, she experienced an increasing sense of discontent, bordering on depression.

The yearning hole of **perceived** unmet unconditional love from childhood could not be filled by the huge amount of recognition she received for her achievements. Though she was not consciously aware of it, it was that perceived unmet need that grew into discontent and depression. This unconsciously driven emotional programming also meant that she did not love herself.

Sarah was not conscious of why she was so driven, why her success brought her only discontent, and why she felt unlovable. A very important part of her path of self-transformation was coming to both consciously understand and experience the unconscious deficit motivation that produced her behaviour and emotional patterns. One of the reasons we deny, suppress or even repress our deficit motives is that they so commonly are based on fear.

Part of Sarah's healing process was to access and understand what empowered her deficit motivated fear. She transformed her 'inner world' so it became driven by conscious, positive emotions rather than fear, and this resulted in a sense of well-being. She was then able to pace herself and as she put it, 'take time to smell the flowers'. She began to experience the sense of satisfaction that had previously eluded her and she felt much better about herself. She no longer had the feeling that something was lacking in her that made her unlovable. She found she was able to accept and even love herself just as she was.

FEAR AND DEFICIT MOTIVATION

All deficit motivation is to one degree or another based on fear:
- The fundamental underlying fear is that the specific unmet need (whether real or just perceived) will never be met. We will never be able to assuage the yearning or driving need.
- The corollary is an additional fear that the reason the need will never be met is because something is wrong with us: either some essential quality or trait is missing or we have some important negative trait or quality.
- The third kind of fear is based on one of the functions of the success treadmills. Many success treadmill activities are ways of resisting and psychologically covering up the distress and negative self-image that results from failed or aborted childhood/adolescent needs that remain emotionally programmed within us. These feelings live just below our

conscious surface level self-esteem. If at any point our strengths begin to fail us, the surface level self-esteem will crack and the old negative feelings will begin to rise. Thus, we must stay on the treadmill.
- Finally, there is a fourth kind of fear that if we stop pursuing our success treadmill activities we may hurt, disappoint or let down parents, family, other loved ones, or authority figures whose respect we have earned, and who have given us great support.

These fears are all drivers of deficit motivation and fear is a powerful, often negative, motivator.

SOCIETAL DEFICIT MOTIVATION

The third source of deficit motivation is the promise that achieving or having certain things will ultimately lead to lasting satisfaction and happiness. Once we come to believe this, and we start to pursue those achievements/things, we get onto the treadmill.

There are two causes that underlie this form of deficit motivation. These causes are so pervasive in our culture that most of us rarely think about them.

THE FIRST CAUSE
The things we have learned to value through our experiences during childhood and adolescence, and which were reinforced by our experiences as an adult, fall within the domain of Maslov's first four motivating needs — the survival, security, relationship/belongingness and self-esteems needs.

The underlying belief system (whether conscious or unconscious) is that doing things that are motivated by those four values should lead to fulfilment and satisfaction. You may have already achieved things such as:
- financial security
- good personal and professional relationships
- many personal and professional successes and achievements
- a sense of belonging

The belief is: *these are all the things that are really worth pursuing. If you just keep pursuing more and more of these activities and goals alone, then you will ultimately find the satisfaction and fulfilment you seek.*

It is true that these pursuits, based on Maslov's first four needs, lay the foundations for the satisfaction you seek. The difficulty here is that each of these needs are finite and can only take you through the first four levels of development. Once your survival, security, belongingness/relationship and self-esteem needs have been met where do you go, what do you do?

Therefore you are on a success treadmill because you are ready for the next stage of growth or self-renewal — whether or not you are conscious of it — and the needs and desires that motivated you previously simply cannot provide the level of satisfaction you seek. You have reached the desired end state for the adult socialised self.

However, there may still be some fear holding you in the treadmill pattern. This is simply the fear of the unknown and is usually accompanied by the fear of leaving your comfort zone.

Moving on to a new level of development means moving into psychologically uncharted territory. It means evolving a new identity: becoming a different self! The questions are:
- Who will I become?
- What will my life be like?
- How do I know this will all work for me?

THE SECOND CAUSE
The assumption is that at whatever our level of development, having an identity structure that rests on a finite, limited state of consciousness, could bring the ultimate satisfaction and fulfilment we seek.

This assumption is a little more complex to explain, but once explained, quite easy to understand. All of us, simply by being human, possess an underlying identity, a state of Being that predates the mental/emotional programming or conditioning which created our adult socialised self.

You can often see young, happy, well-loved and well-parented children in this state of Being. When they are, they live in the present, each moment is sufficient unto itself, each activity intrinsically enjoyable, and there is no yearning or longing for something else. This is precisely the state we have called 'mindfulness'. Of course young children are not in this state all of the time, but with much love and good parenting they can be in this state more often than not.

This state of Being or mindfulness is always there as a potential to be experienced, but the mental/emotional programming or conditioning that created our socialised self identity prevents us from being aware of it. When we are busy on our deficit driven treadmills it is extremely difficult, if not impossible, to experience that underlying state of Being.

This state of Being is our deepest underlying identity. There are a number of ways to cultivate contact with this identity. For example, the regular practice of meditation is one of the oldest and most powerful methods. However, any methodology for facilitating that contact involves a process of penetrating and releasing ourselves from the 'covering up' affect of our socialised self's mental/emotional programming.

In the philosophical system that underlies this book, the state of Being, our ultimate identity, is not a finite entity. It doesn't begin or end. It cannot be defined by any finite set of adjectives. There are no 'degrees' to which it exists. It is just there, whether experienced or not!

We can be more or less in touch with this state of Being — of mindfulness — at any given time. However, the underlying purpose of our existence is to gain deeper and more permanent access to, and experience of, this ultimate identity.

Here lies the true path to happiness: to deep and lasting satisfaction. No amount of finite accomplishments by our socialised self could ever bring the same level of satisfaction or fulfilment. The pathway to lasting happiness and satisfaction always involves pursuing those levels of consciousness that lie beyond the socialised self: the independent self, the transpersonal self and the unitive self — the three higher levels of adult development. As we begin to awaken and gradually realise the potentials for development at each of these levels, we become more deeply and more permanently in touch with our ultimate identity, providing ourselves with a greater capacity for mindfulness.

---

1   BP Hall, *Values Shift: A Guide to Personal and Organisational Transformation* (WIPF and Stock Publishers: Eugene, Oregon, 1994) p 27. A Maslov, The Psychology of Being (2nd edn), (D. van Norstrand Company: Cincinnati, Ohio, 1968), the whole of his book deals with the hierarchy of values, including D-cognition and B-cognition values.

PART 3

THE Q12 MAPPING SYSTEM

A PSYCHOLOGICAL PROFILING METHODOLOGY

CHAPTER SIX

THE Q12 MAPPING SYSTEM

THE purpose of the Q12 mapping system is to assist us in gaining an accurate and in-depth level of self-awareness. It is to assist us to see ourselves from an objective and mindful perspective: to see ourselves, our inner world of thoughts and feelings and the outer world of our behaviour, openly, accurately and without judgement.

Its second purpose is to assist us in gaining insight into people who are very different from ourselves. The Q12 system is designed to help us see how and why people different from ourselves think, feel and behave as they do, and why they see the world as they do. It is intended to do this objectively and without judgement.

At this point, it is important to distinguish between external observable behavioural patterns and our internal patterns of thinking and emotion. Other people recognise who we are as a personality by the external, observable behavioural patterns. But for us personally, the non-visible internal factors of thinking and feeling seem closer to the core of who we feel we are.

The relationship between the internal domain of thoughts and feelings and our external behaviour is a causal one. Our thoughts and emotions create our intentions, which in turn generate our behaviour. It is our inner world that motivates and shapes our external behaviour.

To better understand this we need to make a few distinctions within the inner realm of thoughts and feelings. Our inner world of thoughts and feelings is made up of many things: our needs, desires, hopes, fears, beliefs, values, attitudes and so forth. This list could go on to include many more internal, subjective experiences — yet this internal complexity has an underlying simplicity. Any of the numerous possible internal states or experiences are actually an expression of any one, or some combination of, three core dimensions: our emotions, our will and our thinking.

These three are the core dimensions of our inner subjective life. They are the core building blocks for our motives and intentions, our behaviour and ultimately, our identity.

In the process of growing up, from infancy through adolescence, these three core dimensions were gradually shaped by our experiences. We have called this shaping process a kind of internal 'programming' — using the metaphor of a computer. The result of this programming process is measured by the three maps that comprise the Q12 system.

EMOTIONS AND THE RELATIONSHIP MAP

Our emotions or feelings are the ultimate motivators. The emotional patterns that are programmed into us by our life experiences become the basis of the patterns of our relationships to other people or groups of people. It explains both **how** and **why** our patterns in relationships occur. In the Q12 system, this is conceptualised and measured by the relationship map.

OUR WILL AND THE ACTION MAP

We define the will as: **the active, directed, outcome oriented expression** of our emotions. Our will is that part of our psychology that is programmed to want or intend to achieve certain outcomes. It is what motivates us to achieve those outcomes. Equally it may motivate us to prevent certain outcomes, or to prevent something from happening.

Our will is largely shaped by the socialisation process, so the words 'intend', 'want' and 'should' all apply in the programming of the will. However, whatever it is we want, intend or feel we should do, the programming of our will is always the result of, and driven by, our emotional programming. This includes both what we instinctively feel we want to do or achieve and what we feel we should want to do or achieve.

Thus the patterns of our will are the underlying basis for the patterns of our actions. The will is the core, underlying basis for both how and why we undertake, try to undertake or intend to undertake our actions. Equally, it explains why we intend to achieve specific types of outcomes from those actions. In the Q12 system, this is conceptualised and measured by the action map.

OUR INTELLECT AND THE THINKING MAP

Finally, what are the manifestations of the programming of our thinking? Our style of thinking is programmed to provide the conceptual framework through which we can understand our world. We may be pragmatic or conceptual thinkers, we may be logical or intuitive thinkers, we may be visual or verbal thinkers, etc. Whatever our thinking style, our thinking patterns are programmed to create our (conscious) belief systems about ourselves, other people and our world. They create a certain type of mental interpretation of reality or 'world view' that is unique and specific to us. In the Q12 system, all of this is conceptualised and measured by the thinking map.

These three internal core dimensions are the drivers of our behavioural habits or patterns. By the time we are adults, we become so accustomed to, and identified with these internal and external behaviour patterns that we see them as traits or qualities that define who we are. At the adult socialised self stage, we call this collection of traits or qualities our 'character structure'.

WHY THE 'MAP' METAPHOR?

We use the concept of maps to describe our character structure because of the richness of the metaphor. Terms like 'home territory', 'comfort zone', 'explore new frontiers', 'plot a new course', 'current boundaries', 'shape of the terrain', 'scale', 'axis' and 'orientation' all flow freely and create imagery appropriate to learning. A map also allows us to locate ourselves relative to other people, to appreciate wider horizons of expression and to establish growth paths that will take us where we want to go.

WHAT DO THE MAPS LOOK LIKE AND HOW DO THEY WORK?

All three maps are represented by a square, bisected by a horizontal and vertical axis, resulting in four quadrants. Since there are three maps, each with four quadrants, this makes a total of 12 quadrants — hence the term 'Q12' to identify the instrument.

The following diagram shows the basic structure that applies to all three maps.

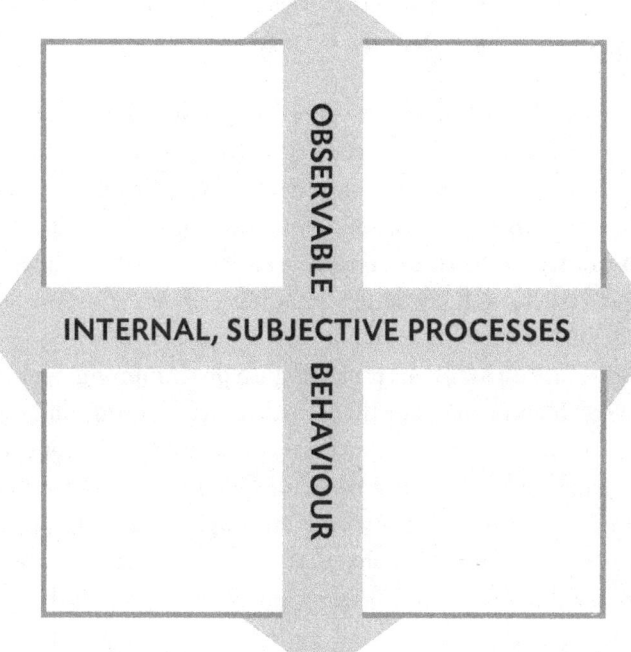

The horizontal axis in each map represents the element of our internal psychological makeup that underpins each of the three maps. For example, in the relationship map, the horizontal axis represents the degree to which the individual prefers to experience, and actually experiences, emotions in relating to others. This is based on the simple but profound fact that we tend to relate to others from somewhere on a continuum that can range from very strong to very little emotion. Thus, the horizontal axis in the relationships map looks like this:

High Emotional Charge   **Low Emotional Charge**

The Q12 relationship map is designed to measure where we fall on this continuum. People who score strongly on the left hand side of the horizontal axis prefer to experience an emotional connection with those to whom they relate. People who score strongly on the right hand side prefer to experience less emotional contact in their relationships. However, this does not mean that they never experience emotions in their relationships, just that in most of their relationships, most of the time, they are not emotional in the way they relate to others.

The above example is from the relationship map. However, the horizontal axis in each of the three maps always represents the psychological programming of our inner, subjective processes — our emotions in the relationship map, our will in the action map and our thinking processes in the thinking map.

By contrast, the vertical axis represents our observable behaviour, including our verbal and body language. It is based on the simple fact that our observable behaviour may or may not directly express what we do (or don't) feel, think or want. As part of our psychological programming, we have learned patterns of speech and behaviour that either directly express and reveal, or do not directly express or reveal, our internal, subjective state. Not expressing or revealing an inner, subjective state can range from simply not speaking about it through to consciously or unconsciously trying to hide or disguise it.

Yet even if our observable behaviour does not directly express and reveal what we are thinking or feeling, there are still subtle cues in body language, posture and subtle aspects of facial expression or voice qualities that do reveal our inner state to those trained to recognise such cues. Thus, speech and behaviour (including body language) which does not directly express and reveal our inner, subjective state does in fact indirectly express that state.

THE RELATIONSHIP MAP

As stated earlier, the horizontal axis represents a continuum from those who experience more emotion to those who experience less emotion when relating to others, while the **vertical axis represents the degree to which each individual directly or indirectly expresses their high or low level emotional state in their relationships with others.** If you are someone who scores high in 'direct expression', your emotional or unemotional state in relationships will be directly observable and obvious to others by your behaviour. Conversely, if you are someone who scores high in 'indirect expression' your observable behaviour will not easily disclose that you are experiencing either more or less emotion in your relationships.

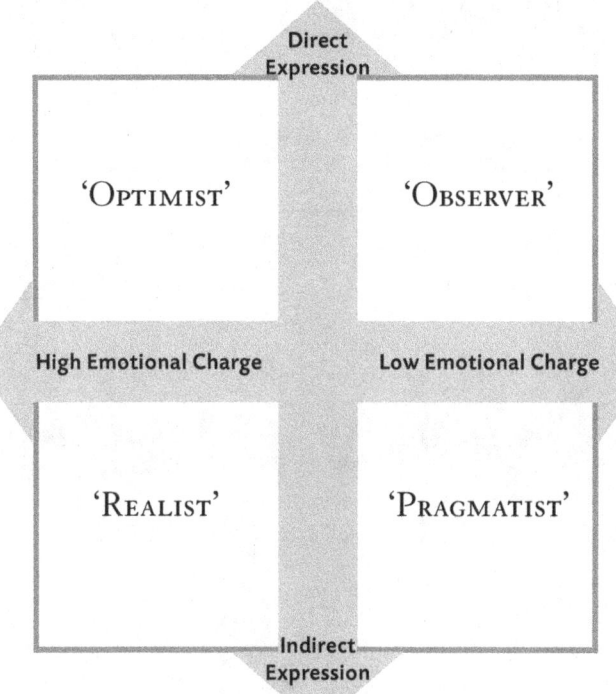

The following are the four basic possibilities that represent each quadrant within the relationship map:
- The **Optimist** quadrant will define the character traits found in people who are usually more emotional in their relationships and who often directly express their feelings to others.
- The **Realist** quadrant will define the character traits found in people who are usually more emotional in their relationships but often do not directly express or reveal their feelings to others (indirect expression).
- The **Observer** quadrant will define the characteristics found in people who are usually less emotional in their relationships and who directly express or reveal this in their relationship behaviour with others.
- The **Pragmatist** quadrant will define the character traits found in people who are usually less emotional in their relationships but whose relationship behaviour does not directly express or reveal this to others.

See Chapter 7 for further discussion of the relationship map.

THE ACTION MAP

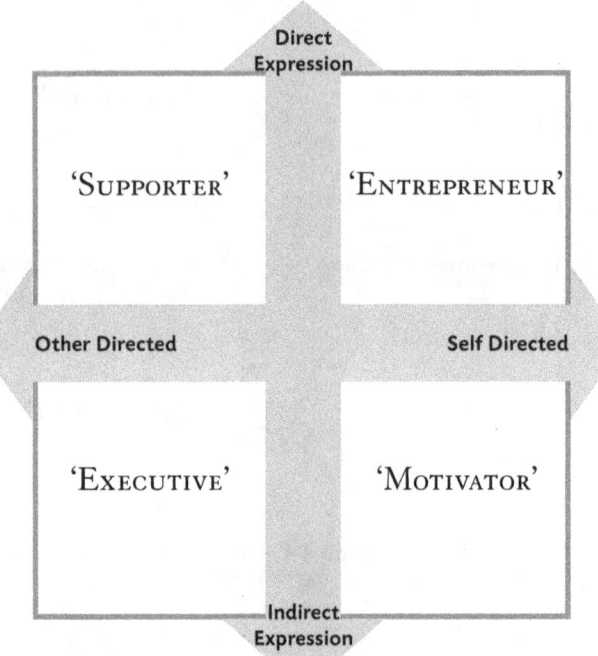

In the action map, the horizontal axis represents the degree to which we are self- or other-directed in undertaking action. Our will is programmed to be more or less self- or other-directed. More 'self-directed' people are those who tend to look within themselves for signals about what values they should embrace and what goals they should pursue in undertaking action. Those who are more 'other-directed' tend to look more to others or to their environment for signals about what values and goals to pursue in undertaking action.

The vertical axis represents the degree to which we directly or indirectly express our self- or other-directedness. If someone scores high in 'direct expression', their self- or other-directedness will be directly expressed in their behaviour and obvious to others. Conversely, if they score high in 'indirect expression', their observable behaviour will not directly express or reveal their self- or other-directedness.

The following are the four basic possibilities that represent each quadrant within the action map:

- The **Supporter** quadrant will define the character traits found in people

who are 'other-directed' and who directly express or reveal this in their daily behaviour.
- The **Executive** quadrant will define the character traits found in people who are 'other-directed' but whose daily behaviour does not directly express or reveal this.
- The **Entrepreneur** quadrant will define the character traits found in people who are 'self-directed' and whose daily behaviour directly expresses or reveals this.
- The **Motivator** quadrant will define the character traits found in people who are 'self-directed' but whose daily behaviour does not directly express or reveal this.

See Chapter 8 for further discussion of the action map.

THE THINKING MAP

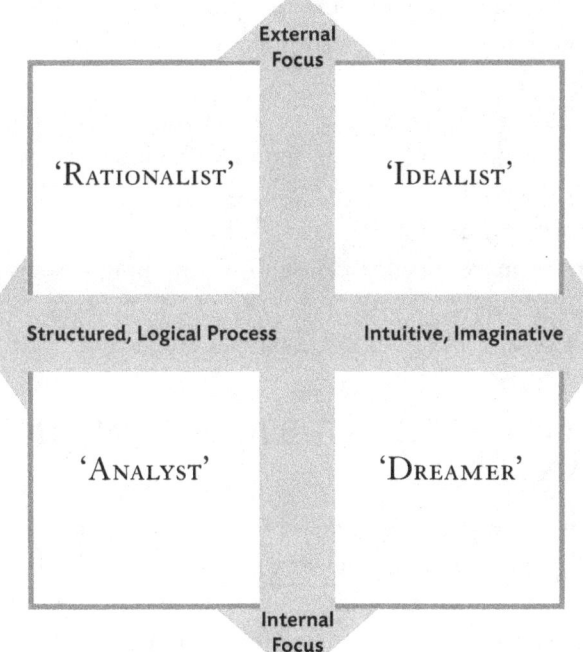

In the thinking map, the horizontal axis represents the degree to which we are more structured and logical versus more intuitive and imaginative in the way that we think. Most of us tend to employ a thinking style that is either more structured/logical or more intuitive/imaginative, though some employ both depending on different circumstances.

The vertical axis focuses on behaviour, but is a variation of the direct versus indirect expression found in the relationship and action maps. It represents the degree to which we are either externally or internally focused during the thinking process. If someone scores high in external focus, they prefer a thinking process which involves much communication and interaction with others, and they tend to have an extroverted way of communicating their thoughts. If someone scores high in internal focus, they prefer to spend time thinking and reflecting alone within their own heads, and their way of communicating their thoughts tends to be more thoughtful and reflective.

The following are four basic possibilities that represent each quadrant within the thinking map:

- The **Rationalist** quadrant will define the character traits found in people who have a more structured, logical thinking process that is more externally focused.
- The **Analyst** quadrant will define the character traits found in people who have a more structured, logical thinking process that is more internally focused.
- The **Idealist** quadrant will define the character traits found in people who have a more imaginative, intuitive thinking process that is more externally focused.
- The **Dreamer** quadrant will define the character traits found in people who have a more imaginative, intuitive thinking process that is more internally focused.

See Chapter 9 for further discussion of the thinking map.

WHAT DOES IT MEAN TO BE STRONG IN A QUADRANT?

If you score as 'strong' or 'high' in a particular quadrant, this simply means that, in terms of the character traits that define that quadrant, you are in the upper 20% of the population. This implies that those character traits are an accurate description of you. If you are strong in a particular quadrant, you should recognise that most of the character traits that define the strengths of that quadrant apply to you. Also, depending on your experiences and your level of development, you may have more or less Achilles' heels or treadmills associated with each quadrant in which you are strong.

THE THREE STAGES OF THE Q12 MAPPING SYSTEM

In the next three chapters we will explore the Q12 mapping system in the following three stages:

Step 1: Identification of the particular quadrant of that map to be explored and brief description of the character traits of people who are strong in this quadrant.

Step 2: Personal stories of four individuals in leadership positions who are each strong in one of the four quadrants in each map. In each case the individual leader has reached their level of success because of the natural strengths associated with the quadrants they are strong in. But in each case they have reached an impasse because of an Achilles' heel or treadmill often associated with those quadrants. (In Part Four we will see how they broke through that impasse, overcoming the Achilles' heels or treadmills).

Step 3: Summary of the main traits or qualities people strong in this quadrant commonly demonstrate:
- A list of the **natural strengths** that people strong in this quadrant usually have
- A list of the possible **Achilles' heels** that people strong in this quadrant may have
- A description of the typical mental, emotional and behavioural **treadmills** that people strong in this quadrant may be on
- A description of the **greatest fear** that people strong in that quadrant at the adult socialised self level often have

IMPORTANT NOTE TO THE READER
As you read through the list of each of a particular quadrant's natural strengths, you may wish to place a tick after each strength that applies to you, two ticks if it strongly applies to you. You may also want to place a tick after any Achilles' heels that apply to you. This will give you some idea of where you are located in the Q12 mapping system.

CHAPTER SEVEN

RELATIONSHIP MAP

THE RELATIONSHIP MAP has two axes; a horizontal axis that represents whether we are more or less emotional in the way we relate to others, and a vertical axis that represents whether or not we usually directly express or reveal our emotions to or around others. The horizontal axis represents all possible emotions — love, joy, happiness, fear, anger, sadness, etc.

As we have seen, our patterns of emotional responses were programmed into us beginning as early as the 5th month in the womb, and this programming continues throughout childhood and adolescence. Since these patterns or habits of emotional responses were learned through relationships with people, they remain throughout our life the underlying basis of our relationships, unless we make a conscious choice and effort to change them.

On the relationship map, every relationship territory has its own natural strengths and possible Achilles' heels, and its own fears or challenges to growth. The intent of the Q12 relationship map is threefold. Firstly, it is to provide a broad understanding of the relationship world map, including four basic patterns of relationships. Secondly, to provide insight into your home territory — how you came to claim it, what its natural strengths and possible Achilles' heels are and how you can master them. Thirdly, it is to provide a *Lonely Planet* guide to territories (quadrants) currently unfamiliar to you and give you access to them.

This means learning to see the world through the perspective of other people's home territory, to understand how they see 'reality', to gain insight into their natural strengths and possible Achilles' heels. It may also mean developing and using some of the natural strengths of other territories.

All of this can have a major impact in improving the quality of your relationships, and thus your life experience by:
- Gaining self-acceptance and the acceptance of others
- Building a balanced self-esteem, starting with self-respect
- Learning 'full heartedness' and appropriate expression of the full range of human emotions
- Building the capacity to give and receive love and support unconditionally
- Learning to meet our own emotional needs
- Learning to remain 'in relationship' with others through emotionally difficult experiences
- Learning to build vital, healthy relationship experiences with people very different from ourselves
- Experiencing a fuller, richer quality of day to day life

The two qualities that are essential for achieving self-mastery in relationships are: **empathy and respect.** Empathy is what gives us the ability to see the world from the perspective of other people's home territory, to understand how they see reality, to understand both what their natural strengths and vulnerabilities are. Through empathy we can come to perceive and treat others with respect. This is absolutely essential for building and maintaining good quality relationships, both personal and professional.

THE OPTIMIST — HIGH EMOTIONAL CHARGE DIRECTLY EXPRESSED

The Optimist is someone who is usually more emotional in their relationships and often directly expresses their feeling to others. Their credo, or the statement which sums up their world view, is *'Where there is life there is hope'*.

People strong in the Optimist quadrant usually appear **warm, open, friendly, lively and outgoing**.

The Optimist has a strong drive and talent for making meaningful emotional connections with others as part of their daily life experience. They are the master of personal involvement; caring, nurturing, spontaneous and fun to be around. The Optimist expresses emotions more freely than any other style, and what they are feeling in the moment is usually obvious. Life is never dull around the Optimist.

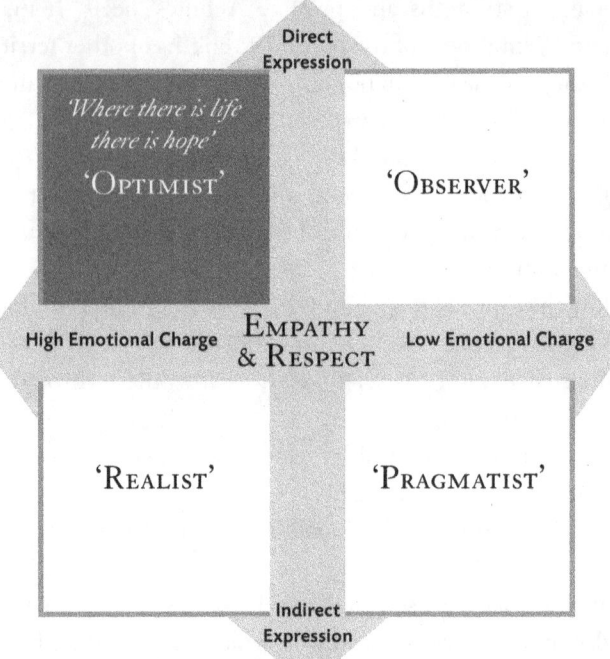

Many sales people, actors, politicians or anyone whose career involves much mixing with people, often have high optimistic characteristics. Optimists have very lively, engaging, outgoing personalities. Their outgoing nature tends to allow them to make friends easily and to mix in anywhere; because of their warmth and optimism, people find them positive, friendly, welcoming and easy to be around. They are usually among the first to introduce themselves to new people and to offer a warm welcome.

Optimists tend to be very trusting of other people. This trust can sometimes be offered too early, before they really know the person. This can easily lead them to be hurt or disappointed at a later stage. Thus, Optimists often have a fear of rejection. Yet after experiencing hurt or disappointment, they will usually rebound into a hopeful, optimistic attitude that next time it will turn out better.

Optimists tend to view both people and situations optimistically. No matter what the current difficulties with a person or situation, they tend to intrinsically believe that all will turn out for the best. In a workplace, this quality in Optimists can help raise the morale of those around them. But people who see themselves as more realistic or pragmatic, sometimes find this quality in Optimists annoying.

Optimists often have an instinctive feeling that someone or something external to them holds the key to their inner fulfilment. The feeling is often that some change in their environment will do the trick. For example, when I have my next relationship, job, boss, life situation, etc — then I will be fulfilled. Or when I retain my current partner, job, boss, life situation and THEY change so that they meet my needs — then I will be fulfilled. This can make Optimists vulnerable to getting into emotionally dependent relationships.

TINA'S STORY

Tina was a warm, friendly outgoing person. She said she was happily married with two children. She loved her work as a GP and said she had more regular patients then she could handle. Her partners in the medical practice said this was because she was so warm and friendly and she showed such a genuine concern for each individual patient, regardless of the seriousness of their condition.

She appeared to be such a happy, healthy, optimistic person that it was easy to wonder what problems she had. However, it turned out that there were two reasons she felt the need to take a personal development course.

The first problem was professional. Tina's practice group employed 12 GPs and several nurses. With the leader of her practice group entering retirement, Tina had been offered the job. Although she had the full support of the other doctors, she had strong reservations about her ability to effectively fulfil the role.

The second problem was more personal. Tina loved her husband deeply, but she did not feel that the love was returned, despite the fact he constantly did little things for her. Every morning he would bring her a cup of tea while she was still in bed. He was skilled at woodworking and would constantly make things for her. He took her out every week to do something that she enjoyed: theatre, films, museums, dinners. In fact, he seemed devoted to her.

The problem was that it was difficult for him to show direct affection to her and equally difficult for him to accept her signs of affection. She hugged him a lot, gently reached out to stroke his face, constantly told him she loved him — and all of this seemed a little embarrassing to him. She felt emotionally rejected even though the things he did for her daily showed great devotion.

Tina had always had a passionate, romantic image of how her marriage would be. She dreamt for many years that her husband would change and become a much more directly affectionate person. In fact one of her reasons for coming on the course was to find out if there was something she could do to help him make that change. She felt if only this would happen she would be content, and while her husband's failure to provide that kind of affection made her at times feel disillusioned, she would always bounce back into a hopeful, optimistic state — again, and again and again!

TYPICAL OPTIMIST CHARACTER TRAITS
Natural Strengths:
- Open and friendly
- Mixes well with people in both social and work environments
- Expresses emotions easily
- Views people and situations optimistically
- Warm and empathetic
- Forms friendships and relationships easily
- Likes contacting people
- Lively, enthusiastic and fun to be with

Possible Achilles' Heels:
- Can be overly trusting of others
- Can be oversensitive and easily hurt
- Can be clingy or emotionally dependent
- Can react to people or situations in an overly emotional way
- Can be extravagant and overly dramatic
- Can easily get into co-dependent relationships

Typical Optimist Treadmills:
- To continually seek out the next relationship (or job, experience, situation) looking for emotional fulfilment; or
- To hope that their current partner (or job, experience, situation) will change, resulting in emotional fulfilment

Deepest Fear and Key to Freedom:
- Fear of rejection

THE REALIST — HIGH EMOTIONAL CHARGE INDIRECTLY EXPRESSED

The Realist is someone who **usually experiences an emotional connection** in their relationships but often **does not directly express** or reveal these feelings to others. Their credo, or the statement which sums up their world view, is *'Free lunches don't exist — there is always a price'*.

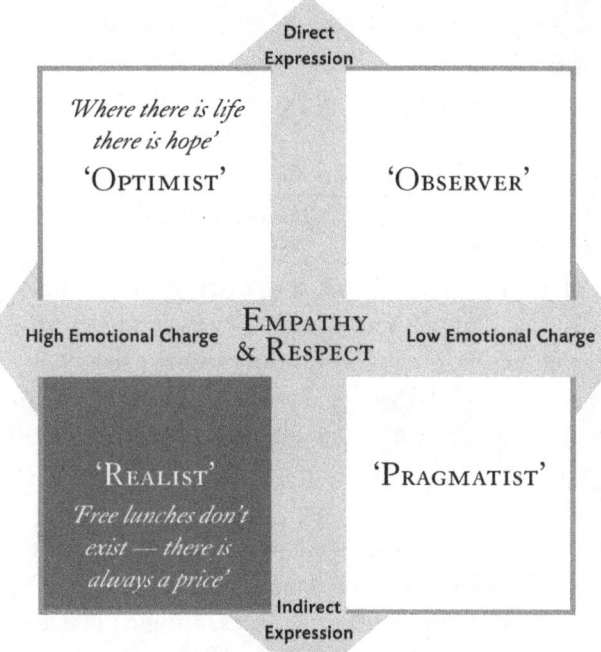

People strong in the Realist quadrant usually appear **strong, independent and self-sufficient.**

The strongest driver for the Realist is to be self-sufficient in all relationships. They are capable of feeling strong emotions, but they tend to contain rather than express them, because they feel expressing emotions might make them vulnerable. They very much want to retain an emotional connection with people or groups, but they want it to be under their conditions so that they can remain independent while connected. Thus, the Realist's emotional charge tends to be indirectly expressed, in contrast to the Optimist.

Realists tend to cultivate one-way relationships in which the Realist remains independent and self-sufficient while the other person depends upon the Realist. They often give the impression that they don't need anyone, yet display a strong need to be needed by others.

As a result, they are often good at and enjoy helping other people develop: mentoring, coaching or counselling. They often find themselves in indispensable positions where others must come to them for help. This way they get to feel needed without having to express their own needs.

Realists have a great need for security both for themselves and for others.

Because of this they are very good at identifying what is wrong (or potentially wrong) for themselves, other people, groups or organisations. This makes them excellent trouble shooters. They often become masters of working out strategies for avoiding things that could go wrong or correcting things that are wrong.

Thus, Realists make excellent auditors, sales managers, journalists, social critics, etc. Where Optimists tend to live in 'hope', Realists externalise those feelings and see them as 'goals'.

Realists often have a quick wit and a dry sense of humour. They are not easily tricked, and are extremely loyal once genuine trust is established. They show caring and nurturing by offering security in some form or other. However, the over-focus on what could go wrong or on the one mistake made, if not managed, can quickly kill off spontaneity and fun in a relationship.

JAMES' STORY

James ran a successful small business employing about 30 people which he had originally bought as a successful ongoing enterprise. He had gradually and carefully expanded the business over five years, bringing in a good income for himself and his family. It was very important to James to have his own business because it made him feel independent and self-sufficient.

James was married and had two children, seven and ten years of age. He was very devoted to his wife and children.

There were two issues that brought James to the personal development workshop. The first was a feeling of insecurity, in spite of continuing success. The second was an ongoing complaint, by his wife, that he was just not emotionally available to her or the children.

James was obsessed with security, both in his personal and business life. He constantly worried about the future, always trying to anticipate what could go wrong. He had a good analytical mind and spent endless hours keeping up with the literature in his industry so he could anticipate any important changes or directions.

He tended to pursue security in the same way at home. He had numerous insurance policies, trust funds set up for his wife and children, and he'd paid off the mortgage on his house early — all of these to ensure security for his wife and children.

James firmly believed that he was doing the right and responsible thing with his family and business. However, he still did not feel secure! He never told anyone about his insecurity because he prided himself on his strength and independence, and his ability to contain these feelings.

This self-containment and unwillingness to express these feelings was also evident in his personal relationships. He was always there for his family and while from time to time he stated ritual expressions of love, it was evident that it was indeed a ritual and not a genuine, direct expression of feeling. The irony was that he really did love his wife and children.

TYPICAL REALIST CHARACTER TRAITS
Natural Strengths:
- Identifying problems and possible pitfalls
- Developing realistic strategies for overcoming problems
- Translating hope into goals and setting realistic, practical goals
- Seeing through scams and inauthentic people
- Being incisive social critics and commentators who can offer realistic alternatives
- Dependable and desirous of being needed
- Slow to trust — but once trusting, very loyal
- Good at mentoring, coaching or counselling others
- Display a wry, witty sense of humour based on an awareness of human foibles
- Generally supportive and helpful

Possible Achilles' Heels:
- Can become overly critical
- Can become exclusively task and goal-focused, ignoring the personal human element
- Can become sceptical or even cynical about people's attitudes and intentions
- Can make people overly dependent on them
- If someone does start to become independent, can psychologically sabotage them so that they lose that independence
- Witty sense of humour can turn into biting irony or sarcasm
- Can be emotionally remote and unavailable
- Can find it difficult to accept support from others as this makes them feel dependent and not self-sufficient

Typical Realist Treadmill:
- To constantly feel a need to be connected to others and yet self-sufficient through cultivating 'one-way' relationships

Deepest Fear and Key to Freedom:
- Being emotionally vulnerable and dependent on anyone or anything

THE OBSERVER — LOW EMOTIONAL CHARGE DIRECTLY EXPRESSED

The Observer is someone who is usually less emotional in their relationships and who directly expresses or reveals this in their relationship behaviour with others. Their credo, or the statement which sums up their world view, is *'Peace is important above all else'*.

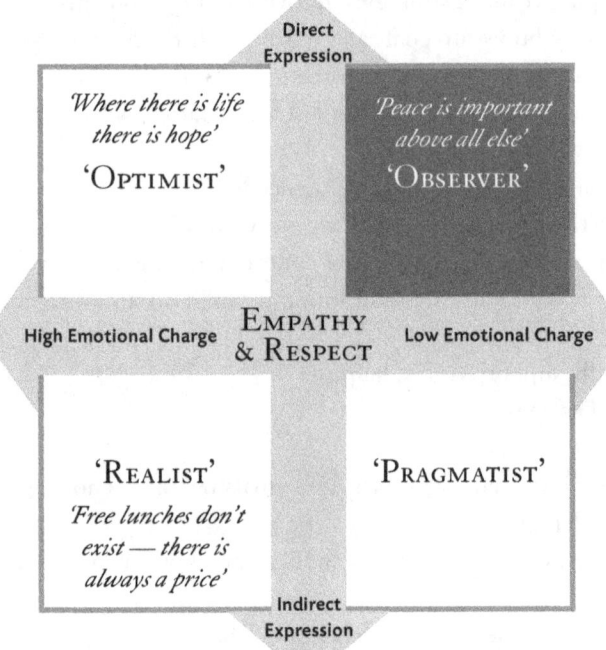

People strong in the Observer quadrant usually appear **peaceful, unobtrusive, quiet, unthreatening and thoughtful**.

Observers have very sensitive emotional wiring and, above all, value peace in any relationship. They intensely dislike conflict in any individual relationship or group. They will usually withdraw, walk away from or just avoid any potential or actual conflict or emotional situation. If they get caught in any relationship or group where conflict or strong emotions arise, they instinctively dissociate from the emotion and withdraw into a quiet, safe, peaceful place within themselves.

Observers have a pattern of minimising their self-expression and contact with others, preferring to operate outside of a group. They usually have very few close personal relationships and prefer those relationships to involve a minimum of emotional exchanges. In one-on-one exchanges, they often prefer discussions about intellectual, artistic or very pragmatic subjects.

Thus, Observers generally have a low emotional charge and this is obvious to those around them.

Observers seek and adapt well to solitary jobs and lifestyles. They can be writers, artists, or craftspeople — anything that can be done alone and that requires attention to detail. When they are part of a team they will often have a job that does not require much interaction with others (eg software programmer, librarian, technician).

Because they are not emotionally involved, they can be very fair and objective observers of group dynamics, a quality that can be of great benefit to a group if they are encouraged to speak. However, if they sense any resistance to what they might say, or any conflict, they will not speak.

Observers often have a very rich internal life. They can spend endless hours listening to music, reading and thinking about a subject, and they often have a vast reservoir of knowledge. Their thinking can vary from very logical to highly creative.

TIM'S STORY

When I first met Tim on our workshop, he was very quiet and self-contained. In his personal life he preferred to be alone most of the time, although he claimed that solitude brought him a kind of 'flat', empty peacefulness. He had a great interest in literature and music, was well read and had a huge music collection. He said that the only time he really lost that 'flatness' or emptiness and experienced emotions was when listening to music, or reading a fine novel. He had a few friends who were academics with whom he spent time having intellectual discussions.

Tim had never married nor had a girlfriend for any length of time. His periodic relationships only lasted three to six months. When women left him they always gave the same reasons: they didn't feel loved by him or felt little or no emotional connection with him. They always said he was gentle, kind and a really good person, but they had no idea what he was feeling. He said each time a girlfriend would leave him, he felt some sadness but also relief — for the emotional demands of any relationship just seemed too great.

Tim had a deep aversion to conflict of any kind. Thus, he avoided being around individuals or groups where conflict of any kind might occur. He said there were times when he knew he should stand up for himself, or disagree with someone, but he almost never did. The fear that this would result in confrontation and conflict was too great.

Professionally, Tim had a PHD in structural engineering and worked for a large building company. Although he was happiest when he could work mostly alone, he often had to work in project teams. This required communication with other team members, but as long as it stayed professional, not personal, he was fine.

Tim sought personal development for two reasons: he had been promoted to a senior management position and felt unprepared for the responsibility, and he was beginning to feel isolated and depressed. He was beginning to feel that there was something wrong with him and he was starting to feel a desperate need to escape this isolation.

TYPICAL OBSERVER CHARACTER TRAITS
Natural Strengths:
The strengths of the Observer derive from their emotionally uninvolved state.
- Can observe and be very insightful and objective about other people's strengths, motives and weaknesses
- Can develop artistic skills, particularly if they can work alone or with minimal interaction with others
- Are often good at working at solitary intellectual tasks for long periods of time —computer programming, scientific or scholarly pursuits, etc
- Often see solutions in problem solving activities that others, who have more at stake emotionally, cannot see (though they usually won't pursue any idea aggressively)
- Easy to be around as long as you don't want emotional contact with them
- Virtually never cause interpersonal clashes because of the fear of confrontation
- Generally very fair-minded in dealing with and making judgements about controversial people or subjects

Possible Achilles' Heels:
- Fearing confrontation they may not speak up about their unusually objective insights
- Being self-contained, they often won't communicate enough with others — which can cause frustration for others

- Taking far too long on a task because their deeply introverted focus causes them to lose track of time
- Difficulty forming or maintaining friendships at work or in personal life
- Not usually being good at tasks that are 'people-focused'

Typical Observer Treadmill:
- To establish and maintain a life free from any emotional involvement with individuals or groups; to avoid all forms of potential emotional hurt or confrontation

Deepest Fear and Key to Freedom:
- Experiencing strong emotions – emotional overwhelm.

THE PRAGMATIST — LOW EMOTIONAL CHARGE INDIRECTLY EXPRESSED

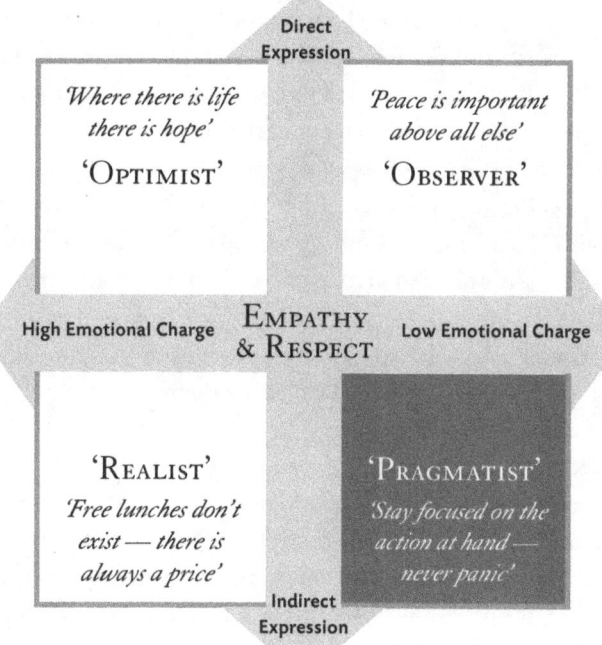

The Pragmatist is someone who is usually **less emotional** in their relationships but whose relationship behaviour **does not directly express** or reveal this to others. Their credo, or the statement which sums up their world view, is *'Stay focused on the action at hand — never panic'*.

People strong in the Pragmatist quadrant usually appear **cool, highly-**

focused, practical and action-orientated.

For Pragmatists, relationships are mainly activity based-rather than involving any emotional connection or exchanges. Pragmatists have the ability to transform any actual or potential emotional energy into action-focused mental and physical energy, and then undertake intense action. By doing this they ensure that they are not affected by their own or other's emotions.

Surgeons, emergency workers, etc, are often strong in this territory. Pragmatists tend to be drawn to careers or professions that require undertaking major challenges or risks that require a cool head, intense focus, and the application of high levels of skill.

Like the Observer, the Pragmatist strives to avoid any potential or actual emotional situations. However, in contrast to the Observer their way of overriding the emotion is by taking action which gives the appearance of involvement while being free of emotional influence. In fact, the more stressful the situation, the cooler and more focused the Pragmatist becomes.

Pragmatists tend to become leaders who take charge, or loners who 'do their own thing'. But even when leading or working within a team, all their relationships are activity-based. In fact, most relationships for Pragmatists tend to be activity-based rather than social or personal.

Friends for Pragmatists are people you do things with, not people you sit around with socialising or sharing personal ideas or feelings. They tend to seek out other action-orientated types and try to avoid conversations that might be either frivolous or personal. Spontaneity, passion or just being 'in a relationship' for its own sake, are all mysteries to the Pragmatist and a source of frustration to those who want to be close to them.

MIKE'S STORY

Mike was head of a large division of a financial services company. Mike was a very focused, hard working and self-disciplined person. In his interactions with people at work he displayed no emotion — except from time to time impatience or anger — which only showed up when he communicated to people about workplace related subjects. Other than the fact that he was divorced and had two children who were in the custody of his wife, most people knew nothing about his personal life.

Mike was well-known for his amazing levels of both mental and physical energy which sustained the long hours he worked. His powers of focus and concentration on the goals and tasks at hand were legendary.

As a division head, he had to run a number of meetings. He was very good at keeping all participants focused on the agenda topics and not allowing off agenda issues to intervene.

He was very cool under pressure and those around him felt that he both enjoyed and thrived in pressured situations. He had to interact and communicate extensively with others in project teams under tight time pressure where the financial stakes of success or failure were very great, but he never seemed to lose his cool in these communications or interactions.

Mike rarely socialised in the workplace and when he did attend the odd office party he would only talk about workplace subjects. He never gossiped and discouraged gossiping in others.

Mike was admired for a number of these traits by those around him. However there were two issues that bothered others. Firstly, people felt that he was so task-focused and impersonal, that they didn't really know who he was. They felt no personal connection to him at all.

The second issue that bothered people was that Mike didn't seem to be aware that an emotional domain existed in human life. He seemed either to have no awareness of his own or other people's emotional needs and he seemed to be unaware of the emotional consequences this had for those around him.

The people around him did not feel that they were really appreciated and valued as people. They also felt they could never show any emotion or spontaneity, fearing they might lose his respect.

TYPICAL PRAGMATIST CHARACTER TRAITS
Natural Strengths:
- High level of mental and physical energy and endurance
- Demonstrate undivided, full attention to the task at hand
- Remain cool, calm and collected in tense, difficult or challenging situations
- Invariably develop and maintain high levels of professional skills and also high levels of skill in action-oriented recreational activities
- Have a strong work ethic and are very task-focused
- Take full responsibility for any project, task or activity
- They do not make excuses for failure, instead, they re-focus their full mental and physical energy on the next task at hand
- They can work on their own for long periods of time
- Can be very competitive

Possible Achilles' Heels:
- Can appear to others to be cool, aloof or uncaring
- Find it difficult or impossible to communicate about personal or emotional things
- Often become workaholics
- May seem remote and unreachable
- Can be incapable of spontaneity and playfulness
- Do not feel comfortable socialising
- If forced to socialise, can only communicate about tasks or activity-oriented subjects, never personal things
- Often not aware of how emotional issues affect the people around them, or how they affect people

Typical Pragmatist Treadmill:
- Intense, focused, emotionally uninvolved, practical action (the more focused and intense the action, the easier it is to keep the emotions under control).

Deepest Fear and Key to Freedom:
- Having their own or other's emotions out of control.

CHAPTER EIGHT

ACTION MAP

THE ACTION MAP dynamics are based on the development of the will. The will shapes our behaviour because it is motivates us to do things which achieve specific ends, it is: *'the active, directed, outcome-oriented expression of feeling or emotions'*.

The fundamental distinction between 'self-directed' and 'other-directed' denotes the reference point from which the motivation and action style are expressed. For self-directed people, the ultimate reference point for their values, beliefs, ideas, goals, etc is within themselves. For other-directed people, the reference point from which their motivation originates and is experienced, lies outside of themselves. They are programmed to directly serve other's needs, desires, beliefs, values, ideals, ideas, goals etc.

As self-directed people evolve through to the socialised-self stage, they build traits and skill sets that empower them to get others to respond to beliefs, values, ideals, ideas, goals that are ultimately sourced from within themselves. They come to experience their value as equated with their ability to get other people to support and serve their broad values or objectives. However, this does not mean there is something intrinsically selfish or self-centred about self-directed people. Their values and objectives can often be idealistic and inclusive.

As other-directed people evolve through to the socialised-self stage, they build personal traits and skill sets that empower them to respond effectively to an external authority. They come to see their value as equated with their ability to effectively serve other people's, a team's or an organisation's needs or goals.

The childhood and adolescent formative experiences that programme our will usually result in our occupying large territories in one or two of the action quadrants in the Q12 system, giving us the qualities and traits of a distinctive action style. The larger the territory we occupy in any one quadrant, the more powerful these qualities or traits will be. This can result in a greater degree of success in areas where our style is appropriate, but it also provides greater challenges in mastering our Achilles' heels and in working well with people who have action styles very different from our own.

The Q12 action map can be used for three purposes. Firstly, to provide objective insight into our own action style, with both its natural strengths, Achilles' heels or treadmills. Secondly, it can provide the methodology required to master these Achilles' heels or treadmills. And thirdly, it can empower us to see 'reality' from the perspective of other territories and provide a pathway for developing alternative traits and skills.

The aim here is not to become the master of every territory, but to break the chains that bind us to a limiting pattern of both perspectives and behaviour. This can result in our being far more adaptable, being able to respond differently and more effectively in various situations, and being able to work more effectively with people whose action styles are very different from our own.

Thus we can expand the range of our ability to respond and gain the self-mastery trait of **responsibility**.

THE SUPPORTER — OTHER-DIRECTED DIRECTLY EXPRESSED

The Supporter is someone who is 'other-directed' in their actions and who directly expresses or reveals this in their daily behaviour. Their credo, or the statement which sums up their world view, is *'Let me help you'*.

People strong in the Supporter quadrant usually appear **reliable, accommodating, loyal, task-focused and service-oriented.**

The Supporters' greatest quality lies in their service to others and in their sense of duty. They are most at home when providing a direct service. In doing so, they usually demonstrate the qualities of patience, steadiness and reliability. They are other-directed in that they focus on following the directions or meeting the needs of others. Yet they can get very attached to a specific way of doing something that can make them inflexible.

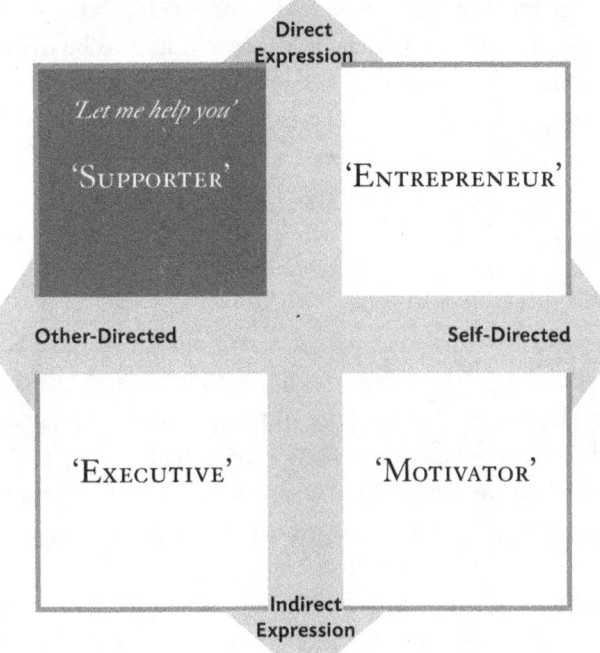

Supporters are classic team players. They are usually very co-operative and supportive. They are very dedicated to achieving the task at hand and willing to carry the load. They bring a sense of harmony to the team.

Supporters usually have a strong task- or people-focus. They tend to accept others' authority and to be very loyal to authority figures and team mates. As part of their sense of obligation to duty, Supporters often have a strong sense of fairness and justice.

Supporters tend to put everyone else's needs first. Because of this, they can develop an underlying resentment, of which they may or may not be conscious.

Supporters often have a strong desire to help others feel happy, loved, valued and cared for. Because of this, many Supporters enter the helping service professions such as nursing, teaching, counselling and social work, where they can help people directly.

TIM'S STORY

As you will recall, Tim was an Observer in his relationship map. He was quiet, self-contained and found it difficult to develop emotional attachments. Tim valued peace above emotional attachments and the pain they could cause. Thus he spent much of his time alone. Tim had come seeking personal development for two reasons. The first was that he was beginning to be depressed by his feelings of personal isolation; the second was that he had recently been promoted to a senior management position and felt completely out of his depth.

Tim's work within the building company was structural design work, which he found endlessly interesting. He was very task-focused and was always careful in his design work. Tim had a creative flair and sometimes he disagreed with a design approach, but he never attempted to argue his case because of his fear of confrontation.

Tim had usually worked as part of a design team and had been a project team leader for several years. He was a good leader and always treated his team mates with respect. He was quiet and only spoke when necessary. All his communication was task-focused and never personal.

Tim had a strong sense of fairness and social justice. It disturbed him greatly when he thought someone was treated badly or unfairly, but he rarely spoke up.

The members of his design teams were technically competent and hard working. Thus, the only meetings he had to lead focused on delegating the various technical tasks for any given project, co-ordinating these tasks and ensuring that his team members got whatever technical support was needed. This did not take a great deal of time and Tim was still able to spend most his day working alone in his office or in the design laboratory.

Tim demonstrated many of the characteristics of a classic Q12 action map Supporter profile, combined with the relationship map Observer profile. Both of these character traits were sufficient to lead to success in his current position as a project team leader. However, they were not when the time came for Tim to step up into a higher leadership position. When he was promoted to a senior leadership position, he hit an impasse.

TYPICAL SUPPORTER CHARACTER TRAITS
Natural Strengths:
Supporters usually have the following natural strengths:
- They can be very patient, steady, reliable and dutiful
- They are usually very co-operative
- They readily accept others' authority and are usually very loyal
- They are usually good team players
- They usually have a strong task or people focus
- They will usually work within the guidelines or rules

- They tend to create stable, harmonious workplace environments
- They are very service-oriented
- They have a strong sense of social justice and fairness

Possible Achilles' Heels:
- They tend to put everyone else's needs first
- They often feel an underlying resentment (because of the above) but feel it would not be right or safe to express this
- They can find it difficult to place pressure on others
- They often find it difficult to work in environments where the authority, rules or norms are not clearly stated
- They often find it difficult to take personal initiatives unless based on someone else's authority or needs
- They find it difficult to say 'No!'
- They hate conflict and will often not speak up because of fear of confrontation
- Their sense of justice can make them too easily hurt or resentful about perceived (or actual) unfairness
- They tend to dislike major or dramatic change initiatives
- Their attachment to routine and authority can hold back their personal creativity

Typical Supporter Treadmill:
To continually seek the welfare and/or the approval of others by putting others' needs first, often at their own expense.

Deepest Fear and Key to Freedom:
Fear of the 'bad' consequences of letting others down or doing something 'wrong'

THE EXECUTIVE — OTHER-DIRECTED INDIRECTLY EXPRESSED

The Executive is someone who is 'other-directed' in their actions but whose daily behaviour does not directly express or reveal this. Their credo, or the statement which sums up their world view, is *'I can handle it — I will achieve this goal for you'*.

People strong in the Executive quadrant usually appear **strong, self-reliant, independent, very capable and/or very professional**.

Executives become successful through disciplined, independent, goal-focused actions. They are strong believers in self-reliance and hard work as keys to success. Executives dedicate themselves primarily to success as defined by an external source. For example, the source could be the requirements or codes of conduct of a particular profession; or it could be the goals or objectives of their team or of an organisation; or it could be achieving a specific outcome for a particular client. In this way executives are other-directed.

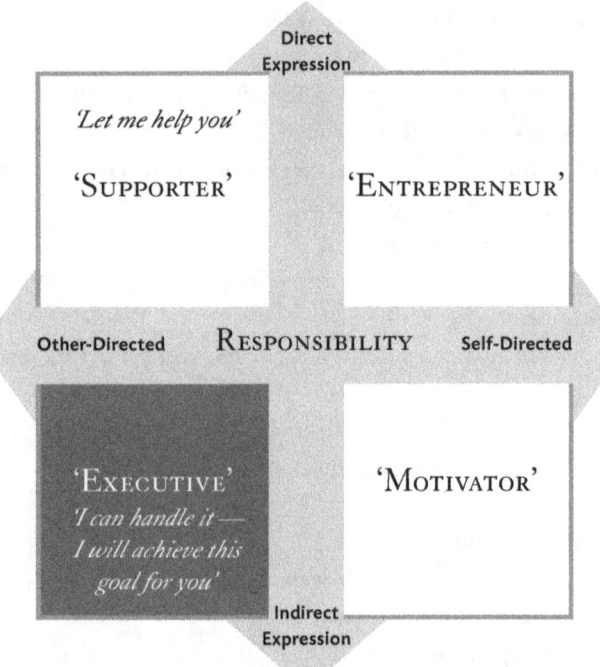

The Supporter, whose task focus is either to directly serve another person or work under someone's authority, directly demonstrates their other-directedness. By contrast, for Executives it is important to be fully independent and self-reliant. They are highly results-orientated, as exemplified by the independent professional who does what it takes to reach an agreed goal. The qualities of independence and self-reliance disguise their 'other-directedness' — so their other-directedness is indirectly expressed.

Executives usually have great endurance and are capable of working for long hours. They are very tenacious and not easily deflected from their pursuit of a goal or outcome. For these reasons they can easily become workaholics. However, this can also mean early promotion to middle and then senior management.

Executives like a systematic, structured, well-planned approach to activities and projects. They are very self-disciplined and are highly responsible and accountable in all that they do. They tend to work within the accepted norms of their profession or organisation.

Executives can be poor delegators, having a tendency to micro-manage or over-supervise. For this reason, they may jump in and do a 'hands on' takeover when a subordinate is struggling or failing. They can also drive a team to achieve goals at the expense of their people. With their strong goal/ task focus they may not be aware of, or may neglect, their people's needs.

JAMES' STORY

You will recall that James was a Realist in the relationship map. The issues that brought him to the personal development workshop were: feelings of insecurity in spite of all the very effective measures he took to create security for his family and small business; and his inability to express his feelings for his wife and children (despite loving them deeply). James, as a Realist, always had to appear to be independent and self-sufficient.

James' desire to be independent and self-sufficient was also an expression of his action map profile — the Executive. James felt appearing to be independent and self-sufficient was a demonstration of his strength, competence and professionalism. For James, appearing vulnerable or in any way dependent was a demonstration of weakness

As an expression of his Executive profile James was very goal-focused. He did everything in a highly systematic and organised way. He was very tenacious and not easily deterred from achieving his goals. He worked long hours, including weekends. He was very self-disciplined, had great endurance and was able to handle these long hours easily.

Part of the reason for working these long hours is that he felt the business might begin to fail without his hand constantly on the tiller. He had succumbed to one of the Achilles' heels of the Executive profile — feeling that he was indispensable.

James was also both a highly responsible and ethical person and he expected the same of others. He always insisted on holding himself accountable for any promises he made to his family, employees and customers, and it was very rare that he did not deliver on what he promised. This basic fairness and consistent ethical behaviour won him a lot of points with his employees. But James had another trait that they felt made him difficult to work with. He had a tendency to micro-manage the people he employed.

From James' point for view, this was simply what a highly professional and responsible business leader should do, to ensure that everyone was getting their job done in the right way and on time. But it made his employees feel that he didn't trust their competence or their commitment to getting the job done. James was a classic Executive.

TYPICAL EXECUTIVE CHARACTER TRAITS
Natural Strengths:
- Great endurance — capable of working long hours
- Highly task- and goal-focused
- Very tenacious and not easily discouraged or deflected from the pursuit of a goal
- Accepts a high level of responsibility and accountability
- Works independently and is highly professional
- Works within the accepted norms or rules
- Highly self-disciplined
- Likes a systematic, structured approach to activities and projects
- Generally a high achiever
- Enjoys being supportive and helpful

Possible Achilles' Heels:
The Achilles' heels are likely to closely relate to the Executive's natural strengths.
- May be a poor delegator, having a tendency to 'micro-manage'
- Can easily become a workaholic
- Can easily take on too many responsibilities
- Can drive the team to achieve goals at the expense of their people
- Can be overly attached to their own skills and abilities
- Because of the high focus on tasks and goals, may not be aware of, or may neglect, people's needs
- May sometimes display the attitude that they feel they are indispensable
- The need to be independent and self-reliant may prevent them from communicating or collaborating across organisational boundaries

Typical Executive Treadmill:
To continually prove themselves, over and over again, through achieving difficult and challenging goals by dedicated, hard working, self-reliant action.

Deepest Fear and Key to Freedom:
Appearing submissive, weak or dependent, or to be a failure – any of which would feel humiliating.

THE ENTREPRENEUR — SELF-DIRECTED DIRECTLY EXPRESSED

The Entrepreneur is someone who is 'self-directed' in their actions and whose daily behaviour directly expresses or reveals this. Their credo, or the statement which sums up their world view, is *'We will accomplish my idea my way!'*

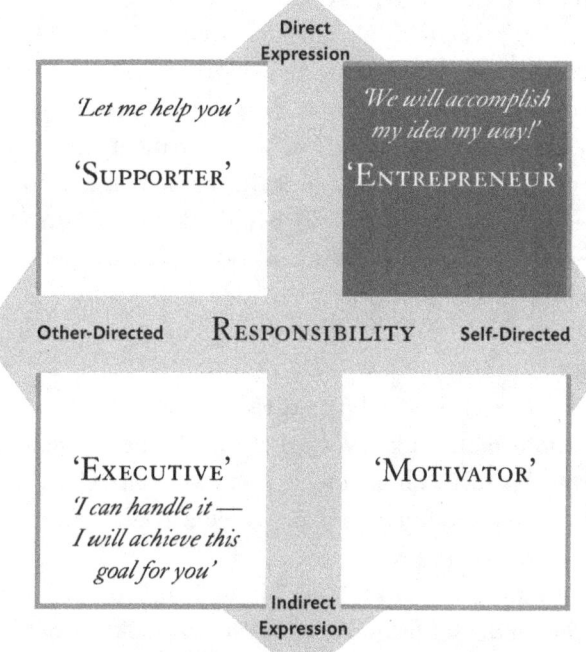

People strong in the Entrepreneur quadrant usually appear **confident, decisive, powerful, creative and dynamic.**

Entrepreneurs often become successful leaders through taking strong personal initiatives, through a strong personal action orientation, and through the ability to get others to take action in support of their initiatives. They directly express their self-directedness in that their goals, ideas and initiatives are obviously sourced from within themselves. Entrepreneurs see the world as a highly competitive place with many win/lose scenarios. They are strongly committed to always having their initiative succeed — to always being the winner.

Entrepreneurs like to undertake big and difficult challenges which inevitably involve a degree of risk. They are very flexible but tenacious and extremely resourceful. They hate being micro-managed and have no intrinsic respect for the status quo.

Entrepreneurs' leadership strength is in seeing the 'big picture' and their preferred method of operation is to delegate the detailed operational or project tasks. At times they may over-delegate and in the process gloss over important details.

Entrepreneurs tend to be restless; they like new and varied activities and dislike routine. They tend to think 'outside the box' and like novel and creative solutions. They see the world as negotiable rather than fixed, which can be a source of frustration to those with more systematic approaches (eg Executives).

Their restlessness can make them very impatient and they can be very blunt, demanding and domineering in their interactions and communications with others. This is especially true if they think that a project is going too slowly or, even worse, is failing. They can also be poor listeners, and may have a tendency to exceed their authority.

MIKE'S STORY

Mike was a senior executive leading a division of approximately 3,000 people. In the relationship map, Mike was a Pragmatist: he viewed emotions as a distraction from his focus on action and achievement. Thus his relationship style tended to be cool and unemotional, particularly under pressure, except for flashes of impatience or anger.

As an Entrepreneur, Mike liked big and difficult challenges. He was never satisfied with the status quo and was always looking for ways to change or improve things. Mike was very 'big picture' orientated and was always quick to set very clear and unequivocal strategic and operational goals with his senior leadership team. While he was very flexible about how these goals were to be achieved, he was equally tenacious in insisting that they be achieved. There was a restlessness and impatience about Mike and he could not tolerate inaction or lack of progress.

Mike liked to structure his day so that it had a lot of variety. Routine tasks he found boring and whenever he could he would delegate them. He was always interested in a new or different way of doing things, a new, different technology, etc. He liked being around people who were highly creative, who liked to think outside the box — provided their ideas would lead to the concrete, practical results that he desired.

Mike had a reputation for taking initiative and getting difficult tasks done quickly and efficiently. But he also had a reputation for doing so at the expense of his people. He had an absolute absence of people skills. His communication style was often tough, blunt and even scathing. The result was that he created a culture of fear and low morale in those around him which filtered down through the organisation. While Mike had all the natural strengths of the Entrepreneur, he also had virtually all the Achilles' heels.

A culture based on fear brings a lot of negatives with it. For example: people try to hide mistakes; they try to avoid placing themselves in a position where they could be held accountable if a failure does occur; they become overly risk adverse and thus create a culture which discourages innovation. Mike was a classic Entrepreneur.

THE ENTREPRENEUR CHARACTER TRAITS
Natural Strengths:
- Strong on taking initiative and willing to take risks
- Very action-oriented and causes others to take action
- Likes big and difficult challenges
- Tends to make quick decisions and expects fast results
- Both gives and expects direct answers to questions
- Makes immediate and full use of authority delegated to them
- Likes many new and varied activities
- Very flexible and yet tenacious in pursuing an idea or goal
- Thinks outside the box
- Can handle crises well

Possible Achilles' Heels:
- Can lack sensitivity to the needs of others
- Can often lack sufficient people focus
- Can be reckless in risk taking
- Can be impatient
- Can be a very poor listener
- Can be blunt in communication
- Can be volatile and use unsystematic approaches
- May exceed their authority
- Can expect outcomes within unrealistic time frames
- Can be demanding and overbearing
- May not be very tolerant of people who have agendas different from their own

Typical Entrepreneur Treadmill:
To continually and repeatedly undertake strong, creative, aggressive actions and to cause others to support those actions.

Deepest Fear and Key to Freedom:
Losing control of their environment or being in a 'fixed' environment and thus not being able to implement their ideas.

THE MOTIVATOR — SELF-DIRECTED INDIRECTLY EXPRESSED

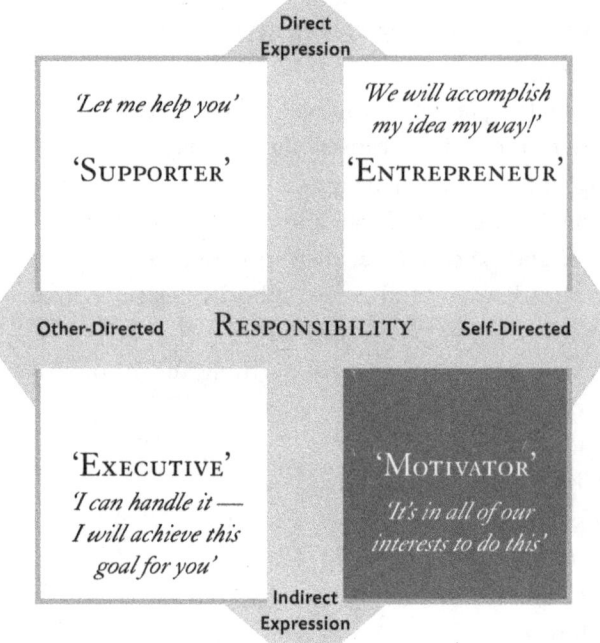

The Motivator is someone who is 'self-directed' in their actions but whose daily behaviour does not directly express or reveal this. Their credo, or the statement which sums up their world view, is *'It's in all of our interests to do this'*.

People strong in the Motivator quadrant usually appear **confident, friendly, enthusiastic, persuasive and verbally articulate**.

Motivators are the masters of influence and persuasion, with the ability to inspire and make a difference to people and organisations. Like the Entrepreneur, Motivators' ideas, agendas or goals are sourced from within themselves, even though they may appeal to external ideas or authority as a means of persuading others.

Motivators are very accomplished in the persuasive arts. They have an ability to appeal to other people's interests and agendas (their needs, desires, values, beliefs and goals), communicating the message that achieving the Motivator's agenda will serve the interests of all. Thus, their 'self-directed' action style is indirectly expressed.

Motivators have the capacity to sense the internal dynamics, mood or agenda of groups or individuals. They know how to pitch the style and content of a message to appeal to both the overt and hidden concerns of people. They sometimes appeal to others directly, using a warm, positive, even charismatic style. But they also often use an indirect, more facilitative style that involves using questions as a tool of persuasion, sometimes called 'speaking in questions'.

Motivators have natural skills in negotiation and diplomacy. This helps them achieve outcomes through people or groups over whom they have no authority. Sales people, human resource managers, non-executive directors, politicians and others who need to get specific results, without direct authority, often have a strong Motivator style.

Motivators can have a tendency to oversell and can talk too much. They can ignore or talk away important details or facts that do not support their agenda.

The Motivator's style has the potential to be used for purely selfish or positive and inclusive ends. However, with positive, inclusive ends, they can make a huge positive difference to individuals, groups, organisations or professions.

TINA'S STORY

Tina was a GP at a community medical practice, who had been offered the leadership position for the practice. She was an Optimist in the relationship map. She was warm, outgoing, friendly, had very good people skills and connected really well with her patients and most of the other doctors and staff.

However, Tina was a Motivator in the action map. She was very self-directed and had a very clear vision for where she wanted to take the practice. She wanted to expand it by bringing in some professionals offering disciplines and therapies that would both complement and enhance traditional allopathic medicine. For example, she wanted to bring in an acupuncturist, a chiropractor, a nutritionist, a specialist in relaxation therapies and techniques, etc. Tina had always believed preventative medicine was as important as treating illness.

Tina believed very strongly that this more holistic approach would be of much greater value to their patients and clients than their current reliance on allopathic medicine alone. But to achieve this, she wanted to gain the unanimous support of all the doctors.

As a Motivator, Tina had very good communication skills and could be very persuasive. Her approach was always to appeal to people's common interests, and to use persuasive, interactive discussion and negotiation to convince people rather than exerting her authority. She very much disliked and distrusted aggressive or blunt communication styles.

Tina was very good at reading people. She had already spoken individually to all of the doctors and, as she had anticipated, eight of them were very open to her ideas for a holistic health centre, with several being quite enthusiastic. However, four of the doctors were implacably opposed. She used all of her very considerable persuasive and negotiating powers with them, but they had very firm and inflexible ideas.

Thus, Tina's dilemma was this: her only reason for accepting the leadership position was to have the opportunity to implement her vision. As a Motivator, Tina had always operated under the assumption that most issues were negotiable. She knew that when she was confronted with implacable resistance, she would tend to get into overselling and endless attempts at renegotiation — both possible Achilles' heels of Motivators. She also knew she would never win over these four doctors this way. She had hit an impasse.

TYPICAL MOTIVATOR CHARACTER TRAITS
Natural Strengths:
- Being good at contacting and engaging with people
- Being verbally articulate and persuasive
- Having good insight into others and using this skilfully in influencing people
- Seeking out, enjoying and being good at group activities
- Creating enthusiasm and motivation in others
- Being skilled at (and enjoying) coaching or counselling
- Projecting confidence when articulating ideas, beliefs, goals, etc
- Asking good questions that draw people out as part of the persuasion process
- Thriving in a free, unconstrained social, professional or organisational environment

Possible Achilles' Heels:
- An overly exclusive focus on people and verbal interaction can lead to lack of tangible results
- Can sometimes promise more than they can deliver
- Can be overly-impulsive
- Can have a tendency to oversell and possibly talk too much
- Can believe/feel everything is negotiable — including plans or goals already agreed to
- Can be overly optimistic about people and life or workplace situations
- Dislikes routine work and highly structured environments
- Can ignore or 'talk away' important details or facts that do not support their agenda

Typical Motivator Treadmill:
A continual need for the development and use of verbal and human interactive skills to persuade people to embrace and pursue their agenda.

Deepest Fear and Key to Freedom:
Using all of their persuasive skills, and yet being powerless to influence a person or group.

CHAPTER NINE

THINKING MAP

THE THINKING MAP horizontal axis represents thinking styles that range from structured, logical processes (the left side of the axis) through to intuitive, imaginative processes (the right side of the axis). Thinking preferences roughly equate with the dominance of either the right or left hemispheres of the brain. The left side is strong in logical process: one step at a time (serial processing), seeing the difference between things, reductionist and detail-focused. The right side is strong in intuitive process: all steps at once (parallel processing), seeing the connections between things, creative and big-picture focused. The horizontal axis of the map represents the dynamic between 'logical' and 'intuitive' patterns.

The vertical axis in the thinking map is somewhat different from the relationship and action maps. It represents a continuum that runs from a highly externally-focused thinking style through to a highly internally-focused thinking style.

For externally-focused thinkers, their observable behaviour is more orientated towards thinking on their feet while interacting with or speaking to others. They also tend to have a vigorous, extroverted style for communicating their thoughts. More internally-focused thinkers demonstrate a preference for spending time thinking and reflecting alone, perhaps within their own heads. When they do communicate their thoughts, their communication style tends to be more thoughtful and reflective.

The four territories pictured represent all possible styles of thinking without referring to the content or subject matter of the thoughts. This depends upon our personal, educational and professional backgrounds and the type of work that we do. The four quadrants define the **way** we think and communicate, not the content.

It is some combination of genetics and our formative experiences that have shaped our thinking style. While the different thinking styles show up to a significant degree in our personal life, they are most noticeable in our professional lives. Each thinking territory has its own natural strengths and Achilles' heels and no quadrant is better or worse than any other.

The Q12 thinking map can be used for three purposes. Firstly, it can provide objective insight into our own thinking style, its natural strengths, Achilles' heels and treadmills. Secondly, it can provide us with both the information and methodology that will enable us to master these Achilles' heels and treadmills. Thirdly, it can empower us to see 'reality' from the perspective of other thinking quadrants and learn to respect people whose thinking style is very different from our own. It can also provide a pathway for developing some of the thinking styles found in other quadrants.

Becoming familiar and comfortable with the thinking terrain of each of the four thinking territories or quadrants is important. However, we do not have to become a master of all of the skill sets associated with each of the four territories.

The self-mastery quality of the thinking map is vision. Mastery of vision is the ability to understand and utilise the role of the four quadrants in bringing an original idea into concrete reality. As we go through each of the quadrants, it will become obvious that at some stage in bringing this vision to fruition, the skill sets of each quadrant are essential.

THE RATIONALIST — OUTWARDLY-FOCUSED STRUCTURED, LOGICAL THINKING PROCESSES

The Rationalist is usually someone with a more structured, logical thinking process, and whose thinking and communication style is externally focused. Their credo, or the statement which sums up their world view, is '*Here are six good reasons why*'.

People strong in the Rationalist quadrant usually appear **highly intelligent, intellectually confident, verbally articulate and intellectually assertive.**

Rationalists have a 'left brain', logical intellectual style that is often expressed in strong, assertive arguments to justify a position (proposed action, plan, goal). The Rationalists' strength is in their intellectual clarity and their ability to create carefully-structured, logically-sound arguments to build a convincing case for their position.

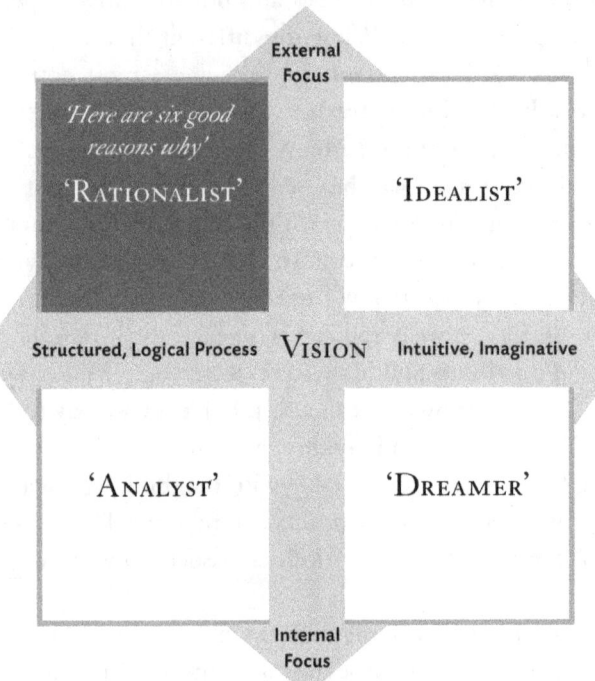

Rationalists generally have a distinctively competitive nature and often see their intellect as a competitive weapon. They usually enjoy competitive intellectual endeavours and debates. They tend to approach their arguments in a competitive style and spirit. While they want to get at the truth or argue for the best position, it is equally important for them to 'win'.

Rationalists are particularly good at critical thinking. If they are debating something, or trying to construct a convincing argument, they depend on their critical thinking to do two things: either, to anticipate the arguments others might offer against their case and then strengthen that part of their case; and/or to plan how they will pick holes in the other person's argument.

A Rationalist's argument is often of essential value for organisations and professions. The Rationalist's skills are of great value to businesses and organisations; facilitating well-structured, logical plans for projects and change initiatives, and debating alternative ideas and strategies, etc. However, Rationalists are often not good listeners.

Rationalists commonly perceive the expression of emotion as inconsistent with their assertive, logical communication style. As a result, their tenacious focus and strong rationality may give them the appearance of being cold and hard, even if that is not how they actually feel.

MIKE'S STORY

Mike was a senior executive leading a division of 3,000 people. His relationship map profile was the Pragmatist and his action map profile was the Entrepreneur.

Mike's thinking map profile was strongly Rationalist, and it strongly reinforced his action map Entrepreneur profile. Mike was highly intelligent and expressed this intelligence with clear, powerful and well-reasoned communications. When he presented his case his arguments always had a strong impact. Part of this impact was due to the clarity and soundness of his logic, and part to the power and authority of his personality.

His communications were usually well-structured, had sound logical coherence, and were very comprehensive. He would often list what he thought the counterarguments might be and then include his own arguments against those possible counterarguments. Yet he was also able to present his case succinctly and he could think well on his feet.

Mike actually enjoyed active debate, provided that three conditions applied. Firstly, those debating must stay focused on the subject at hand — he had no tolerance for wandering off the point. Secondly, those debating him must use the type of succinct but clear, logically well-structured arguments he used. Thirdly, the debate must not go on too long.

Like many Rationalists, Mike also had a phenomenal memory for detail. When making his periodic trips through the organisation, personnel were often astonished at the detailed questions he would ask.

Through the power of his logic, Mike usually won his arguments, but often at a cost. Equally, many people were aware that the power of a logically-structured argument did not by itself guarantee that it was the best case.

TYPICAL RATIONALIST CHARACTER TRAITS
Natural Strengths:
- Very effective in delivering convincing, logically-structured arguments
- Effective in competitive intellectual endeavours or debates
- Good at finding and actively picking holes in others' arguments

- Effective in thinking on their feet under pressure
- Good at developing strategies and plans through active intellectual debate
- Possessing an assertive, tenacious intellectual style that is not easily defeated

Possible Achilles' Heels:
The possible Achilles' heels derive from the over-use of a competitive, intellectually-assertive style.
- Can win arguments but lose people's hearts
- Can sometimes show disrespect for people less intellectually adept — or sometimes just people who are more intuitive
- Can be poor or selective listeners
- Intellectual assertiveness can backfire, alienating people rather than convincing them
- May tend to discount hunches and intuitive processes in favour of logical argument, and can fail to take seriously those whose views and experiences are not based on logic.

Typical Rationalist Treadmill:
To develop and use intellectual skills as an effective tool or weapon to win arguments or debates and/or to prove they have the best arguments or position

Deepest Fear and Key to Freedom:
Not being smart enough; losing the argument

THE ANALYST — INWARDLY-FOCUSED STRUCTURED, LOGICAL THINKING PROCESSES

The Analyst is someone who has a more structured, logical thinking process and whose thinking process is inwardly-focused. Their credo, or the statement which sums up their world view, is *'The answer is 3.45931'*.

People strong in the Analyst quadrant usually appear **cautious, careful, rational, objective and reserved**.

Both the Rationalist and the Analysts have strong preferences for the use of the logical, analytical left-brain. However, their styles and approaches are distinctively different. The Rationalist style is extroverted, very assertive, putting forth strong logical arguments for a position.

By contrast, the Analysts style is more introverted, quieter and more reflective. They use their intellect to achieve accuracy, precision and understanding rather than to win arguments. They feel that the thoroughness and precision of their thinking should speak for itself.

THINKING MAP

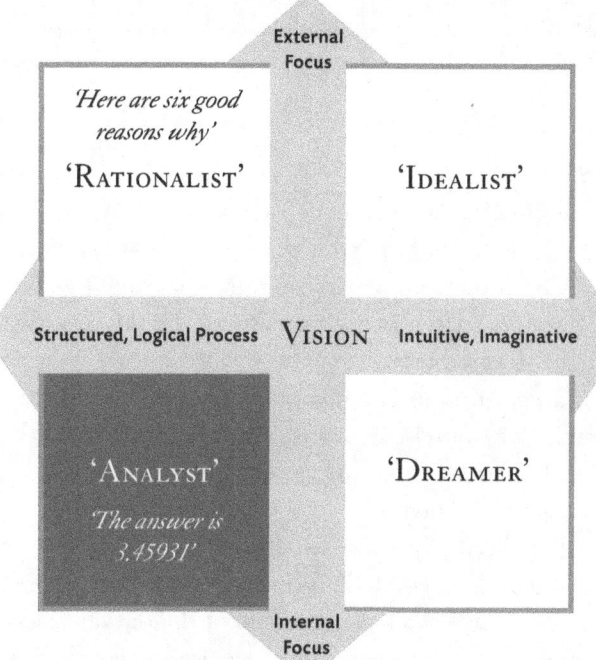

Analysts have the intrinsic ability to make sense out of complexity. They have a firm belief that there is an objective reality out there. They believe that if they can gather all the facts and details, they will discover and understand it.

Analysts have strong puzzle and problem-solving abilities, and they are at home in research, problem-solving and general investigation. They are always thorough in researching all important facts and details. They are often attracted to professions that demand these traits (research scientists, engineering, computer programming, accounting, etc).

They do not like to put forward a position until they have gathered and thoroughly analysed all of the facts, but they will commonly ask very probing questions to elicit all relevant information. They see the value of group discussions as gathering information, not debating.

If they are around verbally-aggressive and argumentative people, they may not speak up even if they have all the facts. This is because, with their quieter, more reflective style, they feel they won't get a fair hearing in an argumentative setting.

Analysts can suffer from 'paralysis by analysis'. They can lose the 'big picture' because of focus on facts and details. They can be poor delegators because they don't trust others to have their standards of precision, accuracy and thoroughness. They also may be overly-critical of themselves and others.

JAMES' STORY

James was a Realist in his relationship map and an Executive in his action map. Security was a major issue for him in his personal life and in the way he ran his company. He always tried to anticipate anything that might go wrong or that might impact the future success of his business. He did this in a very organised, systematic and goal-focused way.

James was a very thorough and systematic thinker and researcher. He enjoyed researching the developments that were occurring in his company's industry. He read a large variety of industry journals and compared and analysed their contents thoroughly.

James was intellectually cautious, careful and reflective in both his research and in the way he presented his conclusions. He never liked to present a conclusion until he felt he had examined all of the relevant facts. He never overstated his case, and always tried to be as precise and accurate as possible.

James' favourite activity was problem solving. The more complex the problem the more he enjoyed working on it. However, his analytical intellect and penchant for critical thinking often caused him to be critical of himself and others. Analysts invariably have very high standards for thoroughness, precision, accuracy – and often high ethical standards for themselves and others.

James was very critical of himself and was often worried that he may not be living up to his own standards. While he could be very critical of others, he would always present his criticism in a thoughtful, polite and respectful way.

James had a tendency to micro-manage his staff. He didn't trust that his staff would have the same high standards as he did. He also had a tendency to put off making decisions because he felt he didn't have enough facts or time to think the issue through thoroughly enough. He was thus overly cautious in a way that actually slowed down the running of the business. James was a classic Analyst.

TYPICAL ANALYST CHARACTER TRAITS
Natural Strengths:
- Very good puzzle and problem-solving skills
- Effective analytical skills—good at weighing pros and cons
- Can place a high value on objectivity, precision and accuracy
- High intellectual standards and values
- Commonly asks very probing questions to elicit all relevant information
- Very thorough in researching all important facts and details
- Can place a high value on intellectually-based expertise
- Tend to be good listeners — but listening mainly for factual and detailed information
- Always think carefully before they speak
- Never overstate their conclusions
- Good at constructing careful, fact-based presentations and arguments

Possible Achilles' Heels:
- Can be pedantic and nit-picking
- Can be a poor delegator (because they don't trust others to have their standards)
- Can be overly critical of themselves and others
- Can lose the big picture because of focus on facts and details
- Can be indecisive because of the need for more analysis (paralysis by analysis)
- Won't speak up until they feel they have all the facts
- Can become so deeply intellectually buried in their work that it isolates them from others
- Creativity may be held back by the need to follow rules for structured processes
- Can have difficulty in both being aware of, and dealing with, emotional and interpersonal issues

Typical Analyst Treadmill:
The continuing need to develop and use intellectual skills and disciplines that enable them to arrive at precise, accurate and objective conclusions

Deepest Fear and Key to Freedom:
Not being able to understand something or being intellectually inadequate for the task.

THE IDEALIST — OUTWARDLY-FOCUSED INTUITIVE, IMAGINATIVE THINKING PROCESSES

The Idealist is someone who has an imaginative, intuitive thinking process and whose thinking process and communication style is outwardly-focused. Their credo, or the statement which sums up their world view, is *'I have a dream'*.

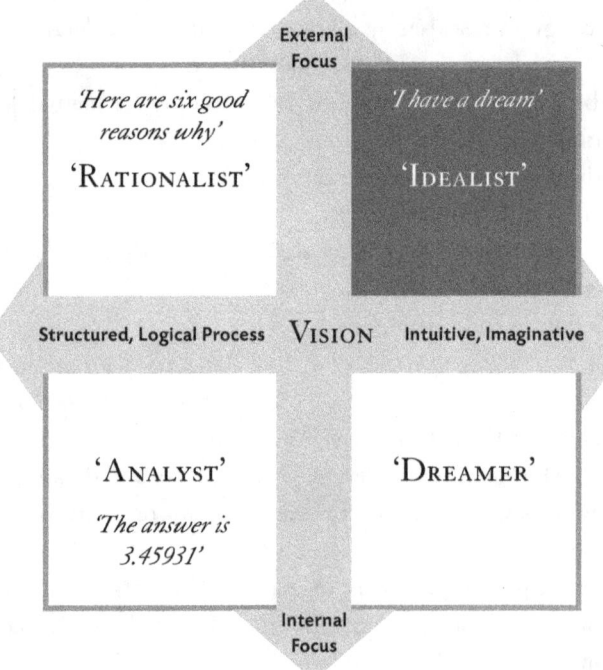

People strong in the Idealist quadrant usually appear **articulate, creative, inspiring, charismatic and visionary**.

The Idealist's cognitive style is one of imaginative, intuitive thinking processes that is externally focused and vigorously expressed. Idealists use their imagination, intuition and creative ideas to paint pictures with words. They have a highly extroverted communication style and speak easily and fluently.

Idealists are charismatic communicators. They are able to inspire us by appealing to what is common to us all — dreams, ideals and a better future. They are able to form and express a common vision that can unite us in our individual endeavours.

Idealists have the ability to connect seemingly disparate ideas in original ways. They fully utilise the 'right-brain's' ability to fantasise and imagine new possibilities, including new ways of seeing old phenomena, new ways of doing things, new ways of creating a better future. And they are able to express these new possibilities in ways that engage, attract and convince others.

Idealists are highly optimistic and their optimism is contagious. They can often inspire a new sense of hope in a group who's moral and sense of possibilities is low. The Idealist's ability to keep people inspired is the key to the loyalty they often attract.

Idealists can make a huge contribution to an organisation or profession. However, they must learn to use their persuasive powers with great care and responsibility. For example, they can be overly-optimistic, causing people to have unrealistic expectations. They can use their charisma and communication skills to seduce and mislead people for purely self-interested ends, or to avoid dealing with harsh current realities.

Thus integrity is critically important for Idealists. At their best, Idealists can be true visionaries.

TINA'S STORY

Tina's vision was to expand the medical practice into a holistic health centre by bringing in professionals from other health-related disciplines to complement and enhance the purely orthodox allopathic medical practice that was currently used. Tina was an Optimist in the relationship map and a Motivator in the action map.

Tina had a very active and creative mind and an interest in a wide range of subjects and ideas. She said her bedside was always littered with books — history, philosophy, biography, art, music, etc. It was her love of bringing together different ideas and disciplines that had been the original motivation behind her desire to build a holistic health centre. While her professional training was in allopathic medicine she also felt that there was more to medicine than just treating illness; she wanted to develop or improve 'wellness'.

Tina was a very charismatic and inspiring communicator. Long before she was offered the position of leader for her practice group she had been on the lecture circuit. She spoke to a wide range of audiences and was always enjoyed and appreciated. Her charisma, idealism and optimism drew people to her even when they disagreed with her views.

One of Tina's main concerns was that she would awaken 'hope' and a desire for this new holistic centre in some of the doctors within the practice group, only to have that hope dashed on the hard rocks of reality if she could not win over the four doctors who opposed her ideas. She understood that her charisma and idealism could lead to false hopes and disillusionment, and that her persuasive powers had to be used responsibly. How could she break the impasse she was in?

TYPICAL IDEALIST CHARACTER TRAITS
Natural Strengths:
- A very effective, engaging and inspiring communication style
- Being good at connecting disparate pieces of information into a whole and communicating those connections and the 'whole' to others
- Very good at developing and communicating visionary ideas and concepts
- Always thinking and speaking in terms of new possibilities; able to convince people that these possibilities can become real
- Very high ideals and the ability to convince others to embrace and pursue these ideals
- Can think in non-linear, creative and open ended ways
- Can inspire others to think and act beyond their usual limits
- Can inspire others to work voluntarily towards a common purpose
- Very optimistic, with the natural ability to spread the spirit of optimism to others

Achilles' Heels:
- Can be impulsive and dislike routine activities
- Can sometimes find it hard to stop being creative when it is time to make decision and take concrete actions
- Often finds it difficult to operate within an environment of highly structured rules and systems
- Can be overly-optimistic — causing others to have unrealistic expectations
- Can talk too much and oversell an idea
- Can use imagination and creative thinking to avoid dealing with harsh current realities
- Can use their charisma and communication skills to seduce or mislead people (groups, organisations, etc)

Typical Idealist Treadmill:
To continually engage in imagining and intuiting new possibilities, new ideas and ideals and, through developing and using the charismatic communication style, to influence and inspire others to embrace these possibilities, ideas or ideals.

Deepest Fear and Key to Freedom:
Not being able to influence people; being in a closed system with rigid rules and limited possibilities; not having sufficient insight.

THE DREAMER — INTERNALLY-FOCUSED INTUITIVE, IMAGINATIVE THINKING PROCESSES

The Dreamer is someone who has a more imaginative, intuitive thinking process and whose thinking process and communication style is inwardly focused. Their credo, or the statement which sums up their world view, is *'Perhaps we could look at this upside down or from a completely different angle'*.

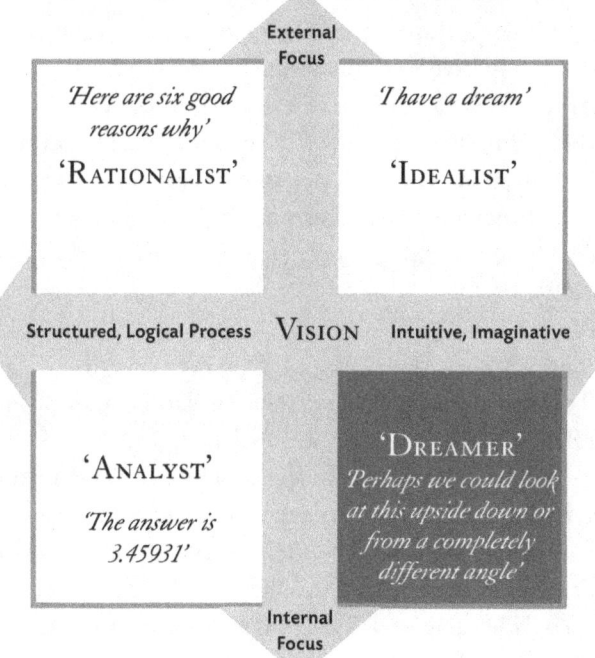

People strong in the Dreamer quadrant usually appear **quiet, reflective, intuitive, unassertive and creative**.

The Dreamer's cognitive style is an imaginative, intuitive pattern. The dreamer has natural access to 'seed forms' of thinking. Through this they are able to form new and original concepts that lead to pioneering and innovative discoveries. These deeply intuitive thinking skills of the Dreamer may range from attempting to understand the workings of the cosmos to the creation of a new art form.

All new ideas come into reality through this territory. Like dreams, at first these ideas often have a symbolic and surrealistic quality, and while meaningful to the dreamer, they are often initially difficult to communicate. For example, Einstein initially intuited all the basic ideas for General Relativity Theory before he even knew the mathematical language (Tensor Analysis) necessary to communicate and test the theory.

The Dreamer's imaginative, intuitive insights are often held within themselves and not expressed – hence they have a strongly 'internally-focused' pattern. They have quiet reflective, introverted natures and are happy spending long periods of time alone. They are also very sensitive to their human environment. For example, in a workplace environment they will only thrive and contribute if their group or team is supportive and respectful of them and their intuitive, imaginative thinking style.

Dreamers can make a huge contribution to any organisation or profession. However, to be useful, their ideas need to be structured in communicable form and then communicated. The Dreamer should be accepted and encouraged to communicate, but they must also take responsibility for communicating their ideas, which means overcoming some of their instinctive introversion.

TIM'S STORY

In his relationships map Tim was an Observer and in his action map a Supporter. Tim's two problems (personal isolation and promotion) were greatly exacerbated by his Dreamer personality.

Tim's natural strengths were the source of his success as a structural design engineer. He had a distinctive approach to his work: first he would saturate himself with information relating to the task and the client before beginning the design work. After completing this, he would spend quiet, reflective time alone until a 'seed' idea emerged. This seed idea would provide a basic strategic direction that enabled him to begin the technical engineering design work. This required a huge amount of detail, yet he did not have a systematic, logical approach to this lengthy, detailed part of the process although in the end it was usually a brilliant piece of work.

The function he enjoyed most and found endlessly fascinating was the creative part of the project. He loved being alone inside a rich but peaceful 'inner space', letting the ideas flow. If at any point he got stuck in a project he said he would simply 'tinker around' with drawings or ideas until a solution suddenly showed up.

Tim's problem was that he enjoyed this quiet, inwardly-focused creative process so much, that it reinforced his tendency to be alone most of the time — even though he had been a project team leader for several years. However, his skill also eventually got him promoted to a senior management position, where he could no longer stay isolated and where the traits and skills he needed were quite different from those of the Dreamer.

TYPICAL DREAMER CHARACTER TRAITS
Natural Strengths:
Some of these are the same as the Idealist, but without the Idealist's externally-focused, easy, fluent, visionary communication style:
- Good at mentally connecting disparate pieces of information into a cohesive whole
- Often see things that other, more aggressive or assertive types, miss
- Think in non-linear, open-ended, creative ways, thinking 'outside the box' — 'lateral thinking'
- Can often have very accurate, intuitive insight into people, groups, situations, problems etc.
- Can have a rich capacity to imagine new possibilities and different alternative realities
- Great patience and mental stamina.
- Can often make huge, useful, imaginative leaps from very little information
- Have the capacity to work alone for long periods of time
- If accepted and valued, they can make profound and truly innovative contributions to the group

Possible Achilles' Heels:
The Dreamer shares a number of the Idealist's Achilles' heels, but not those caused by the Idealist's externally-focused, fluent, visionary communication style:
- Often dislikes routine activities
- Can find it hard to stop being creative when it is time to make decisions and take concrete actions
- Often will not speak up or contribute if more verbally aggressive people dominate a discussion
- Can use imagination and creative thinking to avoid harsh or unpleasant current realities

- Can become so absorbed in the creative process as to lose track of time deadlines
- Can be very dreamy or absent-minded
- Can find it difficult to communicate in a way that can be understood and valued by either highly logical or very pragmatic people
- Can often find it difficult to work within highly-structured environments and systems

Typical Dreamer Treadmill

To experience a constant need, through quiet, intuitive reflection to gain deep insight into the nature of things (themselves, others, groups, society, the world, the universe, spiritual reality etc).

Deepest Fear and Key to Freedom:

Having their imaginative, intuitive ideas or quiet, reflective communication style subject to ridicule.

PART 4

THE DYNAMICS OF TRANSFORMATIONAL CHANGE

CHAPTER TEN

THE Q12 PROFILING INSTRUMENT AND LEVELS OF CONSCIOUSNESS: INTEGRATING THE TWO MODELS

In order to provide a clear, practical understanding of the change process, we need to integrate the two conceptual systems in this book — the Q12 profiling system and the stages of development (or ladder of consciousness) model.

UNITIVE SELF	Level 7
TRANSPERSONAL SELF	Level 6
INDEPENDENT SELF	Level 5
ADULT SOCIALISED SELF	Level 4
ADOLESCENT SELF 12/13 years through adolescence to early adulthood Ends at Adult Socialised Self Stage	
LATE CHILDHOOD SELF Approx 8 years through approx 12 years	Level 3
EARLY CHILDHOOD SELF Approx 21 months through approx 7 years	Level 2
PRE VERBAL 'BODY SELF' Approx 5/6 months in womb through approx 21 months	Level 1

Chapters 4 and 5 have provided an overview of the stages of evolution from ground zero through the first four levels of development (pictured opposite) ending in the adult socialised self, plus an understanding of success and failure treadmills, and the deficit motivation that drives these.

We will now briefly explore the three higher levels of consciousness. Unlike the earlier stages of development we do not automatically pass through these higher stages. Instead we must take proactive steps to develop through these stages. The rest of this book will give examples of these proactive steps through continuing the stories of Tina, James, Tim and Mike. It will also describe the formative experiences that created their Q12 character structure.

When anyone undertakes to use the Q12 profile there may be a wide variety of specific changes that they wish to initiate. The Q12 profile is a powerful tool for identifying specific changes required but the change that facilitates and reinforces all others is 'transformational change'.

Transformational change involves undergoing a change in the 'lens' through which we view ourselves, other people and our world. It involves seeing our 'reality' from a higher and more wide-ranging perspective.

When an individual uses the Q12 instrument, they receive a picture or 'snapshot' of their personality (their socialised self character structure) at a specific moment in time. This snapshot identifies their main characteristics and the core motivating factors that formed, and continue to drive, those character traits. However, what is critically important is that this snapshot is based on a moment in time. At a later moment in time one or two possible kinds of change may have occurred: horizontal or vertical change.

HORIZONTAL CHANGE

In the case of horizontal change, you are still operating at the same adult socialised self level but your Q12 profile may have changed (eg higher in some quadrants and lower in others). Your identity is made up of the new or different defining elements of your specific profile. The statement 'I am the cluster of character traits identified in my profile' will be an accurate description of your self-concept. Those character traits define who you experience yourself to be.

This type of change involves expanding and further developing your socialised self, while remaining at the same level of consciousness. This type of development can occur through a purely skills-based training programme: you can acquire skills that come naturally to other people with profiles different from your own.

Horizontal change allows you to develop a socialised self with a broader skill base, which can result in a better self-image.

VERTICAL CHANGE

Vertical change involves a transformational change to a higher level of consciousness. In this case your Q12 profile may be the same or different, but you will be experiencing and operating that profile from a higher level of consciousness. For example, the deficit motivation that previously drove your profile will have lessened or disappeared. In addition, you will either be free of — or be in the process of freeing yourself from — your Q12 profile's Achilles' heels and success or failure treadmills. Finally, your Q12 profile will now be driven by an entirely different level of motivation appropriate to a higher level of consciousness.

Thus, exactly the same profile can be experienced at four levels: the adult socialised self, the independent self, the transpersonal self and the unitive self. As you evolve vertically to higher levels of consciousness, your Q12 profile may or may not change. Whether or not it does, will depend on the specific character traits and skills that are needed in your personal and professional life.

However, to achieve this kind of vertical (transformational) change requires reversing the emotional programming that originally formed our adult socialised self's character structure: **emotional de-programming**.

In order to address the issue of emotional de-programming, we need to return to Paul McLean's description of the three different layers of the brain: the primitive or 'reptilian' brain, the 'mammalian' brain and the cerebral cortex (see Introduction for more detail). Even though they have different functions, all three layers of the brain are interconnected. These connections include links between the three different layers, but also between the left and right hemispheres of the limbic system and the cerebral cortex. (The 'reptilian' or primitive brain has no hemispheres.)

The primary emotional programming of the relationship and action maps occurs in the limbic system, including the amygdala. This is fairly obvious with the relationship map, since it describes the role of strong and weak emotional charges in shaping our relationship patterns.

The action maps, are of course, shaped by the conditioning of the will. It is important to remember that the will itself is defined as: the *active, directed, outcome orientated expression of emotions*. The self- and other-directed will are in fact also the products of our emotional programming. The will is shaped in response to emotionally charged experiences in childhood and adolescence, beginning in the second developmental stage as we develop and master language.

It is in this stage that our socialisation process begins, with parents and other authority figures providing guidance about should and shouldn't, do's and don'ts, right and wrong, etc. It is also at this stage that we encounter both positive and painful experiences in our environment, resulting from how we respond to that guidance.

It is equally true that our thinking map behaviour — while expressing itself through the cerebral cortex — is also shaped by the emotional programming within the limbic system. To a large extent our thinking map provides the *cogitative behavioural patterns that justify and reinforce the relationship and action map patterns.*

The style of thinking behaviour both gives expression to and reinforces the emotionally-based behaviour patterns of our relationship and action maps. For example, the Dreamer quadrant thinking pattern can both give expression to and reinforce the emotionally withdrawn behaviour of the relationship map Observer quadrant; or, the intellectual assertiveness of the Rationalist quadrant can both give expression to and reinforce the strongly self-directed behaviour of the action map Entrepreneur quadrant.

The thinking map mental and behavioural patterns become increasingly more sophisticated during adolescence and early adulthood. As this occurs, our thinking style can be used to provide good reasons for our self-concept and our view of reality. It thereby provides justification for our beliefs about how we should approach relationships and undertake actions. Thus, our cerebral-cortex-based thinking map is heavily entangled with the emotional and behavioural patterns of our relationship and action maps.

EXPERIENTIAL LEARNING AND EMOTIONAL DE-PROGRAMMING

There are many methods that are useful and effective for facilitating the process of emotional de-programming. However, it must occur, quite literally, by experiential learning processes that are the reversal of the experiential learning that initially created the programmed patterns. This involves three interrelated things:
- De-programming (releasing) the stored emotional energy from emotionally-charged memories of childhood and adolescent experiences

- De-programming old neuro pathways in the limbic system that lead to the compulsive mental, emotional and behavioral patterns of the Q12 Achilles' heels and failure and success treadmills
- Re-programming new limbic neuro pathways, thus opening up a wider variety of mental, emotional and behavioural possibilities

Undertaking activities that result in emotional de-programming can bring up uncomfortable or unpleasant emotions and take you out of your comfort zone. It takes courage and commitment to pursue this kind of change.

Experiential learning is quite different from the didactic classroom teaching that is used to learn technical or specialist skills. This type of skills-based training focuses largely on utilising the higher mental functions of the cerebral cortex. However, cerebral-cortex-based cognitive learning cannot by itself de-programme the emotional programming that exists within the brain's limbic system. In other words, you can't emotionally de-programme by just reading books, attending lectures, although these activities could inspire you to undertake the experiential learning that will result in emotional de-programming.

Experiential learning methodologies used in the stories of the individuals throughout this book include the following:
- Regular daily practice of meditation
- Attending personal development workshops
- Using coaching to assist in facilitating the desired changes
- Attending leadership development workshops and programmes
- Using the Q12 system (with a coach qualified in the system) to provide the deep and accurate self-awareness essential to the transformational change process.

There are other methodologies available but these above are the ones described in this book.

CHAPTER ELEVEN

TINA'S STORY

TINA had the strong characteristics of the Optimist in her relationship map, the Motivator in her action map and the Idealist in her concept map. When Tina came to our workshop she had two issues that she faced — one personal and one professional.

TINA'S PERSONAL ISSUE

In most areas of her life Tina was very happy and had a warm, outgoing and sunny disposition. However, there was a deep core of unhappiness in her marriage because she did not feel that her husband returned her love. Although he was very devoted to her it was difficult for him to show any direct expressions of emotion and equally difficult for him to accept direct expressions of affection from her. She felt like there was an empty hole within her, a continual yearning for her husband to show her direct expressions of love.

Tina was on the hope-disillusionment treadmill:

To continually hope for and seek out the next relationship (or job, experience, situation) that will leave you in a state of emotional fulfilment; and/or to hope that your current partner (or job, experience, situation) will change, resulting in your emotional fulfilment.

Tina had parents who were very warm and affectionate. She received constant daily signs of affection from both of them, but her father was especially affectionate and demonstrative. However, this changed when she was about 11 years of age. By this time his only sign of affection was a perfunctory kiss on the cheek or perfunctory hug. When she tried to be more affectionate with him, he would seem uncomfortable and embarrassed and would move away.

What Tina experienced with her father is not uncommon. Her father had felt very comfortable directly expressing affection to her when she was a child, but as she moved towards adolescence he began to see her as a sexually mature girl. In a way that may have been completely unconscious to him, he may have felt that strong overt signs of affection from him could have sexual connotations and violate the incest taboo. It is not likely that he actually consciously had those thoughts, but subconsciously he started to shy away from direct demonstrations of love.

In any case, whatever her father's actual reasons, Tina underwent the type of formative experience that commonly creates the Optimist profile, including the deficit motivation that drove her treadmill (the need for her husband to make her feel emotionally fulfilled by providing more direct demonstrations of his love).

The source of this deficit drive was the difference between what Tina had experienced with her father in earlier childhood and the dramatic change in his behaviour towards her after she turned about 11. By age 11 she was experiencing 'paradise lost' and this became the source of the subconscious drive, but fully conscious yearning to re-experience early childhood feelings of being intensely loved. The emotional memories, stored in her subconscious, were the source of the emotional hole within her. They were what led to her hope that her husband would behave in ways that would make her feel emotionally whole and fulfilled.

However, the change in behaviour Tina was hoping for in her husband could never provide the state of emotional fulfilment she sought. Her treadmill was deficit driven and could never be satiated by focusing on any external source. Instead there were the three interlinked pathways that she would need to pursue to resolve her dilemma.

- She would need to give up the 'hope' that the behavioural changes she desired from her husband could ever be the source of her fulfilment. She had to learn to give up the larger illusion that someone, something or some change 'out there' could ever be the source of fulfilment.
- She would have to understand and accept that the ultimate reason behind this illusion was the emotional programming, now subconscious, driving her conscious yearning for fulfilment. She would need to find the strength

to give up the general belief, endemic to our society, that anyone else can make us emotionally whole and complete.
- She would have to come to understand that the feelings of inner wholeness and emotional fulfilment she was seeking from outside of herself were actually intrinsic to her true self, her 'Being self' we described in Chapter 5. By releasing herself from the grip of that emotional programming she would begin to experience the fullness that was already there within herself.

Sometimes the releasing of some deeply embedded emotional programming can occur very suddenly, while for others it occurs gradually through the daily use of experiential learning techniques. For Tina the change occurred quite suddenly. I asked her during the next meditation process to emulate or imagine the process of giving up the hope about her husband's possible changed behaviour becoming the source of her fulfilment.

During the meditative process, as she imagined herself giving up this hope (and its associated illusion) Tina felt as if a 'chunk' of herself was melting or dissolving within her. This was accompanied by a feeling of great sadness and she began to sob. These experiences were internal metaphors for losing a part of her socialised self identity which had its roots in her childhood.

Yet the process of letting go or 'surrendering' the emotionally-programmed illusion, meant she was 'born' into a new level of consciousness, with a new, more whole identity. When the internal dissolving was complete and the sadness had passed, she felt an indescribable peace and wholeness.

This new kind of awareness is symptomatic of the beginnings of the first of the higher levels of consciousness: the independent self. It is the experience of seeing our socialised self, with all of its typical responses, as if from a mindful perspective — to see and accept, objectively and non-judgementally, truths about our socialised self that we would normally resist. As one becomes more accustomed to being in that state, four fundamental qualities of experience begin to emerge. They are a deep sense of freedom, wholeness, self-acceptance and intrinsic self-esteem. The critical one of these for Tina was wholeness.

When she returned home, Tina's behaviour was relaxed and accepting of her husband in a way that she had never before known. She could feel the love that was implied in his little gestures. She no longer felt the need to try to evoke demonstrations of affection from him. Instead, she was able to accept him just as he was. After a few days her husband seemed to become more relaxed around her.

What happened after this was quite remarkable. From time to time, he actually began to show direct expressions of affection to her. Tina loved this, but was careful not to make too much of his new behaviour, for she intuitively sensed that this would cause him to feel pressured and revert to his old behaviour.

In addition, she started to let him take the lead in any direct demonstrations of affection. She simply stopped initiating these as she had always done in the past. As a result, her husband found it easier to directly show affection to her. Feeling no pressure to show direct expressions of affection, a naturally affectionate part of him started to emerge.

Tina experienced something that appears to be a paradoxical law of nature in the dynamics of human relationships: *when we no longer have the deficit need for anything from another person, it is more likely that person will give us what we want.*

The key point to remember here is that Tina's new behaviour was enabled by her new state of consciousness. She felt free of the deficit need for constant demonstrations of love. She felt 'whole' and complete. Consequently her behavioural adjustments were easy to make; she could simply choose to make them, since the compulsive deficit drive was no longer there.

TINA'S PROFESSIONAL ISSUE

Tina's professional issue was more related to her action (Motivator) and concept (Idealist) profiles. She was a GP who had been offered the leadership position at a community medical practice. She wanted to take this position, but only if she had the opportunity to implement her vision for the practice. As a Motivator she was very self-directed and as an Idealist had a very clear vision of where she wanted to take the practice group. She wanted to create a holistic health centre by bringing in professionals that would both complement and enhance traditional allopathic medicine: an acupuncturist, a chiropractor, a nutritionist, a specialist in relaxation therapies, etc.

She believed she needed the support of all the practice's partners. As a Motivator, Tina was very good at reading people and had insight into what their concerns and agendas were likely to be. She had already spoken individually to all of the doctors and eight of them were very open to her ideas for a holistic health centre. However, four of them were implacably opposed, despite all of her very considerable persuasive and negotiating powers.

Tina had always operated under the assumption that most issues were negotiable. She also knew that when she was confronted with implacable resistance, she would tend to get into overselling and endless attempts at renegotiation — which are some of the possible Achilles' heels of Motivators.

As a Motivator (and an Idealist), Tina had very good communication skills. Her approach was always to appeal to people's common interests, and to use persuasive, interactive discussion and negotiation to convince people rather than exerting her authority. She very much disliked and distrusted aggressive or blunt communication styles.

Tina had grown up in a warm and loving home environment. Her parents had many good values which showed up in their daily behaviour. They were kind, willing to help others, generous, compassionate. They also held education to be of great importance and encouraged and helped their children to do well in school.

However, while Tina's parents were kind people with many good values, in a number of ways they were also very conservative and conventional. For example, both of them were very conventional Roman Catholics and Tina and her siblings were brought up in the church with the expectation that they would follow the same religious path. Tina's parents also placed a lot of emphasis on socially conventional behaviour, where the specific forms of conventionality were largely determined by their own conservative upbringing and the middle class community in which they lived.

When Tina was around 14 years old, she began to think more independently and have doubts about the church. For example, she could not reconcile the idea of eternal damnation with an all-loving and compassionate God. She questioned the need to have a priest as a mediator between her and God and queried some of the rigid doctrines. This was Tina's first step in becoming 'self-directed'.

Tina's parents' conventionality particularly expressed itself in two rigid rules
- You must never say anything to an individual or group that might challenge them, upset them, or make them feel uncomfortable.
- You must never insist on getting your own way.

Tina said she remembered feeling real fear around these rules. She had witnessed her older brother breaking these rules and her father getting really angry and dealing out harsh punishments.

However, with her new independent thinking, she began to question the wisdom of both of these rules. Although she agreed that there was no need to do or say things that upset people unnecessarily, she also felt that at times you should express what might be uncomfortable truths and not just acquiesce to another's opinions. Tina's way of getting around this, while causing the least upset, was to develop skills in the persuasive arts and to become a very skilled negotiator

As an Idealist, Tina learned to express her own innovative, imaginative and idealistic ideas with great fluency and eloquence. She read widely — comparative religion, politics, sociology, etc — and loved connecting various ideas from these sources into the beginnings of her own personal philosophy. She also joined a debating society in high school where she learned to express these ideas in warm, idealistic but non-confrontational style.

However, the really difficult issue for Tina came from the rule about never insisting on getting your own way. The influence of her parents had left deep emotional roots in her subconscious, causing a conscious fear of doing this as an adult.

Tina had made a number of unsuccessful attempts, using her persuasive, negotiating and diplomatic skills, to win over the four doctors who were opposed to her idea of a holistic health centre. She had come to believe that there was nothing she could do or say that would change their minds. However, she also believed that without the support of all the medical staff she would not be able to fulfil her vision.

I asked Tina what she thought would happen if she held a meeting with all the doctors and she stated something like the following:

> *Creating a holistic health centre has been a dream of mine for a long time and I feel a deep commitment to realising that vision. Therefore there are really only two possibilities for me. Either I accept the leadership position, you agree to accept and align with that vision, and working together we will create a holistic, multi-service centre, or I decline to accept the practice leadership.*
>
> *This vision means so much to me, that I will resign from my medical practice here and find another practice that will agree to establish such a centre. I would much prefer to do this here since I have worked with you all, know you well and respect your medical knowledge and skills, but at this stage in my life I feel very strongly that I must find a way to bring this vision to fruition and that must take precedence for me*

Her first response was fear. This was her Achilles' heel because she would be insisting on getting her own way. She thought the statement sounded like a threat or ultimatum, even a kind of emotional blackmail. She also thought such a statement would contradict her image of herself as an unselfish, reasonable and kindly person.

I asked her to list the reasons why she believed that a holistic centre would be better for the patients. She was able to rattle off at least 10 good reasons in just a few minutes, and as she spoke I could feel the depth and authenticity of her belief.

I then asked her if she thought that her reasons were narrow and selfish or broad and inclusive in intention. She replied that they were broad and inclusive. She had no problem with her intentions, it was making an ultimatum that seemed selfish.

I then asked her if she could see this not as an ultimatum, but a simple statement of fact.

Tina already had many traits associated with the independent self level of development. In most areas of her life she could see herself objectively, accurately and non-judgementally, she felt free and independent, and was accepting of herself — both her strengths and her Achilles' heels. She had very solid self-esteem and the only issues holding her back were:

- The deficit need that drove her feelings and behaviour with her husband.
- The emotional grip of rules programmed into her from childhood about never insisting on getting her own way.

Tina had achieved most of the Maslovian needs that are the main motivational drives through childhood, adolescence and into the adult socialised self stage. For her to simply continue what she was doing professionally would not provide more self-esteem. Undoubtedly she would remain successful just continuing along her current path, but she would be on the kind of success treadmill where one stage of development is complete — she was ready for the next stage.

The drive to undertake the leadership role and facilitate the creation of a holistic health centre had nothing to do with deficit motivation or any of Maslov's first four needs. It was in fact driven by Maslov's fifth level of motivation — the self-actualisation drive. This is the drive to overcome and master your current mental, emotional and behavioural limitations and more fully realise your potential: the drive to achieve a challenging personal vision. Rather than being selfish, this was an essential step she needed to take for her full evolution into the independent self stage of development.

While the outcomes Tina sought were greater benefits for her patients, she came to understand that the inner drive to take the leadership in creating the centre was also essential to her next step of personal development. So Tina decided on a fairly simple strategy:

Step One: She needed some strong allies to provide assistance in gaining the support of the practice group. There were three doctors in the group who were friends and who she knew were very supportive of her vision for the holistic centre. She met with them privately to tell them of her decision, to explain her reasons and to get their active support. They were not overly surprised but they expressed sorrow that she would be leaving the practice if she could not get the support for her initiative.

Step Two: Together they would contact already existing holistic centres in Britain, Europe and the US seeking letters of support from traditional allopathic practitioners who worked in those centres. They would also seek any statistical or scientific data that supported the holistic approach.

Step Three: Tina and each of her three allies would speak privately to the individual doctors they each knew best, to gain as much support as possible before Tina asked for a meeting with all the doctors.

Step Four: Together they created a presentation for the meeting with all the doctors which would have four parts:
- Tina would open the meeting by presenting her vision for the centre. She would begin by speaking about her vision directly from her mind and heart, without visual aids of any kind.
- One of Tina's allies would then present the evidence retrieved from the letters and statistical data collected, using visual aids and documents.
- Then another doctor would provide a presentation covering all the critical practical issues involved, including: the recommended time span for creating the centre; methods for identifying and selecting the alternative health professionals; financial and legal implications; and finally a possible internal structure and organisational operating procedures. A highly consultative approach would be emphasised with regard to planning and implementation.
- Finally, after answering any questions, Tina would conclude by making her 'either/or' statement (described above).

For Tina, presenting her vision for the holistic health centre at the beginning of the meeting felt easy and natural because she would be using all of her natural strengths as a Motivator and an Idealist. However, the closure of the meeting with the either/or statement felt very challenging and brought up a lot of fear.

Tina wanted to know what she needed to do to face this challenge effectively. As a Motivator she had an indirectly self-directed action style; she would look within herself for signals about what ideas, goals or actions she would embrace and pursue. But her approach in persuading others to join her was indirect and diplomatic. **However, her statement at the conclusion of the meeting would need to be very bold and direct, a statement of fact and not a threat.** There was really no way to be diplomatic about this. She would have to be very clear that, while there was room to negotiate about how the centre would be created, the actual creation of the centre was non-negotiable.

I asked Tina which of the four action quadrants embodied the ability to do this as a natural strength and she identified this as the Entrepreneur — the directly expressed, self-directed action style. I asked her to read through and meditate on this action style and then to write out the statement she would make, practising it many times.

This is how it all unfolded.

Tina's opening statement of her vision for the holistic health centre was magnificent. She demonstrated a calmness, clarity, confidence and authenticity that her audience found quite moving.

The other doctors then presented the letters and evidence from Europe, Britain and the US and outlined the practical details of the proposed centre. They then answered all the questions.

When Tina came to make her closing statement she appeared very calm and confident. She thanked her audience for listening and then stated that at this stage in her life she was personally and professionally deeply committed to creating the centre. Her greatest desire was to do it within this practice group because she knew them well and respected their medical knowledge and competency. If they would agree to the creation of this centre, she stated that she would be honoured to accept the leadership of the practice group.

However, if they would not agree to the creation of the centre, she would (with great reluctance) not accept the leadership position. Because of her deep commitment to creating the centre, she felt she would need to leave the practice group and seek out a group who would be willing to create a holistic health centre. She thanked them again for their time and left the room so they could discuss the issue among themselves.

The meeting continued for over an hour and a half. By the end of the discussion two of the four doctors who were originally opposed had come on board and all of those who formerly approved remained positive and supportive.

The two who were opposed were quite upset about what they saw as Tina's 'ultimatum'. They argued that any doctor who believed that a patient might benefit from alternative therapies was free to refer them to an alternative health practitioner outside the practice group. They argued that it was not necessary for the allopathic and alternative health professional to reside under one roof.

The meeting had reached a deadlock and at this point Tina was invited back in. She replied that a holistic health centre was not just about allopathic practitioners recommending alternative therapies. It was about allopathic and alternative health professionals collaborating in their treatment of patients. True collaboration would be much more effective if all the professionals could consult and interact with each other daily. They could also keep each other up-to-date on new and promising research and development within their specialist fields, thus providing greater benefits for their clients.

Tina then asked the following two critical questions:
- Were the majority willing to move ahead with the holistic centre?
- What would those opposed do if the majority did decide to go ahead?

They decided to vote on who would actually support and help with the establishment of the holistic centre and almost immediately 11 hands went up (including Tina's). Tina's strength, the power and authenticity of her belief in the centre and her willingness to negotiate a compromise carried the day.

Tina offered the two others some time to think about what they would do in response to this decision. However, they immediately told her they had decided to leave the practice. They had already consulted lawyers and were advised about how they could seek to stop or at least slow down her project. However, they felt it would be very unpleasant to be in a workplace where everyone would see them as representing a legal threat to the group and a major hindrance to a project that the great majority endorsed.

Tina thanked them for the thoughtfulness of their response and said she personally would miss them as colleagues and professionals. She said that their severance packages would be generous and that they would be given good references — all of which she did.

Tina spent two years in her leadership role — helping to build the holistic centre — and continued as practice group leader for about a year after the centre was fully established, then moved onto a bigger challenge overseas.

The central lessons for Tina were:

- There are certain critical times when a leader must express traits that are not natural to their character structure, and this will inevitably take them out of their comfort zone.
- What may block or prevent a leader from expressing a necessary trait is often not lack of training or workplace experience, but instead experiences within their psychological history that often go back to childhood or adolescence.
- Accurate, in-depth self-knowledge and willingness to accept feedback are essential if a leader is to undertake the necessary steps to master their Achilles' heels.

Tina had fully arrived at the independent self stage of development, one of approximately 25% of adults who reach this stage.

CHAPTER TWELVE

JAMES' STORY

JAMES had the strong characteristics of the Realist in his relationship profile, the Executive in his action profile and the Analyst in his thinking profile. He identified three issues in his life that he wanted to work on:
- He was plagued by insecurity in spite of his continuing success in ensuring the security of his family and business.
- He found it very difficult to directly express his feelings of love to his wife and children, despite being devoted to them.
- He tended to micro-manage his employees. Even though he was very fond of them and treated them well, his management style made them feel that he did not trust their competency or commitment.

All of these were examples of treadmills and Achilles' heels commonly found in his relationship, action and thinking profiles.

James said his parents were very ambitious people, focused on achieving their professional goals. His father became a senior executive in a large international corporation and his mother was a lawyer who had made partner in her firm by her late 30s. They worked extremely long hours and came home late — although each morning they had an early breakfast together.

When they were young, James and his brother were looked after by a nanny/housekeeper who did the housekeeping and cooked meals. She would also put them to bed and remain with them until one of their parents got home. However, when James was eight years old and his younger brother was five, his parents felt he was old enough to take responsibility for looking after his younger brother after dinner, including putting him to bed.

James remembered feeling scared of being alone at home and responsible for his brother, but he never said anything to his parents because he felt ashamed of being scared. I asked him why he felt ashamed to talk about this with his parents and he gave two reasons:

- Both his parents had very strong work ethics and little time or patience for interactions that were not goal- or task-focused. They were both pleasant, even-tempered people who treated their children well but were not emotionally demonstrative or communicative. Thus, James had no role modelling or frame of reference for talking to others about his feelings — so he learned to contain them, rather than express them.
- Both his parents valued being a responsible person above all else. From his earliest years, they communicated this verbally and modelled it in their behaviour. They would occasionally say critical or even scathing and contemptuous things about people they considered irresponsible. Although James, the eight-year-old, could not understand words like 'contempt' or 'responsibility' he could feel what the words implied and it made him feel ashamed to complain or express fear about being given too much responsibility.

Looking after his younger brother taught James to be very aware of things that might hurt or cause accidents, because his brother was quite careless and erratic. This responsibility reinforced James' tendency to anticipate things that might go wrong and correct them before they happened.

Also, James' brother was much more emotionally expressive and more willing to talk about things than either James or his parents. He often came to James to talk and this experience programmed James to begin having one way relationships where others needed him but he did not need others. Thus, as James grew up he acquired the traits of independence and self-sufficiency characteristic of the Realist relationship profile.

In addition, many of the same childhood experiences that shaped James' Realist relationships profile were reinforced by ones that shaped his Executive action profile. Central to this was his need to be independent and self-reliant as well as highly responsible.

James got into the pattern of working long hours, a pattern that was reinforced by the development of his Analyst concept profile which had its origin in two sources:

- The emotional isolation he experienced at home caused him to emphasise using his intellect. He could not talk to his parents about feelings but he could talk to them about academic or factual subjects.
- James was clever and performed really well in school. He took on the characteristics of the Analyst: being thorough, gathering facts, demonstrating attention to detail and in-depth analysis. He excelled at maths and science. This academic performance won him approval which in turn made him apply himself even more.

By the time he was in the last two years of high school, James began hanging around with the top male clique — all of them successful at school and sport and most of them socially adept as well. They all saw themselves as independent, which they equated with physical and mental prowess and the ability to break the rules. They were often critical or dismissive of others.

James said that on the surface, all of this gave him a measure of self-esteem. Yet there was always an underlying fear that he would eventually not be able to hold it all together, that he would fail. This made him work even harder. James said there was always a feeling that if only he achieved enough he would finally have proved himself and his self-esteem would be solid. This is the classic Executive action treadmill.

On the personal development workshop that James attended he was able to access and experience the core issues that comprised the deficit motivations driving his treadmills: feelings of emotional isolation and feelings of insecurity.

During a meditation designed to access childhood memories, James had a powerful, life changing experience. He suddenly remembered being a child at home, feeling intensely lonely and isolated. All these feelings welled up in him with the intensity with which a child feels emotions. He wept like a child as he felt 'wave after wave of emotion' pouring out.

James was completely shocked by these feelings since he always assumed that he had a happy childhood. However, the dynamics were quite simple, though largely unconscious. James had been able to feel a wide range of emotions as a child but was not allowed to express those feelings to his parents or his brother. This influenced him not by anything his parents said but just their actions.

The main conduits we have as humans for making any in-depth contact with others are direct expression of emotions (hugging, kissing, holding hands) and verbal communication. If emotional conditioning from childhood prevents these, we will inevitably feel emotional isolation.

As an adolescent James' feelings of isolation and loneliness were pushed into his subconscious and covered up by his intense activity and the surface-level self-esteem achieved through his academic, sporting and social success. However, these suppressed feelings are actual electro-chemical energy that builds up in the limbic system of the brain.

As this backlog of unexpressed, unconscious emotional energy built up, James came to depend more and more on intense intellectual and physical activity. He would spend long hours at work and then came home and start doing household tasks. The underlying motivation driving his treadmill was the fear that if he stopped the intense activity he would be overwhelmed by the feelings of isolation and loneliness that would surface from his subconscious.

Along with intense activity, the other two factors that kept the powerful feelings of isolation and loneliness subconscious were two characteristics commonly found in individuals like James with strong Realist relationship profiles:
- The tendency to contain rather than express emotions.
- The tendency to cultivate one-way relationships.

By contacting and releasing those stored emotions he achieved a major breakthrough in releasing himself from his relationship and action treadmills.

James could also remember that he felt fear and insecurity about the sudden responsibility of looking after his brother from the time he was eight years old. However, he did not associate those childhood feelings with his current feelings of insecurity as an adult. He was simply unaware that this pattern of emotional response (insecurity) had been programmed into the emotional part of his brain (the limbic system) and was subconsciously driving his security-seeking behaviour now as a mature adult.

Since his security-seeking was created by a fear-based deficit drive, it made no difference how many steps he took to bring security to his family and business. That type of activity and accomplishment would never make him feel secure. Thus no matter what he did he never felt secure. The key to feeling secure was to de-programme the feeling of insecurity left over from his childhood.

James made an ongoing commitment to daily meditation which would continue the process of emotional de-programming and give him greater access to the resources of his Being self.

He also said he wanted to work out strategies for dealing with his family life and his business, but his first priority was to make emotional contact with his wife and children. Because of his emotional breakthrough during the course, he was literally bursting with love that he wanted to express while also being unsure of how to approach it.

James arrived home from the workshop, opened a bottle of wine and had the most important conversation of his life with his wife. He poured out everything he had learned about himself on the workshop. At times he choked up and so did she. He apologised 'from his soul for being so emotionally distant for so long!' And he promised to be there for her in a way he never had before.

Then James took two days off work — a first for him — and he and his wife continued their conversation. She requested that he listen to her and began by acknowledging that she had been thinking about leaving him for at least a year. She felt like she had been living with a robot (a kind and generous one) but nonetheless a robot for most of their marriage.

She now had hope that he had experienced a major emotional breakthrough and was absolutely sincere in the commitments he made to her about changes in his behaviour. But she said that his habits were so deeply engrained that she wanted some assurances:

- She asked for a commitment to see a marriage counsellor on an ongoing basis for at least the next several months.
- She wanted him to spend more time with her and the kids.
- She asked him for a commitment to work fewer hours, to be home by a reasonable time and not to work on weekends.
- She wanted him to get some professional help to support him in making these changes.

James wholeheartedly agreed because he wanted these things for himself, as well as her and the kids. He made good on all of his commitments and his relationship with his family improved to a degree that would have seemed inconceivable before. He still loved his work, but his family life had become far more important to him.

He initially cut back dramatically on his working hours and began seeing the marriage counsellor with his wife. The counsellor helped them both understand many of the ways they were miscommunicating — or not communicating — and to clearly identify the kinds of interactions that were destructive to their marriage. She assisted them in replacing these old habits with much more fruitful and satisfying ones.

James began spending much more time with his wife and his family life became the core of his existence and a source of a happiness he had never known possible. He began talking to his children, asking them questions about what was most important to them, what they felt and thought. He also told them things about his childhood he had never revealed and he began reading them stories before they went to bed.

James gradually came to experience more emotional contact with his children. It took them a while to trust this change in their father, but the payoff came when they began asking their mother when daddy would be home and they greeted him with big hugs. James began to have a kind of metaphoric glow or radiance about him because of this opening up of his emotional life with his family.

JAMES' TRANSFORMATION AS A LEADER

In terms of his professional life James had to focus on things that he could do to get off his Executive action and Analyst thinking treadmills and master his Achilles' heels. His Executive action treadmill was taking on greater and greater responsibility in pursuing business goals and managing his business yet never feeling he was doing enough. His Executive Achilles' heel was the tendency to micro-manage.

His thinking map treadmill was his tendency to overanalyse without ever feeling secure that he had the right answers. What made this more complicated was that he had so many natural strengths within his Executive and Analyst profiles. He was an extremely good planner, organiser and analytical thinker. He expressed some anxiety about overcoming his treadmills and Achilles' heels because he thought he might lose some of these strengths. However, this was not the case.

He would always have the natural strengths associated with his profile. Mastering his treadmills and Achilles' heels would merely make him use these natural strengths in more discerning ways. Plus two things that had been driving his treadmills in the past had been dealt with in his breakthrough:

- The intense mental and organisational/managerial activity had helped keep the early childhood feelings of isolation and loneliness suppressed, and he had an unconscious fear that these feelings would surface and overwhelm him if he stopped the intense activity.
- The feelings of fear and insecurity that were emotionally programmed into him from being given so much responsibility so young.

He was now consciously aware that his need for security came not from the objective needs of his family or business, but from his childhood experience and thus would no longer have the same compulsive grip on him.

James understood that in order to keep his commitments to his wife, he would have to learn to delegate more effectively and stop micro-managing. He would have to learn to trust his people more. Thus he identified three of his senior people with whom he wanted to begin the delegation process. He had to take careful notice of when the impulse to intervene and begin micro-managing occurred and learn to manage that impulse until it disappeared.

James was an extremely competent manager but I asked him to think about the difference between management and leadership. I gave him a list that defined the differences between the two roles (defined in Chapter 1).

James worked hard on the delegation process with his three managers who were shocked, and then delighted, by being given more responsibility. He worked really hard to monitor himself carefully with regard to micro-management because the impulse was still there. His plan was that within one month he would be working 8.00am to 6.00pm and would no longer work weekends. His wife and kids were over the moon about this.

James then outlined the strategic business plan that he had produced in collaboration with his three top people. This plan called for a major expansion of his business over the next five years. When I asked James why he wanted to do this his response was two-fold:

- He realised that the character structure that was formed by his childhood and adolescent experiences made him a natural and very good manager, but he had never developed many of the traits and skills needed to become a leader. Now he realised that he really wanted to become a good leader.
- He wanted to provide an opportunity for his people to grow and develop, and also gain better incomes. His plan was to develop, train and mentor people to manage and lead each of his shops, and when they demonstrated competency and success, he would allow them to purchase shares in the company. To do this he and the other managers would need to build a company culture that would maintain the standards of product knowledge, customer service, teamwork and business ethics that had brought them their current success. He also wanted to offer a profit-sharing plan for all his employees.

Given the scope and size of his vision for the future of his business and the risks entailed, it was obvious something had shifted deep within James. Partly this was because of his willingness to master the insecurity that had so dominated his life and partly it was his willingness to develop some leadership skills and traits that did not come naturally. His new focus was also an indication that he was beginning to experience a level of motivation characteristic of Maslov's higher stages of development, such as the self-actualisation drive.

James already had a vision for the future of his company which he believed in and was deeply committed to realising. He also had high ethical standards, was very service-orientated, was fair and treated his people well, but there were a number of traits and skills that he wanted to develop that were natural to Q12 profiles very different from his.

The traits and skills he was referring to were natural strengths for people with strong Entrepreneur, and Motivator action profiles, plus the Idealist concept profile:

- He wished to develop the traits of strength and initiative, having the flexibility and willingness to take risks characteristic of the Entrepreneur profile.
- He wanted to be better at engaging with people and to have more insight into others — their feelings, moods, fears, desires — so that he would have more empathy and be better at managing and leading. He wished to develop better persuasive skills and to be more effective at communicating his thoughts and ideas: all natural character traits and skills for the Motivator profile.
- He wanted to develop his imaginative and creative thinking skills and to become an inspiring communicator and public speaker: all natural strengths and skills for the Idealist concept profile.

Because this was a very ambitious plan and could not be accomplished overnight James prioritised his list and decided he wanted to begin by developing his public speaking skills. I recommended a very good public speaking course and also suggested that he joined Toastmasters for at least six months. The public speaking course would provide him with the kind of training that would help him deliver major speeches or presentations, while Toastmasters would give him the experience he needed in speaking right from the heart.

James was very committed to his leadership development. Aside from his family, becoming a fully authentic, effective leader was his most important priority.

By the end of five years James had fully realised his vision and had 12 shops operating in three cities with over 400 employees. The whole process of transforming this vision into reality was deeply fulfilling for him.

During that period James became a really fine leader. He managed to develop and master all of the traits and skills he wanted while still keeping the working hours he had promised his family.

James also became a very skilled public speaker. He was invited to speak to many businesses and civic groups. All of his talks emphasised the ideals he stood for: good business ethics; the importance of building a healthy, service-orientated, team-based culture; the critical role of good leadership in building that culture; sharing the wealth with the employees who helped create it; and last but not least, civic and community service for both individuals and businesses.

CHAPTER THIRTEEN

TIM'S STORY

TIM had the strong characteristics of an Observer in his relationships map, a Supporter in his action map, and a Dreamer in his thinking map.

Tim tended to be very quiet and self-contained. He preferred to be alone most of the time, because it felt peaceful, although it was a kind of flat, empty peacefulness. He felt very uncomfortable about emotional exchanges with others and had a very deep aversion to conflict or confrontation of any kind. He had never had a girlfriend for longer than a few months and never felt that he wanted the commitment of living with someone. However, his isolation had started to make him feel depressed.

His other reason for seeking personal development was that he had recently been promoted to a senior management position. Tim was an extremely competent structural engineer who worked alone most of the time. While he had been able to work well as a team leader for a small team, promotion to a senior management position meant he would be in charge of over 70 staff; he would now have to spend much more time dealing with people and their issues, plus he may sometimes have to confront people or deal with conflict. He felt completely out of his depth.

Tim was a single child. Both of his parents were academics. His mother had a MA in English and taught literature at a local college. His father had a PhD in political science and taught at a state university.

By the time Tim was five or six years old, he became aware that his father was increasingly frustrated that his career was not progressing well. His father blamed some of his colleagues and spent endless hours complaining to Tim and his mother. Tim's father also began to drink heavily at this time and show an increasingly bad temper. Other than as a recipient of his anger, Tim had almost no relationship with his father, who ignored him most of the time. He became terrified of his father and tried to avoid him as much as possible.

Though his father's temper was erratic and unpredictable, he had very strict rules about Tim's behaviour: study hard, don't speak unless spoken to, be home from school at a precise time every day, always ask permission if you wish to do something which is not part of the family routine, and always speak with respect to any authority figure.

Tim's mother had always been gentle, soft and loving with Tim until his father began to insist that she should be tougher and more disciplinarian. His mother also became increasingly terrified of his father and Tim could see this pain and fear in her face. it bothered him terribly to see this pain, so Tim also began to avoid being with her as much as possible. By the time Tim was eight or nine, he tried to avoid both parents as much as possible and his pattern of withdrawal was set.

But Tim could not always physically withdraw and so he could often hear his mother being attacked by his father. When he could not physically withdraw he started to 'disconnect' (his words) inside, withdrawing into a safe, quiet place deep within himself. In this inner state there was no fear: he became an unaffected 'observer' of his parent's drama.

This was what psychologists call a 'dissociative state' and it acts like a circuit-breaker. When too much electricity builds up in our household wiring system, there is a circuit-breaker that shuts off the current as a safety measure. Similarly, when a child's nervous system is overloaded with extremely powerful emotions a circuit-breaker affect occurs and all the emotional energy stops. It leaves the child feeling peaceful, but it is a flat, empty peacefulness.

Tim felt shy and did not make friends easily. Although he had a few friends his father's rages meant he didn't feel comfortable bringing them home. He also feared the strong emotions that might come with friendship. Thus, the Observer treadmill of physical withdrawal — or psychological withdrawal (dissociation) —was programmed into Tim.

He found he could spend long hours inside his mind doing intellectual tasks and this helped him become very successful in school and university. However, this solitary intellectual activity also reinforced his tendency for physical and psychological withdrawal. He never learned the social skills of forming good friendships and enjoying group relationships.

While Tim's father was often angry, he also had another side to him that admired academic achievement. When Tim came home with straight As, his father approved and gave him some praise. This made Tim long for those moments of praise and approval and gave him the motivation for obeying authority, keeping the rules and working hard at school.

Tim's mother was an important influence in the development of his Supporter action profile. Tim loved his mother and felt deep hurt when he saw his father treating her so badly. He desperately wanted to rescue her but felt powerless. The psychological legacy of this was that in later life Tim became very sensitive to issues of fairness, social justice and the abuse of authority. Yet while he had strong opinions about this and sometimes desperately wanted to help, he also inherited the psychological legacy of feeling powerless to do anything.

In addition, Tim's Dreamer thinking profile was greatly influenced by his mother — although it was strongly reinforced by the Observer's tendency towards physical and psychological withdrawal that were legacies of his father. When he was small she used to read him stories of magic and fantasy which made him feel loved and safe. Although she stopped when he learnt to read for himself (because Tim's father made her) the love of books and reading was established. He read a wide range of novels, history and books about science, but he particularly loved fantasy and science fiction. Thus, by his late adolescence he had developed the fully adult forms of fantasy and imagination that could be stimulated through reading.

When Tim entered adolescence he also discovered music, especially jazz and classical. He would hide in his room and use earphones so he would not bother his father. Although Tim had earlier learned to enter a dissociative state which was quiet and peaceful, when he began listening to music he also began to experience pleasant emotions without having to subject himself to the possible hurt that might come from interaction or relationships with others. His peaceful, but flat, inner state began to be filled with joy, love, tenderness, sadness, etc, all experienced as completely self-contained emotions.

The extensive reading which stimulated his fantasy and imagination was thus greatly enhanced by the addition of music. By late adolescence he had a very rich but completely private inner life which had the additional benefit of stimulating his capacity for creative thinking.

At university he decided to study structural engineering. He was fascinated by the structural engineering that underpinned and supported large, creative projects — the building of bridges, large shopping complexes and groups of interconnected buildings. His approach was to first thoroughly acquaint himself with all the necessary functional outcomes required for any project and then begin the creative process in his head, letting his imagination flow.

This is the classical approach of the Dreamer and it was a great strength that brought him much success. However, it also strongly reinforced his relationship Observer treadmill because it meant he worked alone, mostly inside his own head. The promotion would change all of this and was therefore quite terrifying to him. He would have to interact with people during a large part of the day and he was completely unprepared.

Tim attended several workshops over a period of time and kept to himself in spite of a number of attempts to draw him out. However, during a sharing session he finally found the courage to speak and told the group about two important insights he had had.

- The first insight was that he had no idea how much the way he was now as an adult was a result of his relationship with his father. He was amazed to discover how much his childhood had moulded his personality as an adult. Tim said the reason he could see no causal connection between his adult personality and his relationship to his father was that he had escaped his father's influence as soon as possible and had broken off all contact with him, not even attending his funeral.
- As an adult, he identified with the positive traits that he developed as an adolescent and adult (not with the frightened child). He identified with his love of reading and music, his imagination and creativity (Dreamer qualities), his skills as a structural engineer, and the strengths found in his Supporter action profile (his co-operativeness and sense of social justice) and Observer relationship profile (his objectivity and non-confrontational nature).

Tim could now see how his adult identity consisted of both elements: his natural strengths and the frightened child who was still there, emotionally programmed inside of him. What was so enlightening to Tim was the realisation that **both his strengths and his Achilles' heels and treadmills had been shaped in response to that frightened child.**

Tim's second major insight was that it was possible to change — deeply, profoundly and permanently. While he did not want to change or lose his natural strengths, he did want to get off the isolation treadmill he was on, both for himself personally, but also so that he could be effective as the leader of the structural engineering department of his company.

The first step in mastering that isolation had been taken when he shared his insights and childhood experiences on our workshops. But there was still some major work to do in releasing the stored emotional energy of that frightened child from his subconscious.

However, Tim had already started to change and develop. During the previous week at work he had witnessed one of the project team leaders speak to one of the female engineers in a very disrespectful way. Normally he would have felt very bad about this because of his Supporter sense of fairness, social justice and the feeling that people should always treat each other with respect, but he would never speak up because of his fear of confrontation. Yet this time he found the courage to explain to the team leader that his behaviour was unacceptable. Tim told him that his role should be to mentor, train and encourage junior employees. He said that treating someone disrespectfully would only lower their moral and confidence. He then asked the team leader to apologise — which he (very reluctantly) agreed to do.

Tim said that after witnessing the team leader's disrespectful behaviour, he felt the impulse to follow his usual pattern and do nothing in order to avoid confrontation. But then he felt another part of himself that was very clear and unafraid. This other 'him' was in the mindful state and was 'watching' his usual self (and its usual avoidance of conflict treadmill) as if that was not who he really was. He identified more with the 'him' that was watching his usual self and it was this experience that empowered him to choose to confront the team leader. This was the first symptom of the emergence of the deeper, richer identity experienced at the independent self stage of development.

Tim continued to work on his personal development and had a breakthrough that was key to freeing himself from the emotional programming of the frightened child within. During one of our processes Tim suddenly felt an emotion that he had never before experienced —rage towards his father. Although as a child he had felt extreme fear and dislike towards his father he had always believed that anger and rage were what defined his father, not him. In fact, he had never felt real anger at anyone in his life. In his mind he physically lashed out at his father, and what amazed him was how good it felt. It made him feel powerful, instead of the usual powerlessness he felt around any aggressive, angry male. However, Tim was then worried that he might turn into an angry man like his father.

Fear, hurt/sadness and anger are all connected. For example, if someone attacks us physically or verbally, or if we're treated badly or unfairly, or lied about by someone, etc, we might initially respond with any one of these emotions: we might feel fear, we might feel hurt or we might feel anger. We might feel these emotions in any sequence (hurt, fear, anger; anger, hurt, fear, etc), but all three are interconnected within the wiring of our emotional brain.

In order to complete the process of emotionally de-programming the stored, negative emotional memories from childhood and adolescence, we need to acknowledge, experience and express all three. However, depending on our genetic makeup and our Q12 character structure, we are more likely to initially respond with one or two of them. For example, highly aggressive people are likely to respond to any threat or attack with anger and they are often unaware that fear and/or hurt underlies the anger. For such people, fear and hurt reside in what Carl Jung called the (subconscious) shadow within the psyche.

Until all three emotions are acknowledged, experienced and expressed, we are stuck with all three because of their interconnectedness. Tim was obviously in touch with the fear and hurt, but now he had discovered and experienced the natural anger. This meant he was well on the road to freeing himself from the effects of his childhood trauma. This was the key to freeing him from isolation and would allow him to develop and express some of the firmer, more assertive traits and skills that he needed as a leader. It did not mean that he would become an angry person.

After this breakthrough Tim identified three priorities that he wanted to focus on:

- To overcome and master his main treadmill, which were the behavioural habits that kept him from establishing relationships of any emotional depth.
- To overcome his fear of confrontation, but also to understand and learn when and in what ways confrontation is appropriate.
- To focus on developing the traits and skills he needed to be a leader at the senior executive level. This task involved overcoming some of his Achilles' heels, but equally it meant developing some traits and skills that did not come naturally to someone with his Q12 profile.

Tim decided that the first thing he would do was to build some personal friendships with people whom he had met on the workshops. He particularly identified three people who were quite different from him: they were all more emotional and one of them had a much stronger, more assertive personality than Tim.

Developing friendships with these people was easier because of the shared experience of the workshops. There is a level of trust and openness that is developed on workshops that is quite rare in our social culture, but still Tim had to make an effort. Forming such friendships may not seem the least bit remarkable to many people – but for Tim it was quite extraordinary. At this point Tim had more in-depth personal contact with these people than he had had with anyone in his entire life. The emotional breakthrough Tim achieved on the workshops, followed by the forming of these friendships, completely erased his feelings of loneliness and isolation.

Although this was fantastic, I cautioned him that sometimes relationships go through difficult periods or even break up. There would be times when he would feel the pull to go back into his old habits of physical and psychological withdrawal. If that happened, it would be very important to have people to whom he could turn for support. Having these solid friendships would make it easier for Tim to take the emotional risks that are always there in any relationship.

TIM'S LEADERSHIP TRANSFORMATION

Leadership development was also a very high priority for Tim. He had never had any management or leadership training, and much of the time he felt he was metaphorically groping in the dark with his new position. The management role did not frighten him. These were things he could learn from textbooks. It was the leadership role that was challenging.

Tim identified several natural strengths he already had that, when balanced with the new ones he wished to develop, would help him in his new role:
- **Strong Dreamer concept profile (creative thinker)** — Up until recently he had applied that mode of thinking to structural design work, but it could also be applied to decision making, strategic thinking and strategic planning. Though he had not previously used his creative thinking skills much in this way, he felt he could learn to do this quickly. I recommended two books of strategic thinking and strategic planning that would be useful for him to read.
- **Objective observer (observer of people and group dynamics)** — Although he rarely spoke up because of the fear of confrontation, this trait was a natural strength associated with his Observer relationship profile. To use this skill as a leader, he had to develop both the confidence and the skill in communicating and coaching.

- **Supporter (strong sense of fairness and justice and genuine care for others)** — He treated people well and fairly, and they trusted him.
- **Expertise (extensive industry knowledge)** — He was generally known and respected for this. He also had very extensive corporate knowledge.

There were two issues that were critical to his new leadership role:
- His relationship with the other senior leaders, and his leadership role in contributing to the development of the company as a whole.
- Managing and leading a department of 70 staff with nine people in middle management positions reporting directly to him.

Beginning with the first issue, there were several qualities that Tim had that were helpful to him in his earlier career. As a Supporter, he had always been a very accommodating and compliant person. This had often been helpful to him in maintaining good relationships with his clients. Plus Tim's non-confrontational character made people feel very safe around him.

Both of these qualities had made him very accepting of, and compliant with the wishes, directives and authority of company managers and policies. For example, he had never vigorously disagreed with his boss. If he disagreed with a decision his boss made or with a company policy, usually he would say nothing to avoid possible confrontation and disagreeable emotions. On the few occasions he did speak up he spoke very tentatively and quietly. If challenged, he would immediately become quiet and compliant.

Now, however, he was part of the senior management team responsible for the long-term growth, welfare, reputation and prosperity of the company. Rather than simply being compliant with company policy, he now had to contribute to creating it. Tim said the CEO was actually a good leader and encouraged vigorous debate amongst his senior management team in an attempt to create the best possible decisions, policies and plans. All but one of the other six members of the team had very strong, assertive personalities and vigorous debate was easy and natural for them. However, Tim's fear of confrontation and his qualities of accommodation and compliance could prevent him from making vigorous, assertive contributions to the team's discussion, debate and decisions. It was clear that he would need to develop some new traits or qualities that did not come naturally to him if he was to be effective as a senior leader.

In addition, Tim identified four traits and skills he would need to develop to successfully fulfil his role as the leader of his department (as distinct from his

role as a member of the senior management team):
- He would have to develop skills in coaching and mentoring his people, particularly his team leaders.
- He would have to learn how to deal effectively with interpersonal issues and conflicts, something he had avoided in the past.
- He would have to learn how to coach or counsel people who were underperforming or whose behaviour was in some way inappropriate.
- He would have to learn how to create a leadership team out of his managers.

The next step was to distinguish the deep character structure traits, abilities and expanded awareness Tim would need to achieve, versus the more specific skills he would need to learn. It was fairly easy to make those distinctions. For example, Tim could take courses in the skills to help him to be more assertive and persuasive (assertiveness training, public speaking), courses that would train him in coaching skills and performance counselling, conflict resolution and team-building.

But the degree of Tim's effectiveness in learning and using these skills would be a function of his level of consciousness and self-mastery. And these would involve deep changes in character structure — transformational change. He would need to develop traits or qualities within himself that would empower him to effectively use the more specific skills listed above. To achieve this would involve the 'emotional de-programming' of certain Achilles' heels and treadmills.

For example, one of Tim's natural strengths was imaginative, creative thinking. However, in order to use this natural strength in communicating his ideas to the other senior managers, he needed to do two things:
- He needed to overcome his fear of confrontation and develop a deep inner strength and confidence.
- He would need to learn to use a highly-structured, logical communication style to communicate his ideas to the other senior managers and other engineers in his division. (Statistically, engineers are more likely to be left brain dominant — in Q12 language, Analysts or Rationalists.)

I asked Tim, what were the deeper character traits he wanted to develop to support him in his leadership role. What traits did he need to develop to more effectively use his natural strengths and to support him in both learning and using the more specific skills listed above?

It did not take long for Tim to identify three:
- Inner strength and confidence — including the ability to take a strong stand on things he believed in, without being inflexible.
- A strong, natural verbal assertiveness and persuasiveness — without verbally dominating or drowning out others.
- An ability to communicate in a way that highly logical, left brain dominant people could understand.

To begin with, Tim started with some in-depth training in the Q12 system for assessing people's character structure. He thought this would create a good foundation for undertaking his leadership development:
- He wanted to use it to help him gain more in-depth self-knowledge, to better understand how his character traits and developed, what his natural strengths and Achilles' heels were, to understand his treadmills and to learn more about how to manage himself more effectively.
- He also wanted to learn about the traits, qualities, natural strengths and possible Achilles' heels of all twelve of the Q12 character structure profiles. He intended to use this to help him gain insight into the people he interacted with daily.

Tim absorbed this information very quickly. He worked out the probable character types of the other senior managers, and he began to use this insight to assist him in learning to interact with them more effectively. He approached this with a degree of humility, understanding that the Q12 profiling system was a dynamic system, not intended to pigeonhole people, simply a tool for gaining greater understanding of ourselves and others.

Tim committed himself to a series of behavioural changes that he knew would be difficult for him at first and take him out of his comfort zone. For example, he screwed up his courage and began to speak up more in the senior management team meetings. To achieve this he used a strategy that involved two things:
- He prepared everything he was going to say ahead of time, being careful to craft his message with words, phrases and verbal constructions that would appeal to highly logical Q12 Rationalists and Analysts — not his usual style of communication.
- He would practise what he was going to say a number of times in front of the mirror to gain confidence before speaking in the meeting, and he committed himself to preparing something of significance to say at every

meeting. He also joined Toastmasters to help him overcome his fear of speaking out.

All this had come to a head when, about 6 months into his coaching sessions, a major event occurred. The senior management team went off site to a conference centre for a three day strategic planning session. Tim prepared by using his long experience in the industry and his highly imaginative, creative mind to come up with some very innovative strategies for how the company could grow its business over the next several years. He then translated these ideas into highly logical verbal constructions, as well as some graphs and charts, that would appeal to the logical, 'left brained' profiles of his colleagues.

Over the three days, even though Tim did not in any way verbally dominate the team meetings, the creative, innovative quality of his ideas gradually emerged as the dominant strategic approach for the new three year strategic business plan. In the end, about 80% of the plan was clearly Tim's ideas. The next day, the CEO asked Tim to his office and gave him acknowledgement for his contribution to the strategic planning process.

Tim also committed himself to a series of changes that, again, would initially be difficult for him and take him out of his comfort zone. For example, he began to have an open door policy in his office scheduled for two hours every day. He announced that his project team leaders or anyone else in his department had access to him during that time. The input from the meetings helped with problem solving and innovation while it also assisted him in maintaining a general level of awareness of moral and job satisfaction. Most importantly for Tim personally, he actually began to enjoy meeting with his people this way. He had truly conquered his isolation treadmill.

Tim also focused on the team leaders who directly reported to him. He took a course in how to facilitate meetings and began holding weekly meetings. He did this mainly to work on workplace issues – but he also wanted to create a strong sense of common purpose, building trusting and respectful relationships within the team. Again, he made use of the Q12 profiling system to gain insight into the profiles of each of the team leaders.

At this time he identified that there were two team leaders whose behaviour was very aggressive and at times even rude to other team members (though their engineering technical skills were good). He knew he had to deal with this, which would be a test of his willingness and ability to undertake action that could lead to confrontation.

I trained Tim in a coaching technique for dealing with inappropriate behaviour and Tim began coaching sessions with the two team leaders. He got very fast results. In his second session with one team leader he found out that he was undergoing a severe personal crisis (his wife was suffering from breast cancer and it was, at this stage, uncertain as to whether she would survive). He said that over the past six months he had felt depressed, powerless, frustrated and angry. He said he knew that this frustration and anger was coming out at work and he felt very bad about it. With advice from me, Tim recommended the manager attend a support group for partners and adult family members of cancer victims. Although the team leader told Tim that he was not usually the type of person who would join groups, he was so on edge emotionally that he agreed to give it a chance. This support group was enormously helpful and within weeks his behaviour in the workplace greatly improved.

The other manager did not respond at all. He seemed to resent the coaching sessions, and in fact after three weeks he refused to continue. His behaviour became even worse and two members of his project team made an appointment to see Tim about this. Tim asked them if they were willing to file a formal complaint and they said 'yes'.

Tim went to see the HR director and told him of the damage the manager was doing and that he felt it was extremely unlikely this person would change. He gave the HR manager the formal complaint and asked what he needed to do, within company policy, to fire the manager. Taking a stance as firm as this would have been unimaginable to him several months before this incident, but Tim felt that his most important responsibility was to provide a safe and positive workplace environment for his people.

Tim took responsibility for meeting the manager in his office to offer him a chance to resign and to tell him that if he did not resign he would be fired. Tim said he had never done anything like that in his life and that he was so nervous he could not sleep the night before. The manager became extremely angry and verbally abusive — but in the end he did resign and was given a generous severance package. Even though Tim knew what he had done was necessary, he felt terrible. However, his spirits were soon lifted when over the next two days every engineer from the project team individually came to him to say 'thanks'.

Tim gave a lot of thought to who the replacement should be. He preferred to promote someone from within his department. He knew from his own experience that the engineer he had in mind combined brilliant engineering skills with very good people skills, however, he had no actual leadership experience. Tim interviewed the engineer and asked him if he would like the job on the proviso he was willing to undertake an intensive leadership and management development program.

Tim then asked that the engineer be interviewed by the members of the project team he would lead because he wanted to ensure that the team had a say in who was going to lead them. The engineer agreed and Tim arranged the interviews. Within the first two weeks of his promotion, it was obvious to all that he was an excellent choice for the position.

Over approximately the eight months of our regular coaching sessions I watched Tim develop into a authentic, effective and mindful leader. Given the personality that Tim displayed when he came to our first personal development workshop, he would be the last person one would expect to become an effective leader. But after his breakthroughs, 'awakenings' and coaching he developed into a remarkably fine leader. Tim was aware of a gradual growing respect from his fellow workmates. It was clear that Tim was truly free of the treadmills and Achilles' heels that would have prevented his leadership development. He had also developed a number of character traits and strengths that did not come naturally to someone with Tim's original Q12 character structure. Tim had grown into a fully authentic, effective and mindful leader through his willingness and commitment to pursue the path of self-mastery.

CHAPTER FOURTEEN

MIKE'S STORY

MIKE had the strong characteristics of a Pragmatist in his relationships profile, an Entrepreneur in his action profile and a Rationalist in his concept profile.

Mike was a very focused, hard-working person, with amazing levels of both physical and mental energy. He was never quite satisfied with the status quo, and was always interested in something new or unique. He liked being around highly creative people and his division of 3,000 people performed very successfully under his leadership.

However, as a leader, Mike had several Achilles' heels that led to serious problems within his division: especially fear and low morale. His people felt that he was so task-focused and impersonal that they didn't really know who he was. Mike seemed completely unaware of his own and other people's emotional needs. Consequently his people did not feel appreciated and valued. He had a reputation for taking the initiative and getting difficult tasks done quickly. However, he also had a reputation for sometimes doing this at the expense of his people. His communication style was often tough, blunt and even scathing.

As a Rationalist, he was capable of putting together clear, powerful, logically-structured arguments for the goals and actions he wished his people and organisation to undertake. Through the power of his logic, Mike usually won arguments, although often at the cost of losing hearts, loyalty and commitment. Many people were aware that a powerful, logically-structured argument did not always guarantee that Mike had the best case — and there were serious problems with his division's culture which he was not addressing. Yet most people were afraid to approach him.

After a series of complaints built up, Mike was forced to do something. As a result, I was engaged as a consultant for a cultural change programme within his division. After interviewing some of his senior staff, I told Mike that it was essential to for him to have a series of one-on-one coaching sessions. He was initially reluctant to do this because he was very confident that he was a successful leader: he had led the division to a high level of financial success and in his mind that was the only real marker of success. I had to convince him that he was responsible for overcoming the fear and low morale within his division's culture. He needed to understand that his patterns of daily behaviour ultimately shaped the culture and that without some personal changes there was little I or anyone else could do to affect a major cultural change.

I began by asking Mike's permission to tell him how people in his organisation saw him, which I had distilled from many interviews. This included his many strengths, but also his Achilles' heels: his personal remoteness, lack of awareness of an emotional domain, his absolute absence of people skills, his communication style and his use of powerful, logical arguments almost as a weapon. Mike's initial response was incredulous because he saw all of these behavioural patterns as part of his natural strengths. It took some time to get him to the point where he was willing to consider that some of this behaviour might be responsible for the cultural problems within his division.

After reflecting on what he had learned about his Achilles' heel behavioural patterns he returned for another coaching session. He seemed very different to his usual very confident, very fluent style: he seemed quieter and more reflective.

It became clear that Mike's relationship pattern emerged from his early family experiences. His father had been a senior federal government executive. He was highly intelligent, extremely hard-working, and very cool and unemotional. Mike's mother was an accountant and consultant. She was equally intelligent, hard-working and rarely expressed emotions of any kind.

Mike had an older brother who quite often bullied him. When Mike was young, his brother would tease him and humiliate him in front of other children, and when he was about seven his brother began to hit him from time to time.

Mike initially went to his mother to complain and express his hurt. She said she did not approve of what his older brother was doing to him, but that crying or feeling hurt would not help Mike at all and would in fact encourage his brother's behaviour.

Mike's father would sometimes discipline his older brother. Yet most of what he said to Mike reinforced his mother's statements that crying or showing that he was hurt were weaknesses and would only encourage further bullying. Mike's father would always say that when he felt weak or hurt, he should get busy doing something he felt difficult or challenging. Doing this would demand so much of his attention that the feelings of weakness or hurt would just go away. Mike said he had been using this approach since he was about seven years old.

As Mike focused more of his attention on his childhood memories he came to remember that his parents were rarely around and he had no relationship with his brother (except being bullied): he realised that he had felt very alone. He never spoke about this because he just thought that this was the natural order of things. However, he did work out that the more he got busy with things, the less he felt fear, hurt or loneliness!

Mike was very smart and much of his time was focused on his schoolwork and sports. He was a natural athlete and virtually every minute of his day was spent studying or playing sport. As he got more and more busy with these activities, he stopped feeling lonely or hurt. This pattern of activity followed him throughout his schooling. He did not join social groups and had no real friends. Social relationships seemed frivolous and a waste of time.

By the end of this session, Mike was very clear about why all of his relationships were activity-based and not emotional. This had been programmed into him at a young age and strongly reinforced by all of his later experiences. This is why no one around him at work had a clue as to who he was and was undoubtedly the reason why his wife had left him — she had found him emotionally remote.

Mike could see how this pattern gave him many of his strengths but he was now also clear about how his behaviour negatively affected those around him. However, he was completely perplexed about how he could change this. Clearly, just changing his behaviour would not be enough. He felt he needed to learn to be more emotionally responsive and personally available.

Mike's Entrepreneur profile also emerged from two experiences that occurred during childhood and adolescence. Not only did Mike overcome his feelings of hurt resulting from his brother's actions and is parents' response by engaging in intense activities, he also became intensely competitive towards his brother. Mike worked hard and loved it when he outperformed his brother in schoolwork. It was also one of the few times when his parents gave him some praise and acknowledgement. Over time, beating his brother academically became an obsession — although his bullying and physical abuse continued.

When he discovered his natural athletic prowess he took up a number of sports including karate. Mike could immediately see the potential in this, for a smaller person skilled in karate could defeat a larger person who lacked those skills. After two years of intense training, Mike felt he was ready to take on his brother. One day walking home from school, when his brother started the usual verbal teasing intended to humiliate, Mike paid no attention and did not respond to the taunts. This made his brother angry and he took a swing, intending to hit Mike very hard in the shoulder. However, Mike was ready, dodged the punch and karate kicked his brother in the leg, knocking him down. His brother got up and tried to fight back to no avail. Finally his brother, badly bruised and limping, walked away shouting abuse at him. Mike's brother told their parents he had been attacked by a bigger kid, thereby escaping any blame or responsibility for getting into a fight and saving face about being bested in a fight with his younger and smaller brother.

A few days later when no-one was around Mike told his brother: 'If you ever hit me or make fun of me, I will use my karate to beat you to a pulp. So don't ever hit me or make fun of me again!' Despite the fact that the threat worked the impact of this powerful experience at such a young age made Mike a hard and ruthless competitor. Mike's extremely competitive view of the world was also reinforced by one of his sports coaches. This coach had two mantras:
- In sport (and in life) nothing counts except winning
- Always be looking for a new way to win — do not be predictable

This coach was a mentor to Mike. Mike had a lot of creative ideas and the coach encouraged him to speak out. He learned to speak out in a clear, powerful way, always giving clear and logical reasons for his ideas. Thus he emerged as the team's spokesman and its natural leader.

Mike now understood that his competitiveness, his powerful verbal dominance, his love of new and innovative methods and tactics, and his tendency to always 'take charge' (all Entrepreneur action profile characteristics) were deeply instilled in him by the time he finished school. These provided the basis for huge success, but also created the qualities that made others fear him and find it difficult to work with him. These Achilles' heels that were contributing factors in the culture of fear and low morale that permeated his division.

However, sport was not the only area in which Mike had been competitive as a child and adolescent. He also felt he needed opportunities to compete verbally and debating provided the perfect opportunity. He quickly learned to be an accomplished debater. Even though he loved new and novel ideas and ways of doing things, his preferred style was to express his ideas in a highly-aggressive yet highly-structured logical style.

I asked Mike how he felt people responded to his style and how it affected them. Mike replied that it was clear people respected his debating ability while also giving the impression that they were afraid of him when he was in intense debating mode. His debating success certainly did not win him any friends. He now understood that his style often lead to his winning at work, but at the cost of alienating people and creating fear. He had to acknowledge that the Achilles' heel of his Rationalist profile had created serious problems in his workplace relationships.

There were two core issues that were tied to all other areas of behaviour that Mike needed to master. Both were based on, and driven by, the emotions of loneliness, hurt and fear that Mike had experienced as a child:

- He had learned that the more focused he became on intense and demanding activities, the less likely he was to actually feel those emotions
- He found he could overcome fear by becoming highly-skilled and competitive, and came to view all life situations as competitive

The limbic system and amygdala in his brain still retained the subconsciously stored, emotionally charged memories of loneliness, hurt and fear from childhood. Despite the fact Mike had been able to remember those emotions, he had not yet accessed and released this stored emotional energy that was the subconscious deficit driver of his action and competition treadmills. Emotionally 'de-programming' this emotional energy was thus the absolute key to change.

There are two fundamental methods. The first is to directly access and release the feelings through meditation, coaching, counselling, various therapies, attending an intense personal development course, etc. The second is by undertaking behaviours and activities that are the opposite of those that serve to keep the emotions suppressed. At this stage Mike felt a degree of urgency about undergoing a deep and permanent transformational change, so he decided he wanted to use both methods.

MIKE'S PERSONAL TRANSFORMATION

Mike decided to attend one of our personal development workshops. During the workshop, Mike made huge progress partly because he had already identified how his childhood and adolescent experience had shaped his adult personality. His rapid progress was also due to his level of commitment and the way he threw himself into the experiential learning activities.

During a guided imagery process (in which music and verbal instructions work together to help participants access memories and emotions while in a safe environment), Mike found himself actually feeling as if he were that lonely, hurt and frightened boy. Later he described not only feeling the emotions, but also feeling the emotional energy releasing and pouring out of his body. He experienced a feeling of peacefulness and saw himself as a boy standing in front of himself as an adult —the boy looked peaceful and happy and as he reached out and embraced the boy he felt his younger self merging with his older self. In one act, Mike reclaimed a part of himself that he had been disconnected from ever since he developed the action and competition treadmills that had dominated his life.

Mike's second important experience occurred during a session of bodywork. Whenever we experience strong emotions that we internally resist and block in some way, we create tension which locks up our muscles. Bodywork sessions are designed to unlock these and thus allow the blocked emotions to flow freely again. Since Mike had used very extreme methods to shut out and block his emotions very early in life, so much of this 'locking' had occurred that it was as if his body was 'armoured'.

During the bodywork session, Mike felt his armouring begin to release and dissolve, crumbling away. Again, this was a surprise, because he was not even aware of his armouring. Mike then became concerned that without the armouring he would feel vulnerable until I explained that this new vulnerability would be of enormous value to him in the changes he may wish to make in both his personal and professional life. Mike had now taken a major first step in his personal and professional transformation, which would be furthered by his commitment to daily meditation.

Mike then decided that he wanted to focus on three areas of behavioural change:
- He wanted to overcome his degree of isolation by making an attempt to develop a social side to his life
- He could see that the greatest potential for developing an ability to

have an emotional connection to another person was through creating a relationship with his sons
- He wanted to change his behaviour at work because he acknowledged that he (as division leader) was the ultimate source of the negative culture

He decided to join a group that undertook regular activities that were not intense, and whose primary purpose was socialising and enjoyment. Mike did some research and found a group that actually had the term 'social club' in its title. Club members would usually spend one night a week together and three or four times a year would go somewhere for a whole weekend. Each evening meeting would involve a pot luck dinner, socialising and a group activity arranged by one of the members.

His natural reaction was to view the whole thing as frivolous, since by far the most difficult activity for him was the time spent socialising. Mike really had no current experiences to talk about except work. I suggested that Mike talk about his children, his marriage break-up, and maybe some experiences from his childhood. Because the group were so accepting and non-judgemental Mike came to share more private experiences them. However, what most surprised him was that he actually began to find the stories other people told about various aspects of their lives interesting and enjoyable. He found that he really began to care about these people and being with them became intrinsically enjoyable; he no longer had the impulse to 'get up and do something'. Mike was beginning to rediscover his humanity.

Mike had been divorced about one year. The divorce was not acrimonious and his ex-wife said she still loved him but just felt no emotional contact coming from him. The divorce gave custody of the children (boys aged six and eight) to his ex-wife, with Mike having the right to have them every other weekend and one evening per week. However, Mike never had them for this whole allotted time because he always claimed he had too much to do at work and simply did not have enough time to spend with them.

As part of his plan, Mike made a commitment to have his boys for the full time allotted. This meant taking much more time off from work. He began picking them up once a week for an evening and spending the entire weekend with them every other week. He did sporting activities with them and took them to games — he even began to teach them some karate. All of this was initially difficult and uncomfortable for him since he had focused so little attention on them in the past that he hardly knew them, and they seemed a little shy, uncomfortable and afraid of him. They did not really trust that he would keep his commitment to them.

The boys and Mike gradually came to feel comfortable with each other and a kind of camaraderie developed. However, Mike knew that just doing active things together would only allow a certain level of relationship to develop because he had always used intense activity-based relationships as a way of avoiding in-depth personal relationships.

To develop a deeper level of relationships with his sons, Mike knew that he had to spend time just communicating with them about personal things. It was difficult but he tried to make sure that they always spent some quiet time together just talking. Eventually the boys did begin talking to him about more personal things. For example, one evening he told them about how he had been bullied as a boy. His younger son then told him that an older kid at school had been making fun of younger, smaller kids in his class in front of the other kids, and had also threatened to beat them up. He said he was really scared of this bigger kid and he admitted that he felt ashamed of being afraid.

Mike talked to his boys about feelings like shame, anger, fear and other emotions. This was a turning point in their relationship. His boys began to be open to him in a way that they had always been with their mother but never with Mike. They felt increasingly comfortable talking to him about anything and their conversations soon covered the whole spectrum of their experiences at school and with other kids, including their private thoughts and feelings.

Mike knew that even though his son had not personally been bullied, he now had to report what was occurring to the school principal. This was both to act as a role model for his sons, but also to let his sons know that if anything like this happened to them, he would be there for them and protect them. Mike took his son with him to speak to the principal. The boy was initially worried and frightened but Mike obtained a promise from the principal that his son's name would not be used in speaking to the offending boy. The school had a zero tolerance policy for bullying and Mike's son never saw the bully pick on anyone again, even though he continued to have a surly temperament. This entire episode permanently changed Mike's relationship with his sons.

MIKE'S LEADERSHIP TRANSFORMATION

In terms of his working life, Mike committed himself to making several important changes. These changes would initially take him way out of his comfort zone and he would have to expect the possibility of some discomfort in this new role.

The first issue was his workaholism — his typical weekly work schedule ran from about 6.00am through 9.00–10.00pm. He would always work at least 12 hours on Saturday and would often work a half day on Sunday. He was now aware that he was on a treadmill and was driven by the deficit motivational drive to avoid emotions, although there were other factors influencing the long hours he worked: namely his management and leadership style.

His leadership style was highly dominant and he alone had always set the basic strategy and goals for building the business. While he did hold meetings to generate new and innovative ideas, he was the sole arbitrator as to which ideas would be used. He alone made the major decisions and he felt he always needed to be at work in case there was a sudden need for an important decision. He would also often create specific project teams to develop and implement new ideas with project team leaders reporting directly to himself. He admitted that sometimes he felt that he was the only truly indispensable person in the division.

In spite of this highly dominant, directive management-leadership style, Mike was actually 'big-picture' orientated. So while he alone set the 'big picture' strategies and goals for developing the business, he never interfered with the details of business activity undertaken to achieve his goals. In this sense he fully delegated operational business matters to members of his management and special project teams, although he was extremely tough and blunt in holding them accountable for achieving the goals he set.

The frustration of his senior management team was threefold:
- They felt they should play an important role in developing 'big picture' business strategy and goals and not have this just thrust upon them
- They felt his blunt, completely impersonal way of holding them accountable for the implementation of these strategies and for achieving these goals was extremely unsupportive and made them live in fear
- They felt his special project team methodology was extremely arbitrary, unwieldy and in the long term not viable

Mike made a commitment to drastically cut back on his working hours even before he had a strategy for how he would do this —he felt that this workaholism was deeply intertwined with his personal and professional issues. He set himself to working a normal professional workday from 8.00am until 6.00pm and to having weekends off. This allowed him to have time to join the social club and to reconnect with his two boys.

Mike felt his first step was to communicate with his personal assistant.

She was extremely efficient, competent and observant, and over the previous ten years he had come to rely upon and trust her completely — even though he did not know her personally. She would always speak her mind even when she knew that he did not want to hear what she had to say.

When she entered his office she said: 'You look really different — something must've happened to you'. Mike told her about his recent life changing experiences and the briefing he was going to give to his senior leadership team. When he finished talking, she gave him a big smile and said: 'I've always had a feeling that there was a lot more to you that what I've seen on the surface, but this is the first time I've had a real glimpse of who you are and who you can be. Thank you for telling me this, I know what you intend to do is right.'

Mike set up a meeting with his senior leadership team to tell them about his change of priorities and his commitment to personal development. He said he would be dramatically cutting back his working hours and thus he wanted to share his leadership responsibilities with them:

- He committed himself to planning and setting the business' strategic direction and its major, big picture goals as a leadership team — the leadership team would undertake periodic strategic planning sessions in a collaborative manner and all final decisions would be made as a team
- He committed himself to sharing his decision-making powers with the senior management team.
- He announced that he would dissolve the complex project team structure by placing the project teams into the existing streams of line management, following the consensus opinion of his senior managers

He told them he had come to realise how impersonally and abruptly he had treated the people around him and that it was clear that everyone he interacted with was negatively affected and feared him or at least tried to avoid him as much as possible. He said he knew that this was a major factor in creating the destructive culture of fear and low moral.

Mike also acknowledged to the team that he personally did not want to be the kind of person who treated people in this way. He told them he had become aware of how and why he kept everyone at such a distance and treated people as he did. As a result of this he wanted to change and was undertaking a series of coaching sessions to assist in making those changes. He also requested that they give him honest, straightforward feedback whenever they saw him slip back into his old communication style. He promised there would be no negative repercussions although he knew it would require some courage on their part to trust that it was safe to give him this feedback.

He then left them to talk it over. Their initial reaction was shock and disbelief. It seemed impossible to them that Mike could change his leadership style so profoundly and so suddenly. They talked and although there was still a significant amount of scepticism, they were pleased with the potential for change. When Mike came back they told him they wanted some concrete promises about how and when this would begin.

Mike had already given a lot of thought to their issues and was ready with answers, making the following three commitments.

- An important decision soon had to be made about whether his division would release some major resources in order to launch a new product. Normally Mike would have made this decision himself but this time it would be made as a team. He said he would provide his management team with all the necessary information and documentation so they could make an informed decision and he committed himself to accepting their collective decision.
- He announced a need to re-evaluate the strategic direction for the division as a whole which would mean undertaking a major strategic planning session. He committed to undertaking a three-day off-site strategic planning session with his senior leadership team. The plan would be a collaborative endeavour and he promised not to exert any undue influence.
- He committed to holding regular meetings to get feedback from his senior team members about his behaviour and communication towards others. He promised that he would use this constructively because he felt such honest feedback was essential, particularly to keep himself aware of how the changes were progressing.

Mike made good on these three commitments. He held the decision-making meeting as promised and while he actively participated in the discussion he did not dominate the meeting. He not only held the strategic planning exercise off-site but he asked two of the senior leaders to write up the results — something only Mike himself would have previously done!

But perhaps most important factor in winning over the senior leadership team were the meetings with the senior leaders to give him feedback on his ways of behaving and communicating to others. Mike's behavioural and communication habits were deeply engrained. In the beginning he had a number of slip-ups where the old communication style appeared before he was even aware of it. He was given polite but very firm and clear feedback and each time he accepted it without trying to deny or defend himself.

Mike came to realise he wanted to treat people as having intrinsic value, as 'ends in themselves', rather than a means to an end. He understood that he had always seen the people he worked with only in terms of their role in the business. This realisation was critical to mastering his communication and interactive style.

Mike also did two other important things. Every morning when he arrived at work, he would smile and say hello to everyone he saw. He felt very uncomfortable and artificial doing this and people initially reacted with shock, but gradually he began to feel more comfortable and eventually to enjoy it. He also committed himself to learning and using the names of all his 3,000 staff (he had a phenomenal memory).

As part of his new leadership style he began wandering around his office building and talking to people at all levels. Previously his only contact was with his assistant, senior managers and project team leaders. Now he would informally talk to groups of people at all levels:

- He would spend some time talking about the division's business strategy and how it was unfolding
- He would ask questions about their work and sometimes about their personal life, and he would always use their names

Mike felt people gradually became more comfortable with him. His staff found this contact interesting and informative and a number of people said it was also inspiring.

Finally, as part of his new leadership style, Mike began holding a lunch hour meeting in a very large ballroom in a hotel next to their office building once every quarter. All 3,000 people were invited even though some had to fly in from other cities. As part of his leadership development, Mike had taken several courses in public speaking, and had developed into a very fine and entertaining speaker. He would always begin these quarterly meetings by delivering a short but very inspiring speech before turning the meeting over to a group from somewhere within the division to report back on some particularly creative or innovative thing they were doing. Mike would then finish the meeting by answering questions. These meetings were very well-attended and they had the psychological affect of creating a more unified culture throughout the division.

Over a six month period Mike transformed himself into a very fine leader. His value system and his communication and behaviour changed so profoundly that he emerged a truly different person. He came to demonstrate all of the qualities essential to the art of mindful leadership.

PART 5

THE LADDER OF CONSCIOUSNESS AND HIGHER DEVELOPMENTAL LEVELS

CHAPTER FIFTEEN

A MODEL FOR THE DEVELOPMENT OF HIGHER CONSCIOUSNESS

THE concept of higher states of consciousness has always been an intrinsic part of many (especially eastern) spiritual and religious cultures, although the concept of **stages** in the evolution of consciousness is much more recent. In western psychology, the idea of structured stages began with the work of American psychologist James Mark Baldwin in the early 1900s.[1] Since then, many western academics and researchers have produced variations on this theme — Erick Erickson, Abraham Maslov, Clare Graves, Laurence Cohlberg, Jane Loevinger, Susan Cook-Greuter and Robert Kegan. Among eastern spiritual thinkers and philosophers, the concept of structured stages or levels of higher consciousness has been presented in the twentieth century in works by Sri Aurobindo and Maharashi Mahesh Yogi.

In creating the model that I am using in this book I have been influenced by six sources, in addition to my own experience over the past 40 years.
- Maharishi Mahesh Yogi (whom I studied and meditated with between 1971 and 1975)
- Ken Wilber (writer)
  — *The Atman Project: A Transpersonal View of Human Development* (Quest Books, Theosophical Publishing House: Wheaton, Illinois, 1980 and 1996)
  — *Integral Spirituality* (Integral Books: Boston, 2006)
- Dr Robert Kegan (William and Miriam Meehan Professor of Adult Learning and Professional Development at the Harvard University

Graduate School of Education)
— *The Evolving Self* (Harvard University Press: Cambridge, Massachusetts, 1982)
— *In Over Our Heads* (Harvard University Press: Cambridge, Massachusetts, 1994)
- Dr Brian P Hall (Professor Emeritus of Pastoral Counselling at Santa Clara University)
— *Values Shift: A Guide to Personal and Organisational Transformation* (Wipf and Stock Publishers: Eugene, Oregon, 2006)
- Dr Abraham Maslov
— *The Psychology of Being* (D. Van Nostrand Company: New York, 1968)
- The work of Richard Barrett and his values centre (www. http://barrettvaluescentre.com)

This model is intended to provide a practical, useful discussion of the levels of development for people without academic background in the subject.

THE LADDER OF CONSCIOUSNESS

It is important to understand the difference between a state of consciousness and structured developmental stages in the evolution of consciousness. In his book *Integral Spirituality*, Wilbur points out that many people have glimpses of higher consciousness that may last for an hour, a day, a week or sometimes longer; for that period of time they experience a higher state of consciousness.[2] Such experiences can be triggered by many things: a personal crisis, listening to a particular piece of music, reading a poem, getting into the 'zone' while playing sport, a deep state of meditation and so on. Maslov called these non-permanent higher states 'peak experiences'.

By contrast, stages or levels in the evolution of consciousness refers to a full and permanent integration of that state into our awareness, a permanent change in the way we internally experience our sense of self (identity), the patterns of our thinking, emotions and motivation, the way we view other people and, in a more general sense, our 'world view'. This permanently transformed internal experience will not be directly observable to others, but as a result of it there will be observable changes in your behaviour.

UNITIVE SELF	Level 7
TRANSPERSONAL SELF	Level 6
INDEPENDENT SELF	Level 5
ADULT SOCIALISED SELF	Level 4
ADOLESCENT SELF 12/13 years through to early adulthood – ends at Adult Socialised Self Stage	
LATE CHILDHOOD SELF Approx 8 –12 years	Level 3
EARLY CHILDHOOD SELF Approx 21 months to 7 years of age	Level 2
PRE VERBAL 'BODY SELF' Approx 5/6 months in womb to approx 21 months	Level 1

The following is a diagram that Wilbur designed. Its quadrant structure provides a holistic conceptual picture which explains the connection between our interior consciousness and the external world — including our observable behaviour.[3]

INTERIOR	EXTERIOR
'I' Singular (Subjective Internal)	'IT' Singular (Objective External)
'WE' Plural (Subjective Internal)	'ITS' Plural (Objective External)

The upper left-hand quadrant describes the interior experiences within our consciousness. To understand the nature and structure of each evolving stage of development, we must rely on individual people describing what they experience. This can be done in a clear and disciplined way and there is a methodology for doing this called 'phenomenology' which had its origins in the philosophy of Edmund Husseral. Inevitably, since these descriptions are subjective, people must rely upon devices like metaphor and analogy: what they describe is very real although other people cannot directly observe it externally.

The upper right hand quadrant focuses on individual living things or objects that are directly observable. This includes individual people, their behaviour and even their organs, such as the brain. These are all objectively, externally observable and therefore can be studied by science, such as neuroscience and psychology.

Modern behavioural science and neuroscience have made much progress over the past 40 years in understanding the connection between different states of consciousness (the interior, subjective 'I' quadrant) and changes in both behaviour and physical changes within our bodies — including the brain (the external, objective 'IT' quadrant). Much of that research has focused on the biological and psychological effects of the regular practice of meditation.[4]

Much scientifically validated information exists demonstrating the biologically positive, health promoting effects of meditation — changes in brain wave patterns, blood chemistry, metabolic rate and so forth. The biological changes indicate that meditation produces a unique physiological state.[5] While this type of research has not yet been done with permanent stages of consciousness, it undoubtedly will be over the next decade, as both behavioural scientists and neuroscientists are showing increased interest in the permanent effects of the long-term practice of meditation. The two lower quadrants in Wilbur's quadrant structure will be addressed in Chapter 18.

STAGES OF DEVELOPMENT AND DIFFERENT KINDS OF INTELLIGENCE

It is important to understand that there are different kinds of intelligence, and that each of these represents different ways we can develop as we grow towards higher consciousness. Howard Gardner was the first psychologist to identify and describe multiple intelligences. In addition to logical-mathematical and verbal intelligences, which are usually measured by IQ tests, he identified five intelligences. They are:

- musical intelligence
- spatial intelligence (eg possessed by architects and painters etc)
- kinaesthetic intelligence (eg possessed by dancers and athletes etc)
- intrapersonal intelligence (an ability to have an accurate and in-depth understanding of oneself)
- interpersonal intelligence (the ability to have an accurate understanding of others).[6]

Over the next two decades other specific intelligences were identified, described and various instruments have been developed to measure them. In terms of our discussions of higher consciousness — where the focus is on leadership — there are four that are significant:

- **Cognitive intelligence** — this is much more broadly defined than IQ (logical-mathematical and verbal intelligence). It includes the ability to use all four quadrants on the Q12 thinking map, ranging from logical thought to imagination and creative thinking. It includes the imaginative ability to see issues from many different perspectives. Thus, given the broader meaning of the term, current IQ tests are not good measures of cognitive intelligence.

- **Emotional intelligence** — this has five components: self-awareness and knowing one's emotions, managing one's emotions, motivating oneself, recognising emotions in others and handling relationships well.[7]

- **Spiritual intelligence** — this is the intelligence involved in pursuing, experiencing and understanding the issues of ultimate importance to people: meaning and purpose in life, transcendent experiences, and living by universal principles (eg do unto others as you would have them do unto you, the Golden Rule). These principles cannot be scientifically proven, but are existential principles found in every major spiritual tradition.

- **Moral intelligence** — this is our 'mental capacity to determine how universal human principles — like those embodied in the golden rule — should be applied to our personal values, goals and actions'.[8]

We can be high in one of these four intelligences and not in another. For example, we can have a highly-developed cognitive intelligence without high

A MODEL FOR THE DEVELOPMENT OF HIGHER CONSCIOUSNESS

emotional intelligence (a technical or scientific genius who has very poor people skills).

Each of these kinds of intelligence plays a role in the development of higher stages of consciousness. However, it is the unfolding of the higher sense of self — the character traits and abilities that emerge and create the core identity structure at each stage of higher consciousness— that ties these intelligences together in our evolution to higher consciousness. Identity is the integrating factor that helps to raise the developmental level of all four intelligences simultaneously. This can be illustrated in a psychograph of the type developed by Wilbur.[9]

The example below is of a psychograph for someone in transition to the transpersonal level.

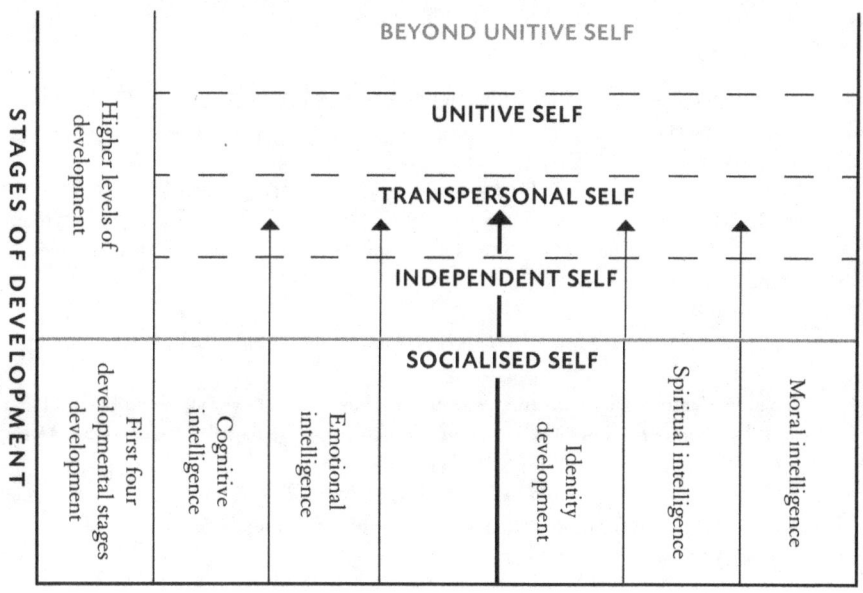

The graph plots lines of development (the horizontal axis) against stages of development (the vertical axis). For the five lines of development I have placed the self (identity) line in the centre of the psychograph, to indicate its status as the integrator of the developmental lines of the four intelligences — cognitive, emotional, spiritual and moral. To have reached full development at the transpersonal level all of the arrow heads must have reached the dotted line that demarcates the transpersonal self level. In this instance, the individual is transitioning to the transpersonal self level, and thus the five arrowheads have not yet reached the dotted line. Notice that the arrowheads are also different distances away from the dotted line at the top of the words 'transpersonal self'. This indicates that identity and each of the four intelligences are not at the exact same level of development, although all have passed the independent self stage.

As this book is not specifically about these four intelligences, I will not refer to them directly in the discussion of the three higher developmental levels. However, it will be clear that at each higher level an individual develops an increasing capability for making better choices and decisions — and operating more effectively — in an environment of cognitive, emotional, spiritual and moral complexity. This capability lies at the heart of mindful, successful leadership.

---

1   K Wilbur, *Integral Spirituality* (Integral Books: Boston, 2006), p 55.
2   Ibid, Chapters 2, 3, 4.
3   Ibid, pp 33–37.
4   M Murphy and S Donovan, *The Physical and Psychological Effects of Meditation* (Institute of Noetic Sciences: Sausalito, California, 1997). Murphy and Donovan provide a synopsis of over 1,000 scientific studies on the subject and there have been many studies since then.
5   Wilbur, p 165.
6   H Gardner, *Frames of Mind: The Theory of Multiple Intelligences* (Basic Books: New York, 1983).
7   The term 'emotional intelligence' was first used by Peter Salovey and John Mayor. It was later popularised by D Goleman in *Emotional Intelligence: Why It Can Matter More than IQ* (Bloomsbury Publishing: London, 1996).
8   D Lennik and F Kiel, *Moral Intelligence: Enhancing Business Performance and Leadership Success* (Pearson Education, Inc, Wharton School Publishing: New Jersey, 2008), p 7.
9   Wilbur, pp 58–61.

CHAPTER SIXTEEN

THE EMERGENCE OF THE INDEPENDENT SELF

I WILL begin by describing a phenomenon which we have witnessed thousands of times on personal development workshops and also in people who have been meditating regularly for at least several months. It is the first symptom of the emerging awareness that is the foundation stone of Level 5 — the independent self stage.

The experience people described was being in the 'fair witness' state: A 'fair witness' is objective, has no agenda and is non-judgemental. Typically, people described finding themselves in a familiar situation where they would usually respond with habitual, Achilles' heel behaviour. Yet instead they find themselves watching themselves from a detached perspective. The socialised self feels the impulse to respond as usual, but on another level they experience being in a quiet, uninvolved state in which they watch their socialised self objectively and without judgement. This is the 'fair witness' state — and is precisely what is meant by being in the state of 'mindfulness'.

When our socialised self is experienced as our identity, as who we are, it is very difficult to respond to people or situations in any other than our usual way. However, when people find themselves in the 'mindfulness' state, their socialised self and its typical, habitual responses, are experienced and perceived as *objects*, rather than their *identity*. Thus a different response is possible.

If you recall, one major issue Tina brought to the personal development workshop was her unhappiness in her marriage. After releasing herself from the emotional programming that kept her on her treadmill, Tina's responses to her husband changed completely. She said she could still feel a mild impulse to do the things she had formerly done to try to evoke some emotional response from him — but that another, deeper part of her could see this old habitual impulse as just a habit and not who she was. Tina's behaviour became relaxed and accepting of her husband in a way she had never before known possible. And with her husband no longer feeling pressure from her, he too became more relaxed and demonstrative.

As each new level of consciousness emerges, it brings with it three things:
1. The awakening of a new type of awareness or ability
2. A new set of motivational factors
3. A newly emerging sense of identity

In the 'fair witness' mindfulness state, the new awareness or ability is the capacity to perceive our usual self quietly, objectively and non-judgementally. We can see our socialised self's belief systems and values and our mental, emotional and behavioural patterns with clarity and detachment. At that moment we are actually *not* our socialised self, we just *have* a socialised self.

The 'fair witness' state of mindfulness is a state of pure Being that is not subject to social-emotional conditioning or programming. This is what (in Chapter 5) we called our 'Being self', our truest, deepest 'unconditioned' identity and can be contrasted with our socialised self, which has been programmed or 'conditioned' by past experience. Thus, from the perspective of this mindful state of Being, we can learn to see more deeply and accurately into our socialised self, and to respond to various life situations in ways that work better for us — and often for those around us.

THE SOCIALISED SELF, THE SOCIAL MATRIX AND THE INDEPENDENT SELF

The socialised self both results from out interaction with other people and our environment during the first four stages of development, while it equally causes our patterns of relationship with people and our environment in our current day to day life. In this sense our socialised self is 'enmeshed' or 'embedded' in our past and present social context.

The following diagram is intended to provide a visual representation of our embeddedness in our social/cultural matrix:

Threads tying us to individuals, events and institutions in the present, which bring out our strengths, successes and our Achilles' heels and treadmills.

Psychological threads tying us to individuals, institutions and events in the past, which shaped our socialised self.

Simply stated, whatever we may believe, at the socialised self stage of development **we are not free and independent beings**. Our sense of identity is deeply tied in with our past and present social matrix. The building blocks for that identity are the socially and emotionally programmed beliefs about ourselves, other people and the world that shape our relationship, action and concept maps. Put quite simply, our social context tells us who we are — and we believe it!

Our socialised self brings with it our Q12 natural strengths, which may have lead to many personal and professional successes and positive outcomes. A reasonably healthy socialised self is itself a major evolutionary accomplishment.

However, there is a **deep impulse within all of us to periodically self-renew**. Even if our Q12 natural strengths greatly outweigh our Q12 Achilles' heels, bringing us much success, there inevitably comes a time when this impulse will demand to be expressed — even if this takes us out of our comfort zones.

Evolution towards higher consciousness requires us to become truly free and independent of our past and present social matrix. It means giving up or 'dying to' our socialised self identity, in order to recreate a new identity at a new level of consciousness. This **'independent self'** is the new structure of identity and consciousness that emerges as the first level (level 5) of higher consciousness.

However, there is an important distinction to be made in the way the term 'independent self' is used, and the way the term 'independent' may be used by people with certain Q12 profiles. For example, people with strong 'Realist' relationship map profiles have a strong need to be emotionally (or otherwise) independent. Similarly, people with strong action map Executive profiles have a strong drive to be independent and self-reliant. However, these are emotionally programmed characteristics for Realists and Executives rather than expressions of the 'independent self' stage.

With the emergence of the independent self this compulsive need to always be — and to appear to be — independent and self-sufficient diminishes and disappears. Thus, for a Realist who has fully achieved the independent self stage, there would be no fear of being dependent, and thus no compulsion to pursue only one-way relationships where they help or support others, but deny a need for help or support themselves. Similarly, the Executive, at the full independent self stage, would have no compulsive need to always act as an independent, self-sufficient person and would find it easier to ask for and accept help, and to delegate tasks.

THE CREATION OF THE INDEPENDENT SELF IDENTITY

The underlying process that begins the creation of the new identity structure for the independent self is learning and practising the art of mindfulness. There are many ways to do this, but all involve choosing the path of personal development towards self-mastery — and the one basic precondition for any path we choose is having accurate knowledge of where we are starting from. Without this we cannot plot the course that will lead us to where we want to be (this is the function of the Q12 Profiling System).

There are many methodologies that can facilitate growth and development towards self-mastery and its ultimate expression in higher consciousness. In addition to the Q12 profiling system, the four identified in this book are meditation, personal development workshops, coaching and leadership development programmes — and there are many more.

While the state of mindfulness is a state of Being and cannot be defined by any finite set of adjectives, repeated experiences of that state gradually create certain core internal experiential qualities:

- **Freedom** — the experience of an essential me that is not limited by any

set of socially-emotionally programmed beliefs, mental, emotional or behavioural patterns, social roles I play, social class I belong to or the social culture I live in.
- **Wholeness** — the experience of being complete within myself, of not needing any one or any thing to make me more complete or whole
- **Self-acceptance** — the experience of a me that does not desire or need to be anything other than what I am. We may still want to change aspects of ourselves, but we can approach this in an easy, relaxed way because we are deeply self-accepting.
- **Intrinsic self-esteem** — esteem that is not dependent on external sources

The more actively we pursue a path of growth towards self-mastery — whatever path or method we choose — the more our identity will be anchored in the 'fair witness' state of mindfulness. This has three effects:
- Firstly, this helps us to cultivate and sustain the internal experience of freedom, wholeness, self-acceptance and intrinsic self-esteem, which become the core traits of our new identity.
- Secondly, this facilitates the process of social-emotional de-programming and frees us from the deficit-driven mental, emotional and behavioural patterns that define our Q12 Achilles' heels and treadmills, giving us greater flexibility, adaptability and effectiveness in how we respond to a whole range of issues in our life and work.
- Thirdly, this frees us from being exclusively bound by the values and beliefs of the social culture we live in. When viewing our environment in the 'fair witness' mindful state, we make no assumptions, have no agenda and thus can see our social culture with objectivity and clarity. This perspective is not available to us at the socialised self stage because the socialised self — in accordance with the resistance/absorption principle — either directly absorbs and accepts or reacts against our social culture's values and beliefs. Neither of these options involves free choice. In the 'fair witness' mindful state we no longer need to accept, or react against, the values, beliefs or rules that define the cultural paradigm of our society our values and beliefs become self-chosen or self-developed.

Because of this, at the independent self level we have a trans-cultural view of our environment. We see the culture or sub-culture in which we live with the quiet objectivity of the 'fair witness' mindful state. Thus we can adapt more easily to living and working in many different social or organisational cultures.

For individuals in leadership positions, a trans-cultural view makes them naturals to introduce organisational change programmes of any kind (restructuring, new systems, etc), but especially for the most difficult kind of change — culture transformation programmes. Leaders at the independent self stage have no attachments to current culture norms and values — and because of this, they can more easily create and live in accordance with new norms and values which will generate a new and healthier culture. Thus leaders at the independent self stage can be referred to as 'cultural creatives'.

In summary, the net result of a shift in our identity from socialised self to the newly-emerging independent self is: the socialised self becomes something we **have** while the independent self becomes who we **are**! The natural strengths and skills that have evolved with our socialised self become tools to be used by the independent self, but do not define that self.

The following is a diagram illustrating the structure of consciousness at the independent self stage:

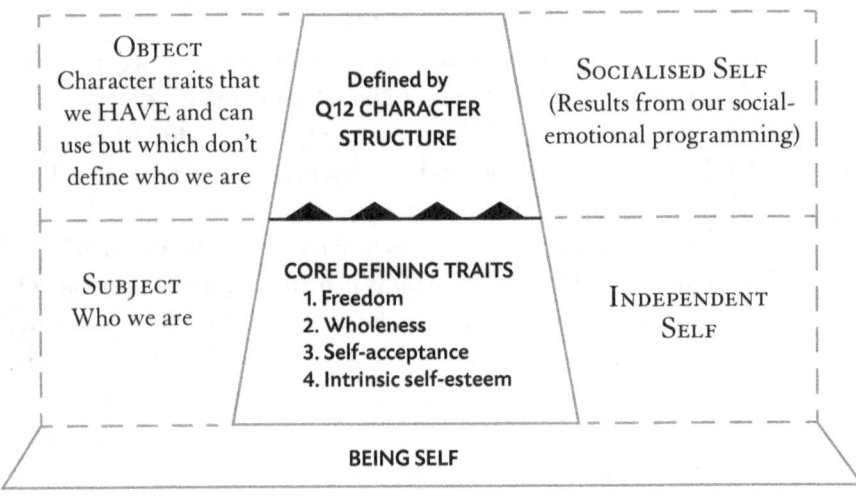

In the above diagram the arrows that extend from the independent self into the socialised self indicate that the four deep core traits of our independent self interpenetrate and influence our socialised self. This assists us in using our socialised self's Q12 strengths in creative and positive ways — and makes us much less likely to slip into Achilles' heel and treadmill behaviours. Underpinning the entire structure of consciousness at the independent self stage is our Being self (our deepest identity) because experiential contact with the Being self is the ultimate basis of each stage in the evolution of consciousness.

NEW MOTIVATIONAL FACTORS AND DEVELOPMENTAL POSSIBILITIES

When we enter each new stage of development, a new set of motivational factors arise. For example, in the second developmental stage the child learns the socially-defined concepts of 'belonging' and 'relationship', and Maslov's relationship/belongingness need becomes a major motivation that continues through adolescence and into adulthood. At around six or seven years of age the child begins to have a sense of how well they stack up against others in terms of their skills, accomplishments and others' perceptions, and they start to feel good or bad about themselves in accordance with this. This is the emergence of Maslov's 'self-esteem' need, which remains a major motivating factor through late childhood, adolescence and into adulthood. Similarly, as the independent self stage emerges new motivational factors arise. In Maslov's terminology the basic motivator at the independent self stage is the **'self-actualisation drive'**.

Once we enter the personal development path and begin to develop the ability to see and understand ourselves mindfully — and we gradually identify less and less with our socialised self — achieving further social self-esteem quickly ceases to be deeply motivating. Doing more, differently or better in those activities that previously gained us the esteem of others becomes self-limiting and loses its attraction. The new and growing self-awareness makes us much more conscious of both our current personal limitations and our great reservoir of unused, unrealised potential. Inevitably, a great drive arises to overcome and master these limitations, and more fully realise our personal potential. This is precisely what is meant by the 'self-actualisation' drive.

THE SELF-ACTUALISATION DRIVE AND INDEPENDENT INTENTIONALITY

As an important part of the self-actualisation drive, a new quality emerges: **'independent intentionality'**. All human beings are intentional beings; as part of our daily life we have intentions.

At the socialised self stage, many of our intentions are defined and driven by our Q12 profile success treadmills and result from our emotionally-programmed mental, emotional and behavioural patterns or habits. It follows that these intentions are not freely chosen.

At the independent self stage, being free of our past and present social matrix, we are empowered to choose the intentions that provide purpose and direction in our daily activities. We call this capability or quality 'independent intentionality'. As we approach the independent self stage, this includes the intention to realise a personal life vision for our future growth and development.

If a professional or a leader at, or approaching, the independent self stage is working in an organisation, they must find a way to realise their personal life vision by contributing to the organisation's success. If the organisation's vision and values are inconsistent with their personal life vision, or does not give them the opportunity to realise their full potential, they will invariably feel a strong need to leave.

Over many years, I have found that people at this stage, who have been employed in organisations as professionals or leaders, will often leave to start their own business. This is often very risky, but they are willing to take that risk because they feel they won't be able to realise their full potential in their current employment. For example, Tina reached the point where she was willing to resign and leave her successful practice if she was not given the opportunity to realise her vision of building a holistic health centre.

This has important implications for public or private sector organisations that want to hold onto their best people, including especially those with leadership potential. It is imperative that these organisations find a way to support these valuable people in realising their potential and achieving their personal vision. This requires building an organisational culture that, on a collective level, embodies many of the traits which define the independent self stage of development — including the opportunities to self-actualise and pursue their personal vision.

The 'self-actualisation' drive now causes people to focus on self-development rather than external achievements. It's not that they no longer have any impulse for external achievements. Rather, these achievements are no longer 'ends unto themselves'; or ways of gaining greater self-esteem; instead they are markers of internal progress (degrees of self–mastery). Each external success is a marker of internal growth.

Tina, James, Tim and Mark all initially identified their current limitations and awakened the new potentials within themselves that they were committed to fulfilling, both in their personal and professional lives. For example, the things they were each attempting to achieve as leaders were worthy and important to them as ends in themselves, but their motivation was not based on typical rewards (prestige, money, promotion, etc) that belong to Maslov's self-esteem (deficit) needs. Rather, their focus was on the developmental steps they needed to take.

This shift in motivation applies not just to the social self-esteem needs (usually tied in with our skills and achievements), it applies equally to all of Maslov's earlier needs hierarchy and includes the (physical and psychological) survival and security needs and the (socially-defined) relationship and belongingness needs.

THE SELF-ACTUALISATION DRIVE AND RELATIONSHIPS

It is not that we do not pursue relationships or join groups at the independent self stage. Rather we do not do so because of Maslov's relationship/belongingness needs: we are no longer influenced by fear-based deficit motivations (fear of rejection, fear of not being loved, the need for someone else to emotionally fulfil us, fear or not 'belonging', or the compulsive need **not** to belong found in some Q12 profiles).

The deficit drives underlying our Q12 relationship profile gradually disappear, as does the socialised self's tendency towards co-dependency. The problematic behavioural patterns that often characterise both personal and professional relationships fade away. As we evolve into the independent self stage, we relate to each other as whole, independent persons. Instead of each person in the relationship compulsively trying to get something (or avoid something) from the other person, we can share our wholeness with each other.

This experience creates entirely new possibilities for the quality of relationships, both personal and professional:

- Each person is able to take responsibility for their own communication and behaviour, rather than projecting blame onto the other
- Each person is more likely to focus on the positive traits and qualities of the other person, rather than those perceived as negative
- Each person can participate in the relationship as an equal, rather than getting involved in power games
- In both personal and professional relationships true co-operation between independent equals becomes the norm
- Not feeling threatened by the other, each person is able to both empathise with, and respect the other person just as they are

While this applies to all relationships, it is obvious this would be of greatest value to people in leadership positions. Most of what leaders achieve is contingent upon their ability to establish good quality relationships with those they lead. Just as the self-actualisation drive causes people to focus on self-development and-self mastery rather than external achievements, that same drive causes people to focus on the co-operative and sharing quality of their relationships. Again the focus is now internal rather than on other people as external sources of need gratification.

How Tina mastered her relationship issue has been discussed above. However, James, Tim and Mike also all had relationships issues. Although James loved his family and was very devoted to them, he was not able to directly express his emotions. Also, while as a leader he treated his staff well, he had difficulty delegating responsibility and tended to be a micro-manager, which made them feel he did not trust their competency or commitment. Tim initially avoided relationships as much as possible in both his personal and professional life. He had a rich internal life and, as often as he could, would withdraw into solitary activities. Mike's relationships were all activity-based and devoid of any emotional or personal contact. In both his personal and leadership life he lacked any relationship skills, was blunt in his communication style and only placed value on those relationships that were necessary to achieve a task or outcome. Many people were afraid of him.

Yet through their intense participation in workshops and coaching, and their dedication to developing as individuals and as leaders, James, Tim and Mike overcame and mastered these relationship Achilles' heels. The quality of their personal and professional relationships improved immensely and became deeply fulfilling, rather than the source of frustration and/or anxiety they had previously been.

Did these four leaders evolve to full independent self status?

In Tina's case, she was already very close to completing the transition from socialised self to independent self. Her only major obstacle was the emotional treadmill she was on with her husband. When she freed herself from the childhood emotional programming that drove that treadmill she made the full transition to the independent self level of development. James, Tim and Mike were initially much further away from development at the independent self level than Tina. They had more issues to work on, over an extended period of time — but they did eventually complete that transition.

By the end of the period I was working with them, all four had developed the main characteristics that define the independent self:

- The major Achilles' heels and treadmills that were causing the problems in their personal life and that were responsible for serious deficiencies in their leadership were completely gone. They had emotionally deprogrammed their deficit motivations and created very positive,

productive and much more deeply satisfying and effective emotional, thinking and behavioural patterns.
- Their motivation had definitely transcended Maslov's (physical and psychological) survival and security needs, the relationship/belongingness needs and the self-esteem needs. Their primary motivation became the self-actualisation drive.
- They had freed their socialised self from its embeddedness in the past and present social matrix. The choices they made were not compulsively driven in response to the expectations, desires or beliefs of others or their past social-emotional programming. This did not mean that they were not aware of, or considered, the desires, beliefs and expectations of others. Out of that awareness and consideration they sometimes provided what was desired or expected, and sometimes agreed with other's beliefs and the dominant beliefs of their social culture. However, they would do so only if it was consistent with their personal, self-constructed values and beliefs. Their responses were freely taken and not compulsive, mentally/emotionally programmed in responses to others (or their social culture's) desires, expectations and beliefs. They all developed a trans-cultural view and became 'cultural creatives'.
- The core of their new identity was built around the four deep structure traits of the independent self stage of development. All of their emotional responses, thinking and behaviour now derived from the core sense of freedom, wholeness, self-acceptance and intrinsic self-esteem characteristics of the independent self.

The other character traits that made them unique remained quite different. In most cases these were the same as the Q12 character traits of their socialised self with its natural strengths — but mostly without its Achilles' heels and treadmills. However, there were several important changes in their Q12 profiles. For example, Tina took on some of the more direct, assertive behaviour of the Entrepreneur in her action profile, while not losing the softer, more indirect and persuasive Motivator communication style. She still relied much more on the latter but could use the former when necessary. James took on some of the more directly affectionate traits of the relationship Optimist profile while retaining many of the more careful, reserved traits of his Realist relationship profile.

So, what percentage of the adult population actually fully achieves level 5 independent self-development? Robert Kegan (Professor of Adult Learning and Professional Development and Chair of the Institute for the Management of Lifelong Education at the Harvard Graduate School of Education) and Dr Brian P Hall (Professor Emeritus of Pastoral Counselling at Santa Clara University and chair of Values Technology) offer models for higher development stages and statistical research on the percentages of adults who reach these higher stages.

Though Kegan and Hall use different terminology to describe the socialised self and the higher developmental stages, I find that there are sufficient similarities in their models to feel comfortable in using the statistical results they have uncovered in their research. This does not mean that they have endorsed my model of higher consciousness. But given this qualification, Kegan and Hall's statistical results are summarised in an article by Bob Anderson (who actually does use the terms socialised self and independent self):

- From professionals returning from work for further higher education, who on average are more wealthy and educated than the general population, approximately 40% fully achieve the level 5 independent self stage.[1]
- From the general population, the percentage who fully achieves the independent self stage is approximately 25%.[2]
- The majority of people reach the level 4 socialised self stage, but many of these do not make the transition to the independent self stage, whether they are fully conscious of this or not.
- Research also suggests that approximately 15% of adults in the general population have poorly socialised personalities. They have not made successful transitions from infancy through adolescence, and are driven by needs unmet at those stages. These are people with strong deficit motivation drives and people who have developed mental, emotional and behavioural patterns that make them very difficult to relate to and work with. They are typically people who are quite aggressive, rebels or those who see themselves as victims.[3]

The next level (level 6) or the 'transpersonal self' is discussed in the next chapter.

---

[1] B Anderson, *The Spirit of Leadership*, The Leadership Circle <www.tlccommunity.com> accessed 11 June 2012, p 22.
[2] Ibid, p 9.
[3] Ibid, p 8.

CHAPTER SEVENTEEN

THE EMERGENCE OF THE TRANSPERSONAL SELF

AS the transpersonal self begins to emerge, the mindful state of Being plays an increasingly important role in its development. The state of Being is our deepest, truest identity but it is not something with a tangible structure and it cannot be defined by any finite set of adjectives. There are many ways we can directly experience the state of Being (eg during meditation) — but since this is an internal, subjective state, we must rely on metaphor to describe our experience.

For example, the state of Being can be imagined as a large body of water. As the state of Being is just undifferentiated Being and nothing else, the water is just undifferentiated water and nothing else. However, the water can be experienced at different levels, different depths. Your experience will be different the deeper you go: different currents, different degrees of pressure, different temperatures. Although the water is still just water **your personal experience of it will change the deeper you go**.

Similarly with the Being self — you can experience it at different levels. The surface level is the 'fair witness' state of mindfulness: calm, fully present, objective and non-judgemental. At the independent self level you perceive your socialised self objectively and non-judgementally, it is something that you have but not who you are.

As you begin to evolve towards the transpersonal level, you will begin to experience the state of Being at a deeper level. At this deeper level you will transcend the surface level calm or objectivity and begin to develop an entirely different identity and reality. This identity and reality will no longer have the sharp boundaries that define the independent self. Instead it will be infused with feelings of empathy, compassion and a perception of interconnectedness. You will then have entered the realm of the transpersonal self.

What distinguishes the transpersonal stage of development is that it begins the process of breaking down the sharp distinction between subject and object. The first five stages of development were all based on our experience of being a separate self. Indeed, our entire concept of 'reality' in the first five stages is based on this distinction. At the independent self stage the boundary between subject and object becomes the clearest and most precise. As we begin to approach the transpersonal level we begin to see this boundary between subject and object as an 'illusion' rather than the basis of reality. It is the capacity to begin to see through this illusion that provides the basis for the emergence of the new level of awareness/ability.

At the transpersonal stage the newly emerging level of awareness/ability is the ability to see and experience people and things as if they are part of who we are: other people and nature itself become as intimate to us as our own self. This requires being able to identify with a multitude of human traits, qualities and viewpoints that are not part of our fully developed independent self.

At the fully developed independent self stage, one of four core identity traits is a high level of acceptance of ourselves just as we are, with our individual qualities as a person. At the transpersonal self level, as we begin to identify with a vastly broader variety of traits, qualities and viewpoints, our self-acceptance also broadens. Our sense of identity broadens to include qualities, traits and viewpoints not part of our independent self — and we become as accepting of them as if they were our own.

INTIMACY AT THE TRANSPERSONAL LEVEL

In personal relationships, this means experiencing a degree of intimacy not available at earlier stages of development. With this newfound intimacy the boundaries between ourselves and others blur and cross over. At the socialised self level, people with some Q12 profiles have a tendency (as one of their Achilles' heels) to lose their identity to others. This can result in their identity being absorbed into the person from whom they are seeking love. At the socialised self level 'identity theft' can also happen in the other direction, with some people able to seduce others into virtually giving over their identity. These are classic cases of mutually interlocking, deficit driven treadmills.

THE EMERGENCE OF THE TRANSPERSONAL SELF

However, at the transpersonal self stage of development, the crossing over of our personal boundaries with others is not driven by a deficit need to absorb, or to be absorbed by, someone else.

At the transpersonal level, the immense capacity for intimacy can enrich personal relationships. There is no longer the need or desire to protect or even maintain our personal boundaries. Indeed, the intrinsic impulse in personal relationships at the transpersonal level is the drive towards intimacy.

For example, shortly after Tina had her breakthrough she experienced herself as whole and complete. She no longer had the compulsive need to try to get her husband to behave in ways that would make her feel 'whole'. This made him feel more relaxed and comfortable around her. At this point in her relationship with her husband, she was at the independent self stage of development. Shortly after this occurred, she noticed something that she at first found difficult to understand. She started to feel as if she could actually feel his love for her. She felt as if she were inside him feeling the love that he was feeling towards her. It was as if she within herself became part of that feeling within him. She didn't feel any compelling need to tell him this because she found the experience so fulfilling in itself. Without intellectually knowing what it was, Tina had awakened and slipped into the transpersonal self level of consciousness and entered a state of transpersonal relationship with her husband. At the transpersonal level of development, this type of relationship can best be represented by the following diagram. Each circle represents the boundaries around the individual's personal, internal, psychological space.

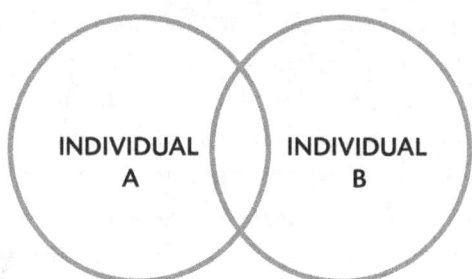

The personal boundaries between ourselves and others begin to intersect and cross over. In Tina's case, she was experiencing that part of herself (circle A) was part of her husband (circle B). She experienced her husband's feelings as her own. At this moment she was not an independent self relating to another independent self. Her actual experience of selfhood or identity included what at earlier developmental levels would be seen as part of another separate self.

I-THOU, BEING TO BEING RELATIONSHIPS

The German existential philosopher Martin Buber described relationships of this kind as 'I-Thou' relationships. While in English the term 'thou' is no longer in use, in German the distinction between the intimate and non-intimate form of the pronoun still exists — 'du' meaning 'thou' and 'sie' meaning 'you'.

For a full I-Thou relationship to occur, both parties must have entered the transpersonal state. The level of mutual trust must be very high for both people to surrender their personal boundaries and share their 'inner world' so deeply. However, someone who has entered the transpersonal state, can still experience their half of the I-Thou relationship with someone not at the transpersonal level, although out of respect for the other person's personal boundaries, they may not communicate what they are experiencing. In Tina's case, she felt she needed to respect her husband's boundaries and not tell him of her experience because she felt that telling him might make him feel psychologically invaded.

In professional relationships this natural impulse towards intimacy needs to be expressed in a different way. There is a need to maintain and respect certain personal boundaries, particularly on the overt communication and interaction level. In professional or workplace relationships, within our consciousness, the ability to see and experience others as if they were part of ourselves is a natural expression of the transpersonal state. However, in workplace or professional relationships, where the need to respect boundaries is crucial, this experience provides the basis for deep insight into others and can be the basis of establishing deep rapport with them. This can be of immense help for people in leadership positions.

I have chosen to use the term 'Being to Being' relationship rather than 'I-Thou' because of a distinction that is essential to understand at the transpersonal level of relating. The distinction is between the **form** and **essence** of the relationship. For example, in relating to any individual, both I and that person can be identified by the many personal character traits we each have, the various roles that we play with each other, and the ways in which we interact and communicate. All of this defines the form of the relationship. However, while the form of the relationship may be important in many ways, at the transpersonal level the essence of the relationship is experiencing the other person in a way that transcends its form. **It is as if we are seeing and touching their soul, their spirit, their being, the essence of them that lies behind the form.** What provides us with the deep feelings of fulfilment at the transpersonal level is experiencing this essence — and the form is just the platform or playground on which the relationship occurs.

For Martin Buber, I-Thou (Being to Being) relationships can also be experienced with nature and with works of the human spirit (great works of science, art, philosophy etc). For example, when you are standing under a magnificent tree, looking at a beautiful lake, watching an animal in the wild or playing with a pet that you love, your inner being may penetrate and experience their living inner essence. In that moment, it is as if this part of nature becomes part of you. Similarly, this can happen when you are reading a novel, listening to a piece of music, looking at a piece of art or watching a play or film. You can be transported beyond the usual boundaries or your socialised or independent self and feel that the work has become part of who you are. It has touched your essence, your soul, your deepest self. Anyone who has had these kinds of experiences has touched the transpersonal level of awareness, even if they are not yet fully developed at the independent self state.

EMERGING MOTIVATING VALUES AND BEHAVIOURS

At the transpersonal level of consciousness, the world is seen as an open-ended mystery, where everything is interconnected and subject to unending change. While change is inevitable, humans can intervene in the change process to create better or worse outcomes. At the transpersonal level the deep, ongoing natural impulse is to intervene in ways that will result in the common good. This is the motivation that drives how we think, feel and act at the transpersonal level. Successfully intervening to achieve the common good also brings with it a profoundly deep and lasting fulfilment.

This definition implies that the deepest motivating factor at the transpersonal level is to make a difference by facilitating outcomes that contribute to the common good. What exactly is meant by the term 'common good'? This term has a very broad meaning which includes the welfare of all that are affected by the leader's activities and decisions. For example, leaders in a corporate setting making a transition to this level would feel a strong sense of responsibility to all the company's stakeholders: its employees, customers, suppliers, shareholders, and the communities and ecological environment within which it operates.

The style of leadership that emerges at the transpersonal level has one overriding value: contributing to the common good. All other values and activities of the leaders are subservient to that one overarching value. However, it would be a mistake to assume such leaders are soft headed idealists. Leaders at the transpersonal level need to possess many skills including good strategic and systems-thinking skills:

- Strategic thinking skills are needed because such leaders not only have a long-term focus in their vision for their organisation's future, but also because they would need to consider the many stakeholders involved. This requires a comprehensive scope in thinking about the future and also great strategic and tactical flexibility in planning.
- Systems-thinking skills are needed because of their basic world view that everything and everyone is highly interconnected. Any decision they make may have affects on many or even all of its stakeholders. With sophisticated systems thinking, all of the 'rippling out' effects of any decision can be anticipated.

Thus, utilising the most cutting-edge strategic and systems-thinking methods, technologies and management techniques, the leader at the transpersonal level will demonstrate a strong commitment to accomplishing their goals and achieving their vision. Their reasons for doing so are not the recognition and rewards of the 'socialised self' motivational level, nor primarily the opportunity to overcome their personal limitations and achieve greater degrees of self-actualisation and self-expression, the motivating values of the independent self stage. Instead, their primary motivation is ensuring that they and their organisation add value to and contribute to the quality of life for all whom they effect. Their primary marker of success is how well and successfully they and their organisation achieve this.

The pressures that are often aligned against leaders at, or transitioning to, the transpersonal level, within our present economic and political institutions, are enormous. In large, publicly traded companies, by far the single greatest pressure on CEOs, senior management and the board of directors is short- or medium-term increases in profitability, share price and return on investment. Financial outcomes for shareholders, under corporate law, are the legally-mandated top priority. This often puts great pressure on a CEO or senior manager, operating at the transpersonal level, who might want to place equal emphasis on community, social and environmental contributions.

Similarly in the political sphere, the primary pressure on those who wish to be career politicians is to be re-elected. Even if their initial reason for running for office was broad, inclusive and idealistic, the pressures of the continuing need for re-election often cause them to gradually sacrifice these ideals. This is complicated by the enormous influence of wealthy corporations and individuals both through lobbying and direct or indirect contributions to campaign funds. And finally, another pressure on politicians is the enticement of lucrative private sector jobs when they leave office, because of their political connections and influence they achieved while in office.

These pressures have two intertwined effects. Firstly, these financial and political priorities can inhibit a leader's development to the transpersonal level. To the extent that they focus only on these pressures and priorities, they will not be doing the kinds of things that will help them rise to the transpersonal level of development. Secondly, if a leader is at, or transitioning to, the transpersonal level, they will find it extremely difficult to operate inside an environment where only money, power, prestige and political influence really count.

Many leaders who are at, or transitioning to, the transpersonal level solve this problem by leaving the organisation they work in and doing one of three things:
- They start their own business, based on transpersonal vision and values
- They become a leader in an NGO, a charity or some kind of organisation that provides a not-for-profit service of some kind
- They manage to gain a leadership position in one of the increasing number of companies that actually do operate from a transpersonal level values system. One of the positive aspects of the business culture that has emerged since the late 1990s is the corporate social and environmental responsibility movement. Many corporations are now beginning to include positive social and environmental impacts as part of their business vision, values and strategy.

THE TRANSPERSONAL SELF IDENTITY STRUCTURE

As we begin to move towards the transpersonal level of development, there are four qualities that emerge as the deep structure of our identity: deep understanding of other's 'reality perspective'; unconditional empathy and compassion; recognition of, and a deep appreciation for our interdependence; and a co-creative approach to all important activities.

As we develop towards the transpersonal self level, these core qualities gradually come to interpenetrate the qualities distinctive of each individual quadrant in our Q12 profile. Thus, a Pragmatist or an Executive or a Rationalist or people strong in any other quadrant will find: firstly, that their natural strengths will tend to be used in accordance with these four qualities; secondly, that these qualities will make it less likely that the Achilles' heel behaviour of a given quadrant will occur; and thirdly, that the strengths of the most appropriate quadrant will be used in any specific situation — which may mean assigning the task or responsibility to someone else who is strong in that quadrant.

When fully developed and integrated within our consciousness, these four traits are what empower us to be effective, as individual leaders, in contributing to the common good. All four are directly due to the breaking down of the experience of the sharp distinction between 'self' and 'other' characteristic of earlier developmental levels.

For most people making a conscious choice to transition to the transpersonal level, these qualities or traits begin as things that we value. As we gradually transform to the transpersonal self level, these qualities transform from being valued to being a major part of who we are, they become the core traits that define our identity.

DEEP AWARENESS AND UNDERSTANDING OF OTHER'S 'REALITY PERSPECTIVES'

This ability derives from the expansion of our awareness beyond the sharp boundaries of the independent self, to include the many possible selves that lie within us. Equally, this same expansion of consciousness makes us aware of the common humanity that we share with others, providing the experience of seeing other people (and nature itself) as if they were part of who we are.

Being able to see the world as others see it is enormously empowering in all relationships, but it is especially empowering to a leader. For a leader to inspire people to embrace and pursue a shared vision of a new possible future requires appealing to many types of people in terms that are both meaningful to them personally and which remind them of their common humanity.

Tina already had strong communication and negotiation skills when I first met her, simply because of the natural strengths associated with her Q12 profile, while James, Tim and Mike did not initially have those skills at all. They developed them, over several years, through much practice and dedication. However, it is important to understand that this ability is not a skill that can be learned through academic study or through following a set of instructions. Rather, this is an ability intrinsic to our transpersonal self and lies dormant within all of us. It must be 'awakened' through the right kind of experiences, and once awakened, cultivated and developed by much practice. Meditation can be an invaluable tool in helping to awaken and develop this ability.

Learning to use the Q12 model can also be very helpful with this process. The expansion of consciousness at the transpersonal level empowers us to embrace and identify with a whole set of different ways of seeing the world that are not naturally available to us at the socialised self or independent self stage. Thus, our new transpersonal self identity structure will have more 'building blocks' than our independent self because it is created by integrating within ourselves many possible other selves.

As the transpersonal state emerges, we begin to reach a stage where we can embrace, own and identify with all 12 quadrants in the Q12 system. In a specific sense, building a transpersonal self identity requires integrating all 12 quadrants within our self structure. This means we are equally at home in the territory of all quadrants. We may not be a master navigator within every quadrant but we have a deep feeling for, and understanding of, all important aspects of the basic terrain. It's as if we have a sense of 'intimacy' with that quadrant. Stated more literally, we can gain the natural, intrinsic ability to see the world from the point of view of any given quadrant. We gain a natural empathy for, and understanding of, the personal beliefs, values and qualities that are part of any one quadrant's concept of 'reality',

While it is highly unlikely that we will develop all of the natural strengths of all quadrants, if for any good reason we need to develop specific traits, qualities or skills, associated with a particular quadrant, at the transpersonal level we will find it much easier to do so. The sense of familiarity and intimacy with the quadrants terrain, with it's, 'world view', will facilitate the process of developing a new character trait or learning a skill that comes naturally to that quadrant.

Again, it is not just the intellectual study of the Q12, but the ongoing practice of using it that helps in awakening and developing the transpersonal self. Thus, awareness and understanding of how others see 'reality' is one of the core traits of the transpersonal self identity structure, and of inestimable value to anyone in a leadership position.

UNCONDITIONAL EMPATHY AND COMPASSION

This empathy and compassion will help ensure that we use our insight and understanding of how other individuals or groups see the world in ways that will empower them, that will lead to the common good.

All of us, at whatever level of development, have felt empathy and compassion for others. For example, seeing someone we love being hurt; seeing someone who is suffering and who has no capacity to overcome the suffering; seeing people starving in third world countries. In these cases, our feelings are based on a specific set of conditions being present.

However, as we transition to the transpersonal level, these kinds of feelings become unconditional. For example, we feel empathy and compassion for anyone who is undergoing any form of loss, hurt or suffering, under any circumstances. These feelings will not just be a state of our inner consciousness, they will strongly motivate us, if it is at all possible, to strategise and take action to either prevent or mitigate that loss, hurt or suffering.

The unconditional nature of these feelings is further demonstrated by the fact that at the transpersonal level, we experience these feelings even towards people who act against us or violate some principle we believe in very deeply. It is true that we may also have some feelings of hurt, anger or outrage, but those feelings are more the surface level feelings of our socialised or independent self. At a deeper level, the empathy and compassion are still there. It is important to understand that this empathy and compassion will not prevent a person at the transpersonal level from taking strong action against others if such action is genuinely needed. Rather it means that whatever actions are taken, that the empathy and compassion will remain.

This unconditional, empathic and compassionate state ensures three things:
- Firstly, that such strong action will never be for personal or selfish reasons
- Secondly, that all reasonable steps will be taken to resolve the issues, making any strong action unnecessary if at all possible
- Thirdly, that such action will not be taken unless truly essential and will be of the minimal degree necessary to achieve the 'common good' outcome

Both Tina and Tim had to take actions that caused people to leave their organisation, but they handled it in ways that met all of the three conditions described above.

In the samurai warrior tradition in feudal Japan, the spiritual disciplines undertaken by every samurai were to ensure that when they fought, they did not hate or seek vengeance, that their motives were never personal, and that they fought for an outcome which they believed was for the common good. This meant achieving justice in which a kind of ethical harmony and balance was restored within the world. Through their Buddhist meditation and spiritual practices, they sought to be in the transpersonal state when they fought.

From time to time, all people in leadership positions have to take strong action in relation to others. This state of 'unconditional empathy and compassion' makes it highly likely that such situations will be handled in a way which is truly for the common good.

RECOGNITION OF, AND A DEEP APPRECIATION FOR, OUR FUNDAMENTAL INTERDEPENDENCE

At the full independent self stage of development, we freed ourselves from all forms of emotional dependency. Yet it is only because of the inner security brought by this achievement that we can recognise and actually begin to appreciate how interdependent (not co-dependent) we all are. Most aspects of our lives are highly interdependent. In a complex network of personal, family, social and workplace relationships, we are constantly giving and receiving, serving and being served , and in dozens of ways, relying on each other!

At the transpersonal level, this interdependence is seen as an essential and positive aspect of life. Rather than resisting or submitting to it, the transpersonal self embraces it and makes full use of the rich network of interdependencies that can be found everywhere. People at the transpersonal level instinctively prefer doing things in interdependent networks within groups (families, teams, organisations, groups of organisations, communities, etc). Leaders at the transpersonal level instinctively also like to work closely as part of an interdependent leadership team. They would also tend to form networks of relationships, both within and outside their organisations, in a way that is not based on hierarchical status.

Also emerging from this consciousness of our interdependency is a world view in which mutual support plays a major role. A leader at the transpersonal level seeks to build a culture in which both individuals and teams are supportive of each other. For example, it might mean an individual helping or providing support to another team or individual in an area outside their allocated task or area of responsibility. It might also mean being willing to ask for support or help from leaders, colleagues or other team members.

A leader at the transpersonal level instinctively models this kind of behaviour by being willing to both ask for and provide help and support when needed. They demonstrate this by the way they act as part of a leadership team. The deepest psychological message behind this is: whoever you are and wherever you are, you are not alone and you are always supported.

Finally, leaders at the transpersonal level emphasise systems-thinking in both leadership and management. Their consciousness of the interdependence and interconnectedness of all things is of no practical use within a large, complex organisation, if they can not predict within reasonable bounds, how changes in one part of an organisation will effect people and systems in another part, or how it will effect external stakeholders.

THE CO-CREATIVE APPROACH TO ALL IMPORTANT ACTIVITIES

At the independent self stage, the culture that a leader would naturally favour would be a reflection of how they behave and manage themselves. Their leadership approach would be one that strongly emphasises building a workplace culture in which:

- Each individual member of a team and organisation is personally fully responsible and accountable for their behaviour, for the tasks they undertake and responsibilities assigned to them
- Each individual approaches their task or area or responsibility using their full individual initiative or creativity
- Each individual works in a highly co-operative fashion with other individuals and teams
- Different parts of the organisation work co-operatively and in a well co-ordinated fashion with each other

The emphasis in such a culture is on individuals achieving a collection of individual accomplishments in co-operation with each other.

As an individual makes the transition to the transpersonal level, a subtle but major transition begins to occur in the approach to both individual and common endeavours. This can best be described as the co-creative approach. The emphasis is now on the 'we' of our personal and team accomplishments, rather than you, I and others each doing our individual task in co-operation with each other. The focus is on collective accomplishments, rather than a collection of co-ordinated individual accomplishments.

Leaders at this level tend to see the team members and themselves as part of a single organism. The leader's strong sense of interdependence causes them to rely much more heavily on a 'living organism' model to describe the ideal team (or organisation). In a living organism, the individual organs are not just independent entities with independent functions that operate in a co-operative manner. In their bio-electrical and bio-chemical interactions with each other, they directly affect each others functions.

Thus, the interdependent relationships within a team, group or organisation are seen more as collaborative partnerships at the transpersonal level. The result of all of this is that a leader at the transpersonal level perceives themselves as a co-creative partner in the team, organisation or community — not just an individual leading other team/organisation/community members in a co-operative fashion.

In accordance with this the transpersonal leader would quite naturally focus on building a culture that embodies this co-creative partnership model. This culture would need to be built around a mission, vision and values that would reach beyond co-operation to full collaboration.
- Its central values would be mutual trust and respect
- It would make full use of the principle of synergy
- It would embody the principles of co-responsibility and co-accountability, creating a 'team of teams'

Virtually all organisations now express their purpose and aspirations in very brief mission and vision statements, and almost all have some kind of values statement that defines the kind of culture they wish to build or maintain. Yet these statements are of practically no value in themselves. Indeed, if these statements simply sit on the wall and are not used or referred to on an almost daily basis they can actually become a source of cynicism.

For leaders at the transpersonal level, the deepest, most natural expression of their consciousness is to influence and inspire others to embrace, own and embody the mission, vision and values. This is done through an enormous amount of face-to-face dialogue with people at all levels, and within all parts of an organisation. But by far the most important influence will be the leader's authenticity in 'walking the talk'. The deepest instinct and natural ability for leaders at the transpersonal level is to be a living embodiment of the organisation's mission, vision and values in all that they do!

The reasons for this are partly humane and 'soft' and partly practical and 'hard'. As groups of people embrace and own a common purpose and values, they bond and become, in the truest and best sense, a team: a group of people working co-creatively and interdependently towards a common purpose within a framework of commonly-held values. When this happens at a whole organisation level, the organisation itself becomes a team of teams. Obviously such a team or organisation would be a pleasure to work in (the human, soft side), but it would also be far more resilient, productive and successful in all of its activities and in the final outputs and outcomes it achieves (the hard side).

However, for this to work, several conditions must apply:
- The team members must have a common purpose or goal, to which they

are more committed than they are to their own individual agendas
- There must be input from a wide variety of points of view and types of people — leaders at the transpersonal level instinctively seek out variety and instinctively recognise the danger of 'cloning' or 'group think'
- There must be a healthy relationship dynamic between team members (good levels of mutual trust and respect, good communication etc)

Leaders at the transpersonal level tend to have highly facilitative leadership styles, making full use of the expertise and inputs of many team, organisation or community members. They instinctively understand that no one individual or group must have undue influence. The most common people exercising undue influence are (a) more senior people in a hierarchical organisation; (b) people with stronger, more aggressive personalities; and (c) people with an expert technical agenda.

Leaders at the transpersonal level instinctively understand that to get the optimal outcome, the final decisions to be made must not be imposed by any individual or group. Rather, the decisions must be facilitated by active debate and discussion. Only in this way does positive 'synergy' occur in which the outcome is greater than the sum of the individual inputs.[1]

At the independent self level of culture, there is much emphasis on fully accountable individuals working co-operatively with each other, with each person being responsible and accountable for some part of a task. This requires good co-operation and co-ordination — but this is not the same as true partnership. To accurately define the co-creativity of a true partnership requires introducing and defining two rarely used terms: 'co-responsibility and co-accountability'.

'Co-responsibility and co-accountability' means that we are each interdependently responsible and accountable for the individual and collective outcomes to be achieved by ourselves and other members of the partnership. This requires a very high level of mutual trust, respect and communication between members of the partnership. Each member has to be willing to communicate difficulties they are having that might lead to failures and be willing to ask for help or support. Each partnership member must also be equally willing to help or provide support that goes beyond the task or responsibility that they are focused on.

A culture of this kind would have many of the traits found in good (highly functional) families: a high level of interdependence, mutual trust and respect, mutual support, openness and honesty in communication. It would also be resilient, effective and very productive.

To fully achieve the transpersonal level of development, using some form of spiritual or transformational discipline is almost essential. If you are not currently practising such a discipline, learning and practising meditation would probably be the easiest and most effective method for helping to cultivate the transpersonal level of awareness. There are many kinds of meditation, so you would need to find one that suits you.

IDENTITY AT THE TRANSPERSONAL LEVEL

The following diagram illustrates the structure and dynamics of the transpersonal self identity structure:

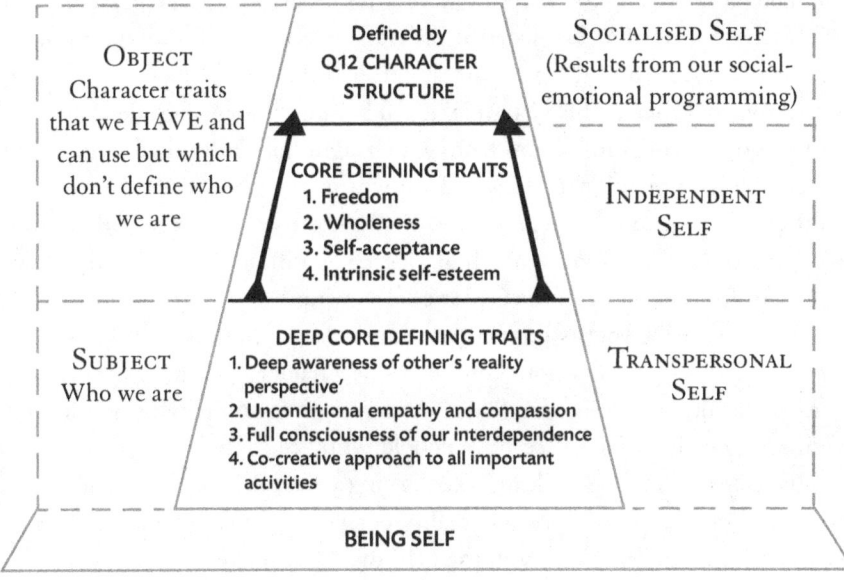

In the diagram you can see that the four core traits of our transpersonal self are experienced as who we are (identity). The arrows extending upward from the transpersonal self penetrate the independent self and the socialised self. These arrows indicate that the four core traits of the transpersonal self interpenetrate, influence and integrate all of the other traits that define our independent self and socialised self character structure. The socialised self and independent self are now resources within our total self that can be used by the transpersonal self. However, they will be used at the service the transpersonal self. The transpersonal self's core traits and intended outcomes act as integrating factors to help bring the character traits of the other selves into harmony with each other. Underlying these is the undifferentiated state of Being that is the basis of all higher stages of development.

THE PATHWAY TO THE INTEGRATION OF MANY POSSIBLE SELVES

It is critically important to understand what is and is not meant when we speak of the fully developed transpersonal self as being made up of many possible selves. For example, a person at the transpersonal level of development is not a social chameleon, showing different sides of him/her self to fit in any situation. They are certainly not people with multiple personality disorders. Such behaviour is simply the result of very poor personality integration at the socialised self level. The key word at the transpersonal level is **integration**.

Daily use of the Q12 profiling system can help us perceive the 'reality perspective' of others. This system is useful because it identifies, describes and measures the 12 core dimensions from which all unique individuals are shaped. Indeed, the combination of these 12 dimensions, expressed or unexpressed to different (measurable) degrees, results in approximately one half million possible profiles. This allows for a high degree of 'uniques' in each individual's overall profile and is one of the Q12 model's strengths.

Equally, its strengths lie in providing a description of only 12 types of building blocks that, in various combinations, create each individual's unique character structure. This simplicity underlying the complexity of different profiles makes it easier to see how people who are high or low in different combinations of the 12 building blocks might see the world. Each one of these combinations represents the 'reality perspective' of a possible self. As we become thoroughly familiar with the Q12 model, it makes it easier to see and understand the reality perspective of many possible selves. When we can see and understand other perspectives we find it easier to embrace and accept them as part of our own way of seeing the world.

Thus, we can gradually learn to have a huge internal reservoir of different 'reality perspectives', expanding way beyond the perspective provided by our own original Q12 character structure. Since each reality perspective represents a possible self, what this amounts to is being able to integrate many possible selves into our own self. We can learn to experience other selves as if they were part of who we are — the experience that defines the transpersonal stage of development.

However, for this integration to have any depth, we must extend ourselves to being beyond just having an intellectual understanding of other reality perspectives. In fact, we must be able to understand and accept the emotions of other reality perspectives. This requires integrating the 'shadow' aspect of our character structure.

The shadow consists of two layers within us although much of it remains subconscious.

The first layer consists of painful memories, fears or yearning needs or drives that result from the social/emotional programming which shaped our socialised self. In the process of development from the adult socialised self to the independent self, most of this level of our shadow would be emotionally de-programmed. As a fully-developed independent self, we would be mostly free of the deficit motivation that shaped our socialised self.

Yet there is a second, deeper level of our shadow which consists of all the unconsciously existing but unexperienced, undeveloped and unexpressed parts of our total possible psychology. During the first four stages of development (from infancy through adolescence) both our genetically inherited qualities and our social/emotional programming facilitated the development of certain traits and discouraged others. In Q12 language, this resulted in us occupying a great deal of terrain in some map quadrants, a moderate amount in some and very little in others.

Those map quadrants where we occupy very little terrain identify where we are likely to find the deeper level of our shadow. It is here that the unexperienced, undeveloped and unexpressed qualities or traits will be found. Yet to embrace, own and integrate all Q12 quadrants, we must be able to experience and express some of the major traits and qualities — both light and dark, empowering and limiting — commonly found in our weak quadrants. Using the map metaphor, we must explore and become familiar and comfortable within that terrain — a terrain in which we are initially uncomfortable.

The process of finding and expressing these shadow traits and qualities is intrinsically daunting, uncomfortable and often infused with fear. The Q12 instrument can be of great use in identifying where to find our shadow qualities. In addition to this, the use of some of the basic tools for facilitating transformational change described in this book — coaching, counselling, transformational growth workshops and the ongoing practice of meditation — are very useful.

INTEGRATING THE SHADOW OF AGGRESSIVE PROFILES

Many Q12 Entrepreneurs and Rationalists and some Idealists and Pragmatists can be very aggressive. If they are, they usually perceive being compliant and accommodating as weaknesses and aggressiveness as a strength.

However, learning to be compliant and accommodating in certain circumstances, and allowing oneself to be seen that way, is essential to gradually overcoming the feeling of weakness or humiliation felt when being compliant and accommodating. The process of experiencing and integrating this shadow of themselves is essential if they are to embrace, own and integrate all Q12 quadrants.

Mike was a classic example of this: very hard-edged, extremely competitive and exhibiting a very cool, blunt communication style. His early formative experiences made any form of accommodating or compliant behaviour seem weak and humiliating. His commitment to developing a close and deep relationship with his children was his path to integrating and accepting the soft, loving and accommodating emotions that defined his shadow. Over many months he gradually opened the door to both sharing and expressing his softest, most tender feelings with his boys. This was extremely difficult for him in the beginning, and progress was often two steps forward, one back.

However, the ultimate test for fully integrating this shadow aspect of Mike was with adults in his leadership role. He committed himself to holding meetings with his senior leadership team just to receive feedback on how he was communicating and behaving towards others, promising he would be accommodating and open to what they said, even if he felt hard and defensive inside himself.

Mike's behaviour and communication habits were very deeply ingrained. In the early months he had a number of slip ups but each time he was given firm and clear feedback. Each time he accepted the feedback without any defensiveness, though he often felt anger which covered other feelings of weakness and humiliation — the emotions that defined his shadow. But Mike stayed with it, and gradually the feelings of weakness and humiliation disappeared.

This, of course, does not mean that people with the naturally more aggressive profiles will become primarily accommodating and compliant. The more aggressive Q12 types will still retain and primarily use their natural strengths although in a more balanced and nuanced way. However, they will be able to act in accommodating and compliant ways when it is truly appropriate and useful to do so.

INTEGRATING THE SHADOW OF COMPLIANT, ACCOMMODATING PROFILES

A reverse process is essential for those Q12 types that are often compliant and accommodating. For example, very commonly Observers, Supporters, Dreamers and Analysts are compliant and accommodating, and also some Optimists. They generally dislike aggressive behaviour in others and would hate it within themselves. Yet to integrate their shadow they must learn to experience and express the capacity for aggressiveness that lies within all of us.

For people with strong accommodating, compliant Q12 profiles, learning to genuinely experience and express aggressiveness can be daunting task, uncomfortable and often fraught with fear. Because of this, the process should always occur with the help and advice of an experienced coach or counsellor to ensure that this is done in appropriate ways and appropriate circumstances, so as not to damage careers or relationships.

Tina was a classic case of someone who had to give expression to a character trait that she saw as very negative and highly aggressive. Her social/emotional programming was that any type of behaviour where you demanded getting your own way, was absolutely unacceptable. The emotional capacity for this kind of behaviour resided in the shadow part of her self.

In her professional career, Tina had come to see that there were only two options for her. Either her practice group would agree to creating a holistic health centre and she would accept the practice group leadership; or she would leave the practice group. She realised that presenting this choice to the practice group was delivering an ultimatum and this felt like she would be aggressively demanding her own way. However, she came to see that her vision for the holistic health centre was not selfish — she genuinely believed it would deliver a better service for her clients.

Thus, at the conclusion of the meeting with her practice group there was really no alternative but to make a very bold and direct statement of ultimatum. She remained calm and dignified, but basically she took an uncompromising stand for what she wanted, something that she had always previously felt was a selfish and aggressive thing to do.

She maintained this personal stand even when two of the doctors decided to resign rather than be part of what she was trying to do. And most importantly, she did not feel guilty. This was the ultimate indicator that she had integrated this ability to take a strong, uncompromising stand (with dignity) whenever truly necessary. It was still never her preferred option, but that capacity to do so was fully, consciously available within her when it was really necessary.

Integrating the stronger, more aggressive character traits of the shadow does not mean that people with naturally accommodating Q12 profiles will become primarily aggressive. The more accommodating and compliant Q12 types will still retain and rely primarily on the natural strengths of their Q12 profile, but they will gain two things:
- Firstly, they will be able to take a strong, uncompromising stand in those (rare) situations where it is appropriate or even essential
- Secondly, they will no longer feel weak, overwhelmed or compliant when they are around highly aggressive people, and will be able to stand up to them without fear

Did Tina, James, Tim and Mike ultimately attain the transpersonal level?

It was clear that all were strongly motivated by the 'common good'. This was not just something they valued, rather it had become part of their very identity. All had taken many steps to ensure that their professional and leadership activities would result in the best possible outcomes for all of their organisation's stakeholders. They had thus fully integrated the motivational level into their inner psychology and outer actions.

All had experienced and expressed the four traits that define the core of identity at the transpersonal level, although these traits had not yet become fully integrated into their identity structure. Nonetheless they all made sufficient progress with this that much of their leadership was an expression of the level of self-mastery defined by the transpersonal level. From my own experience I would say that all of them were in transition to the transpersonal level from the (fully attained) independent self level by the time I had completed my work with them. Approximately 14% of the population are making this transition — and about 1% have fully attained the transpersonal level on the ladder of consciousness.[2]

It is now time to explore the Unitive stage.

---

1   See J Surowiecki, *The Wisdom of Crowds* (Abacus: Lancaster Place, London, 2005). This book addresses the synergistic effects achieved when the conditions I set out are achieved.
2   B Anderson, *The Spirit of Leadership*, The Leadership Circle <www.tlccommunity.com> accessed 11 June 2012, p 22.

CHAPTER EIGHTEEN

THE EMERGENCE OF THE UNITIVE SELF

WRITING about the unitive stage brings with it some very significant difficulties.

Firstly, there is very little information available about exactly what a person would be like at the unitive stage of development. The Buddhist and ancient Vedic texts provide an abundance of information about higher **states** of consciousness — including the unitive state — but very little about **permanent developmental stages**. What sort of identity and motivation would a person have at the unitive stage? How would a person at that stage approach a leadership role?

The second difficulty is how few people actually achieve the unitive stage or beyond. Approximately 20–30% of the whole population (about 40% of individuals returning from work for further higher education) achieve the independent self stage. In addition, only about 1% fully arrive at the transpersonal self stage, while about 14% of individuals are in transition to that stage and thus experience many of the qualities that define the transpersonal self.[1] But as far as I know there are no statistics for those who have achieved the unitive stage. I have no doubt that many of the great mystics from the worlds major spiritual traditions had at least attained that stage or beyond.

Because this book is about leadership and thus focuses on people who live fully in the world, playing major leadership roles, who are at, or transitioning to, the unitive stage, we must look beyond these traditional spiritual figures. I would especially like to focus on leaders that most people will have some familiarity with because of the major roles that they played in modern history.

Individuals I believe have attained this stage of development, or who are in transition to this stage, include:

- Dalai Lama — I have heard him speak and watched with great interest how he has lived his life. I believe him to be a superb role model for how a leader at the unitive stage might carry out their leadership role.
- Maharishi Mahesh Yogi — I studied with him for five years (1971–75). During that time I was able to witness both what he taught about the unitive stage, how he acted on a day-to-day basis in his efforts to raise individual and collective levels of consciousness.
- Other great leaders who were probably at least transitioning towards the unitive stage include: Mahatma Ghandi, Dr Martin Luther King Jr and Nelson Mandela. While they all had some human flaws, one needs only to weigh these imperfections against their massive accomplishments in creating positive collective change, and the degree of awareness and self-mastery they achieved in extremely difficult and dangerous situations.

Someone at, or approaching, the unitive self level of consciousness has a world view that is inclusive on a global scale. They no longer simply experience the interconnectedness and interdependence of all things, characteristic of the transpersonal stage. At the unitive self level, all people and nature itself are experienced as expressions of the same non-dual oneness.

But what exactly is non-dual oneness?

To reach the unitive stage it is usually essential to have undertaken a long-term daily practice of meditation, or some spiritual or internal discipline that approximates the meditative state. Indeed meditation is enormously helpful for developing all the higher stages. Through meditation anyone can begin to experience the 'state of Being'.

There are many forms of meditation — but (for example) if you are sitting down doing mantra meditation, repeatedly thinking a mantric sound, you will notice that thoughts will be going through your mind. As long as you just let the thoughts flow and do not resist them your mind and body will gradually slow down. Your breathing will slow and become very quiet and you will experience the mentally repeated sound at subtler and subtler levels. Then at a certain point your thoughts and the mantric sound will disappear and yet you will be awake and conscious. This is the state of pure, undifferentiated, non-dual consciousness (non-dual meaning no subject and object).

In this state your mind or emotions are not doing anything — you are just in a state of Being. Thus the state of pure (non-dual) consciousness is exactly the state of undifferentiated Being. In this internal state, time and space have no application, there is no yearning desire for anything — the state of Pure Consciousness or Being is sufficient onto itself. With regular practice this experience will occur more often and for longer periods. You will also find that over time you will go deeper into the state of Pure Consciousness or Being and your experience will change. At the deeper levels during meditation the experience is richer and more fulfilling. But the real point of doing meditation is most evident after coming out of meditation and entering into daily life activities. It is the leftover affects of meditation during daily activity that bring about the gradual unfolding of the permanent higher stages of consciousness.

It is important to make a distinction at this point between the 'foreground' and 'background' of your internal consciousness. The **foreground** is the thoughts, feelings, images, ideas and emotions that flow through your mind while the **background** consists of the gradually increasing amount of Pure Consciousness that remains within your mind while outside of meditation during your daily activity. With the regular practice of meditation (or other spiritual or transformational practices) this background of Pure Consciousness (or the 'state of Being') becomes gradually more permanent, more intense and more dominant.

Maharishi Mahesh Yogi used a simple metaphor for this phenomenon. A piece of pure uncoloured cloth is dipped in a dye and then laid out in the sun. The sun fades most of the colour. The next day the cloth is dipped in the dye again and laid in the sun where it fades again although a little more colour remains behind this time. This process is repeated many times and the cloth gradually takes on the colour of the dye more permanently and intensely.

Similarly, each time we meditate we briefly experience the state of Pure Consciousness or Being. Then we go into out daily activity and most of the experience fades away. Yet if we keep doing our daily practice, gradually over time, the state of Pure Consciousness (or Being) starts to remain in the background of our inner consciousness more permanently and more intensely, while at the foreground of our mind we continue to have active thoughts, feelings, images and ideas as we go through our daily lives.

TRANSITIONING TO THE INDEPENDENT SELF LEVEL

As we transition to the independent self stage, we increasingly experience the surface level of the state of Being more and more permanently in the background of our mind. This surface level has a quiet, balanced evenness about it, which allows us to view our socialised self, other people and life situations fully, objectively and non-judgementally — the surface level of mindfulness. When fully developed at the independent self stage, this experience becomes permanently integrated into our consciousness, and is the foundation stone for the four character traits — freedom, wholeness, self-acceptance and intrinsic self-esteem — that define that state.

TRANSITIONING TO THE TRANSPERSONAL SELF LEVEL
As the independent self stage consolidates, and we continue our daily meditation or other spiritual practices, a deeper, more intense experience of Pure Consciousness begins to emerge and become more dominant and permanent as the background of our consciousness.

This deeper dimension of Pure Consciousness is experienced as having more of a warm feeling tone to it — in contrast to the emotional quietness and evenness of the surface level experience of Pure Consciousness experienced at the independent self stage. This warm feeling tone radiates outward towards other people and the environment; this is the source of the feelings of unconditional empathy at the transpersonal stage. This feeling causes us to feel interconnected and interdependent with others, bringing with it a deeper sense of intimacy and insight into other people's emotions and their ways of thinking and ways of seeing the world. This experience and our feeling of unconditional empathy impels us to want to seek the 'common good' — and because of our sense of the interdependence and interconnectedness of all things, enables us to have the wisdom to contribute to the common good in ways that will not create further problems.

TRANSITIONING TO THE UNITIVE SELF LEVEL
As the transpersonal self stage consolidates, a new awareness emerges that begins the process of developing towards the unitive self stage. As we continue with our meditation and/or other spiritual or transformational practices, the state of Pure Consciousness becomes even more dominant and intense in the background of our mind. We begin to experience it with such intensity that we ourselves, our thoughts and our feelings, other people and nature itself are all experienced as individual manifestations of the non-dual oneness of the state or Pure Consciousness or Being.

This does not mean that we can't recognise our individuality, or that of other people. Indeed, in the unitive state we have a cognitive and perceptual sensitivity to make finer distinctions about individual differences than at any earlier stage of consciousness. However, within our internal consciousness we experience every thought and feeling we have, every person, every sentient being in the world, as individualised expressions of Pure Consciousness — and thus we feel at one with everything. The development of the unitive stage begins with glimpses of the unitive state that occur periodically as the result of our daily meditation or other spiritual or transformational practices.

In the unitive state, we see the essence of everyone and everything as that pure state of Being, while each individual person, sentient being or object also has a form. All individual forms have structure, are unique, and are all located in time and space, with a beginning and an end. In the unitive state this timeless essence in the background of our mind is so dominant in our awareness that it creates the 'at oneness' we feel with all the unique forms that surround us.

At the unitive stage, relationships with individuals take on a new dimension. At the transpersonal stage we gained the natural ability to experience the I-Thou, Being-to-Being relationship. In I-Thou relationships our psychological space partially overlaps with another's psychological space, creating a level of intimacy not found at earlier levels. However, at the unitive stage it is not just that I have a psychologically overlapping relationship with 'Thou'; at the unitive stage *I am Thou*. Indeed, at the unitive stage we experience ourselves as being at one with all others.

As the unitive stage develops four traits begin to emerge as the core of our identity. These traits empower leaders to operate on an entirely new level, to focus on large-scale, deep change of a kind that easily transcends all borders: groups, companies, communities and nations. Such leaders are less concerned with the position they hold than with their ability to influence others to make the specific changes necessary for the outcomes they seek.

These traits are not beliefs or belief systems, nor are they skills. Rather they are a world view anchored deep within our consciousness that defines who we are. At the unitive stage, all of our thoughts, feelings and actions come from and are expressions of, this identity, which consists of the following deep core character traits:

- Universal, unconditional love and compassion
- A strong, natural inclination to perceive problems, issues and people from a global, holistic, long-term perspective
- A strong focus on creating change through raising levels of individual and collective consciousness
- Advocacy of universal spiritual and moral principles that transcend different social/cultural and religious beliefs and practices

UNIVERSAL, UNCONDITIONAL LOVE AND COMPASSION

When an individual has achieved the developmental stage of unity consciousness, this experience becomes permanently anchored within their consciousness. Universal, unconditional love and compassion towards the world and all its inhabitants become a daily reality. So, what would a person be like for whom this experience is a daily reality?

At the unitive stage, universal, unconditional love and compassion would be expressed by unceasing daily acts of compassion and caring for others: a life lived in service to others. A leader at or approaching this level would become the embodiment of 'servant leadership'.

One individual who I believe is at this stage is the Dalai Lama. He has lived a life which is the fullest expression of servant leadership. He has devoted his life to attempting to reclaim his Tibetan homeland as an independent country and he has travelled the world speaking to groups of people from a variety of countries and religious traditions. He has also devoted himself to attempting to help people everywhere understand the deeper spiritual dimension within themselves, to overcome suffering and find greater happiness through living a life of mindfulness, and his acts have been acts of unceasing love and compassion for as many people as possible — acts of servant leadership.

Maharishi Mahesh Yogi worked 18 hour days for over half a century until his death at 91 years of age in 2008 spreading the message and philosophy of meditation to millions of people throughout the world. He saw this as a way to relieve suffering and improve the quality of life for people — individually and collectively — everywhere. In his unceasing acts of love and compassion for over 50 years, he was an exemplar of servant leadership.

During that part of their life where they lead major social changes, Ghandi, King and Mandela were all embodiments of servant leadership. Although their leadership brought with it a great deal of danger their compassion and care for others were so central to their identity that they were willing to risk their lives. Being willing to put your life on the line for your people is an act of unconditional love, and perhaps the greatest possible act of compassion and servant leadership.

SEEING PROBLEMS, ISSUES AND PEOPLE FROM A HOLISTIC, LONG TERM PERSPECTIVE

At the unitive level, it is not just that the world is interconnected (as it is at the transpersonal level) — rather it is all experienced as one: all individuals and the natural world are experienced as unique expressions of the timeless, non-dual oneness of Pure Consciousness.

This does not mean that individuals at this level cannot focus on individual people, events, problems or opportunities. Quite the contrary, the greater perspective provided by their higher state of consciousness allows them to focus on individual people, groups and issues that those with less perspective might not see. For example (using a metaphor), the higher up the mountain you are, the easier it is to see things that you might miss at a lower level. At the highest level of the mountain (equivalent to the unitive state) you have a full 360 degree perspective of the landscape. This allows you to see how whatever you are focusing on fits into the larger landscape (the global whole), opening up opportunities for creativity and problem solving. People at the unitive level are more empowered than at any previous level to identify and focus on individual people, groups, issues, problems or opportunities because they are seen within this holistic perspective.

Leaders at the unitive level intuitively sense, within the larger whole, those factors that shape and effect what they are trying to change, and what will be effected within the larger whole by the change process.

People who are developed to the unitive level often tend to prefer more of a statesman-like role, establishing coalitions of institutions, groups and communities to work towards large-scale change that leads to the common good. Mahatma Ghandi was a perfect example of this, preferring not to occupy a formal position, relying on his personal authority rather than positional authority.

In the unitive state, time is experienced in two ways simultaneously. Because of the dominance of the state of timeless Pure Consciousness in the background of their mind, leaders at the unitive stage live in the eternal now. At each moment they can focus entirely on what they are doing without being distracted by concerns about the past or future. They are not psychologically attached to any given period of time, no matter how intense or important the activity. This is a deep and extremely pure form of mindfulness.

While at the unitive self stage we experience time as the eternal now, yet we can simultaneously and intuitively step back and see the long-term

perspective, stretching way into the past and far into the many possible futures. Thus a leader at the unitive level, while focusing on current issues and changes:
- Implicitly understands that the history of cultural, social and economic forces that lead to the current situation often stretch back many decades and even hundreds or thousands of years
- Always keeps in their awareness the long-term envisioned future they intend to create, all the while realising that the full and complete change process may stretch far into the future, often much longer than they will live

A STRONG FOCUS ON RAISING INDIVIDUAL AND COLLECTIVE LEVELS OF CONSCIOUSNESS

Maharishi Mahesh Yogi always said: 'ultimately, you can only create or sustain a better world — for both humanity and the rest of nature — by raising people's level of consciousness'. The focus of his training programme was on raising individual people's level of consciousness through daily meditation practice. However, Maharishi also spoke of the positive synergistic effects when groups of people, actively raising their level of consciousness, join together with a common purpose. He believed that within groups, a higher collective level of consciousness could have an enormous impact in improving collective behaviour and thus collective socio-economic conditions.

The Dalai Lama, Mahatma Ghandi, Dr Martin Luther King Jr and Nelson Mandela all demonstrate a similar deep conviction. Their lives were a testament to this conviction even though they may have used different language and terms to describe it. Ghandi, King and Mandela spoke of changing people's values, beliefs, assumptions, attitudes and behaviour rather than raising their level of consciousness, but the intention was the same.

To understand this we need to return to Wilbur's quadrant system, and discuss the two bottom quadrants.

The lower left hand quadrant is the home of the internal subjective plural 'we'. This quadrant represents a way of recognising that there is an internal chemistry of subjective experience whenever two or more people relate to each other. These consist of shared thoughts, feelings, perceptions, ideas, attitudes, intentions and beliefs that are the result of two or more people being together. These can be positive, negative or neutral (or any mixture of the three). However, they are the collective internal states of consciousness, the shared internal results of the relationship.

THE EMERGENCE OF THE UNITIVE SELF

INTERIOR	EXTERIOR
'I' SINGULAR (Subjective Internal)	**'IT'** SINGULAR (Objective External)
'WE' PLURAL (Subjective Internal)	**'ITS'** PLURAL (Objective External)

When larger groups of people are involved — an organisation, institution, community, nation — the lower left quadrant refers to a culture. More specifically, it refers to the non-visible, subjective collective consciousness. This consists of the values, beliefs, attitudes, assumptions and norms that are shared by most people in the larger defined group. These are interior to the collection of people within the group and not directly externally observable. This interior cultural phenomenon is like a collective state of consciousness. It is the internal collective consciousness that drives the external behaviour of the defined group. The patterns of external directly observable behaviour is represented by the lower right hand quadrant — the exterior, social collective.

In creating transformational change in the social practices and behaviour patterns within any collective (lower right quadrant), there must be a sufficient number of people within that collective who have reached the required developmental level (lower left quadrant). Authors differ on the percentage of the population within the collective who must have achieved this stage in the evolution of consciousness, for a major social transformational shift to occur.

However, whatever the number, once that more conscious percentage is reached, a tipping point occurs. Within a short time the majority of the population are sufficiently affected by the more conscious minority to actively or passively accept the new culture, or at least the new external social practices and behaviour. This does not mean the majority have yet reached the developmental level of the minority who have led the change. In addition, there is usually a sizable minority who will strongly resist the internal values and beliefs and the external social practices and behaviour of the new culture far into the future. Thus a long-term focus is essential, requiring active participation of those who have been won over to the new culture to complete the full transformation.

The black non-violent civil rights movement under the leadership of Dr Martin Luther King Jr provides a good example.

By the time Dr King had emerged as the well-known leader of the Southern Christian Leadership Conference in the early 1960s, there were numerous African Americans and whites who were moving up the ladder of consciousness — in our model in transition to, or at, the independent self level, and perhaps some transitioning to the transpersonal level. The critical tipping point in the civil rights movement occurred in the early to mid 1960s, consisting of non-violent civil disobedience activities and numerous marches and demonstrations, including the famous march on Washington in 1963 where Dr King gave his powerful and deeply moving 'I have a dream' speech. The mid-point occurred when both Houses of Congress passed the Civil Rights and Voting Rights Acts during the Johnson administration in 1965. The latter part of the tipping point was the voter registration drive in the American south and the enacting of other federal and state legislation to support equal treatment in the workplace and elsewhere for African Americans and other minorities.

Since the tipping point in the 1960s, huge progress has been made in changing the individual and collective internal mindsets concerning racial beliefs and attitudes, and in changing daily social and workplace practices and behaviour for the majority of Americans. It is probably true that the majority or Americans at this point in history are not racially prejudiced. However, it is also undoubtedly true that there is still a large number who are. Thus there is still a long way to go to complete the transformation that began with the 'tipping point' in the 1960s.

In summary, leaders at the unitive stage of development lead by facilitating the evolution of consciousness on an individual and collective level. They understand that for lasting transformational changes to occur on any collective level there is a necessary level of consciousness that a certain portion of the people within that collective must have achieved.

Evidence abounds that change initiatives are likely to fail in important ways if enough people (especially those leading the change) are not at the right developmental level. Classic examples of this are revolutions — often fought in the name of high ideals such as freedom and justice — that descended into bloodbaths and tyrannies: the French revolution in 1889, the Russian revolution in 1917, the Chinese revolution of 1948.

The leader at the unitive self level thus understands the need to help individuals to develop all the critical elements of higher consciousness, to create a new sense of self, a new identity. They may seek to do this through personal contact with people (mentoring, coaching) or through ensuring that training and a wide range of direct experience are readily available.

In summary, people at the unitive stage experience a universal, unconditional love and compassion towards all people and all sentient beings. They perceive their ultimate mission as the reducing of human suffering and the creation of a world in which every individual has the opportunity and encouragement to achieve their full individual and spiritual potential. They posses a deep conviction, as a natural expression of their level of development, that the permanent evolutionary changes within human society that will achieve this ultimate mission can only be brought about by raising individual and collective levels of consciousness.

ADVOCACY OF UNIVERSAL SPIRITUAL AND MORAL PRINCIPLES THAT TRANSCEND DIFFERENT SOCIAL AND RELIGIOUS BELIEFS AND PRACTICES

Cultural diversity has enormously enriched the lives of millions of people around the world and continues to do so. However, it is obvious that diversity can also be very threatening. Tension, intolerance, anger, hatred and even violent behaviour can arise when people with deeply embedded but conflicting cultural behavioural norms and religious beliefs and practices encounter each other. The ultimate expression of this is found in war or acts of terrorism.

Cultural norms and religious beliefs are often deeply intertwined and there are two aspects that are relevant to our discussion. The first relates to belief systems about our human relationship with a transcendent Being or transcendent Domain of some kind. Judaism, Christianity and Islam are all monotheistic religions with different names for a single God. For Buddhists and various forms of Hinduism there is a transcendent Domain of experience — often referred to as the 'Absolute' — but not personalised in anthropomorphic form as in Christianity, Judaism and Islam.

The second area of importance relates to beliefs about how people should live their lives individually and with each other. This involves both the spiritual and moral domains. The critical question is: **are there any beliefs and practices** that are universally advocated in all cultures and all major religious traditions? In other words, are there any universal spiritual and moral principles?

But what exactly are universal spiritual and moral principles? How many of them are there? And how do we know that they are indeed universal? While the focus of most cultural anthropologists has been on identifying and describing differences in cultural norms, values, belief systems and behaviour, there is actually an extensive body of literature on human universals that can be summarised in the following brief list from Doug Lennick and Fred Kiel's book *Moral Intelligence*:

- *Commitment to something greater than oneself*
- *Self-respect, but with humility, self-discipline, and acceptance of personal responsibility*
- *Respect and caring for others (that is, the Golden Rule)*
- *Caring for other living things and the environment* [2]

Lennick and Kiel later identify twelve possible candidates as universal principles:
- Integrity
- Responsibility
- Compassion
- Forgiveness
- Generosity
- Commitment to a transcending power
- Justice
- Temperance/self-discipline
- Humility
- Caring for living things and the environment
- Wisdom
- Courage[3]

Whatever their actual number, there are two critical points that apply to leaders at the unitive stage of development:
- They are outstanding exemplars of these universal spiritual and moral principles. While they are not perfect, their leadership goals and behaviour are consistent with these principles.
- They perceive the world through the lenses of these universal spiritual and moral principles. For example, they actually see different cultures and religions as having an underlying unity, found in these principles,

that is more fundamental than the differences. And through this they recognise the sisterhood and brotherhood of all mankind.

However, I would add to one more principle: **inclusiveness**. Each of the five leaders listed at the start of the chapter were strong advocates of inclusiveness.

Maharishi always spoke of all the world's religions as having a core of spiritual truth that was exactly the same, even though their orthodox dogmas and teachings were often different. He was always totally accepting of people practising their own faith even though his own cultural and religious tradition was Hindu ('the Vedic tradition').

The Dalai Lama is especially a strong exemplar of inclusiveness in his spiritual teaching. He comes from a Tibetan Buddhist background but can relate very easily to people of all cultural and religious backgrounds. He has explicitly stated that there are many paths to the ultimate spiritual goal of unity with the divine — and 'at their best' each religion provides different paths to the same goal. At its best a religion does not claim to have the exclusive truth or the exclusive path to spiritual fulfilment or enlightenment. In its deepest and most authentic form a religion should be inclusive rather than exclusive.

The Dalai Lama has met with leaders of all the world's religions: Catholic, Jewish, Anglican, Mormon, Eastern Orthodox, Muslim, Hindu, Sikh and he is currently a member of the Board of World Religious Leaders. This is a demonstration of inclusiveness at its best. He advocates human rights, women's rights, wildlife conservation, and non-violence, to name a few. He also has stated that when scientific truths are in conflict with a religious dogma, the dogma should be rejected.

Dr Martin Luther King Jr was also a strong advocate of many universal spiritual and moral values, including inclusiveness. For example, in his most famous speech, his 'dream' was blacks and whites being together as brothers and sisters.

> *I have a dream that one day this nation will rise up and live out the true meaning of its creed: We hold these truths to be self-evident that all men are created equal...I have a dream that one day, down in Alabama...little black boys and black girls will be able to join hands with little white boys and little white girls as sisters and brothers. I have a dream today!*[4]

He never taught hatred — and forgiveness (another of the universal spiritual and moral principles listed above) was at the centre of his teaching.

Similarly with Nelson Mandela, a lawyer and political activist. Mandela had always been a person of deep integrity, courage and commitment to the service of his oppressed people. During his many years in prison he underwent a deep personal transformation which I believe was what brought him to or approaching the unitive developmental stage. He emerged from almost 27 years of unjust and sometimes brutal imprisonment without a trace of anger, hatred or resentment.

As President of South Africa his inclusiveness was demonstrated by his strong support for the 'truth and reconciliation' process. In this process white South Africans who had committed torture and murder against black South Africans under the Apartheid regime were not prosecuted if they simply and honestly confessed their crimes. This was intended to prevent a potential blood bath because of the enormous anger and hatred that had built up under Apartheid. But perhaps more importantly it was intended as a pathway to bringing blacks and whites together into a single unified South Africa.

The ultimate symbolic expression of this occurred with the following action undertaken by Mandela:

> *In 1995, Mandela symbolized the unity of a new South Africa when he attended the Rugby World Cup game in which the Springboks, the South African national team, were playing. Rugby had been the bastion of white supremacy, but Mandela attended the game. He walked onto the pitch wearing the Springboks' jersey so hated by black South Africans, at the same time giving the clenched fist salute of the ANC, thereby appealing, almost impossibly, both to black and white South Africans. As Tokyo Sexwale, ANC activist and premier of South Africa's Gauteng Province, said of him: 'Only Mandela could wear an enemy jersey. Only Mandela would go down there and be associated with the Springboks...All the years in the underground, in the trenches, denial, self-denial, away from home, prison, it was worth it. That's all we wanted to see.'*[5]

The following diagram provides a visual picture of the identity structure that culminates in the unitive self.

In the diagram you can see that the four deep core traits of our unitive self are experienced as who we are (identity). The arrows that extend upward from the unitive self into the transpersonal self, the independent self and the socialised self indicate that the four core traits of the unitive self interpenetrate, influence and integrate the transpersonal, independent and socialised selves.

THE EMERGENCE OF THE UNITIVE SELF

At the unitive stage, these are all experienced as resources that we can use, but do not define who we are. They are experienced as 'object'. Who we are is now the unitive self.

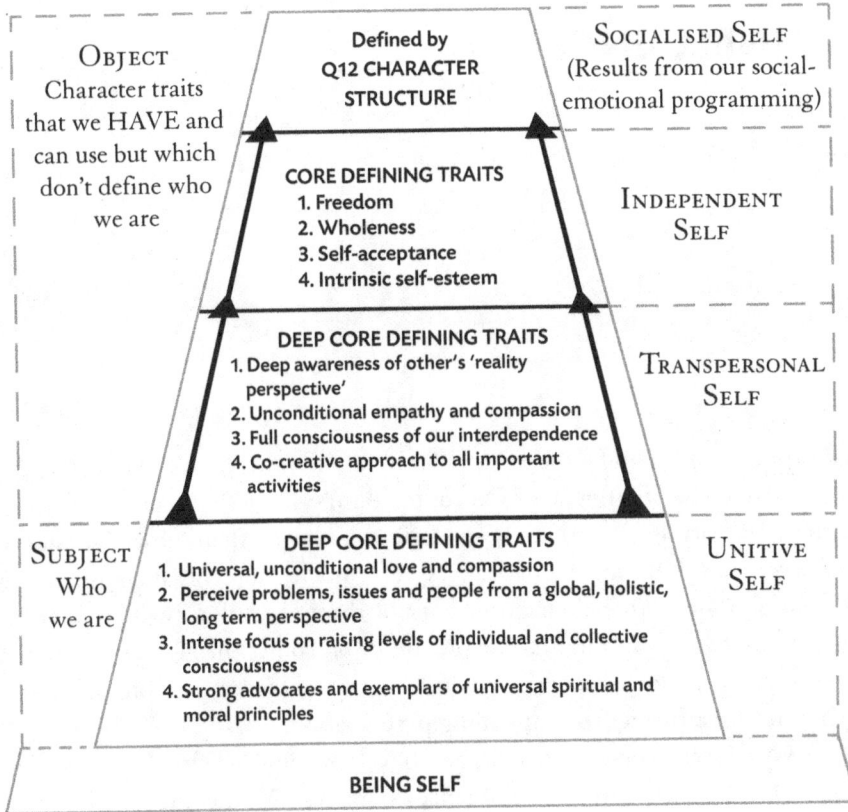

---

1. B Anderson, *The Spirit of Leadership*, The Leadership Circle <www.tlccommunity.com> accessed 11 June 2012, p 22. Anderson uses the term 'integral self' for what I have called the 'transpersonal self', and the 'sacred self' for what I have called the 'unitive self'.
2. D Lennik and F Kiel, *Moral Intelligence: Enhancing Business Performance and Leadership Success* (Pearson Education, Inc: New Jersey, 2008), pp 33–34.
3. Ibid, p 41.
4. *Speeches that Changed the World* (Murdoch Books Pty Ltd: Sydney, 2005), p 152.
5. D Rook and W R Torbert, 'Seven Transformations of Leadership', *Harvard Business Review* (April, 2005), pp 6–7.

CHAPTER NINETEEN

LEVELS OF DEVELOPMENT AND CIRCLE OF INFLUENCE

IT is important to make the distinction between someone's 'circle of control' and their 'circle of influence'.[1] One of the things the circle of control includes is the authority leaders directly exercise because of their official position. However, mindful, successful leaders rely much more on their ability to influence others rather than direct control through authority. This kind of leadership involves facilitating the pursuit of outcomes through and with the willing participation of others: mindful, successful leaders rely on expanding their circle of influence to gain willing participation.

As leaders evolve to the higher developmental levels, the scope and timeframe of their circle of influence increases. At the independent self level, the scope of a leader's influence is usually within the boundaries of the organisation, institution or field in which they work. As a leader evolves towards the transpersonal level, they will have the natural impulse and ability to exercise influence beyond these boundaries. This is a natural expression of their level of development. The deeper motivation at the transpersonal level is to contribute to a common good that includes their organisation, but also reaches beyond it.

There are many ways in which leaders can exert influence at the transpersonal level:
- Facilitating strategic alliances between other organisations and their own
- Encouraging co-operation and collaboration between different organisations or institutions

LEVELS OF DEVELOPMENT AND CIRCLE OF INFLUENCE

- Entering into good faith dialogues with local communities, exploring ways the business or organisation can be a positive influence
- Joining forces with organisations or businesses within an industry to create higher standards for all aspects of industry performance and ethics — thus helping to create a better industry culture

As with the transpersonal level of development, at the unitive level the world and the universe are seen as an open-ended mystery, in which our interconnected world is subject to unending change. While this change is inevitable we can intervene in the process to achieve outcomes for better or worse. And as with the transpersonal level, the natural ongoing impulse at the unitive level is to intervene in ways that will result in the common good.

However, at the unitive level the scope of the desired changes and the timeframes envisioned are enormous. Leaders at this level have a deep natural impulse to expand their circle of influence way beyond their circle of control in which they have direct organisational or institutional authority. They ultimately seek huge outcomes that would often not be achieved in their lifetime. Thus, leadership at the unitive level is more like statespersonship.

The following diagram illustrates the expanding circle of influence at each higher developmental level.

It is my hope that this book will inspire as many of you as possible to begin the journey towards higher developmental levels and higher levels of mindful and successful leadership. It is likely, given the statistics collected by Kegan and Hall, that at least 25% of you are already at the independent self level of development — and perhaps as many as 14% transitioning to the transpersonal level. If this is true it is an excellent start, given that only 50 years ago the percentage of people at these higher levels of development would probably have been much less.

However, we live in a world that, while highly interconnected by globalisation, is also deeply divided in many ways. Conflicts between different ethnic, cultural and religious groups abound — and some of the beliefs and practices within each group are deeply divisive. Thus, we have a profound need for leaders at the transpersonal and unitive levels to influence the process of healing these many divides. Leaders at those levels have a deep and compelling need to ensure that wherever they are — and whatever organisational setting they inhabit — they are contributing to the common good. Their capacity for mindful, successful leadership can often influence people, events and institutions in ways that we would not commonly suppose possible because at those levels of consciousness their circle of influence can extend far beyond any actual positional authority they have.

The Dalai Lama is clearly one of current voices unceasingly calling for the healing of those divides. But this task will require thousands of leaders over generations who are at the transpersonal or unitive level. So where will such leaders come from?

Every kind of organisation can be a breeding ground for mindful, effective leadership if it has a culture built around the right kind of vision and values. Most of us work in or engage with at least one kind of organisation if not more. If an organisation provides the right opportunities, experience, training, development and encouragement, many aspiring leaders will undertake the internal climb up the ladder of consciousness.

This process will create highly self-aware, mindful and very effective leaders who will make major contributions to the success of their organisation or profession. Eventually their influence will also broaden beyond the organisation or profession and they will contribute to building a world without ethnic, cultural, religious or economic divides.

Thus, the Ghandis, Kings and Mandelas of the future who have a global focus may emerge from almost anywhere. And who knows — provided you have a deep commitment to undertaking the journey up the ladder of consciousness — you may be one of them.

---

1   The first time I saw the term 'circle of influence' was in Steven Covey's *'The Seven Habits of Highly Effective People'*. (New York: Simon & Schuster, 1990) but he used it in conjunction with the term 'circle of concern' — not 'circle of control'.

INDEX

abstract thinking 59–60
accommodating profiles 221–2
Achilles' heels 13–14, 16, 18, 41, 84, 85, 191, 193, 195–6, 210
    Analyst 123
    Dreamer 139–30
    Entrepreneur 111
    Executive 108
    Idealist 126
    Motivator 115
    Observer 96–7
    Optimist 90
    Pragmatist 100
    Rationalist 120
    Realist 93
    Supporter 105
action map 82–3, 101–15
    will and 77–8
adolescent self 45, 57–60, 132, 186
adult socialised self 43–4, 45, 61–2, 132, 186, 189, 192–4, 217, 237
advocacy 233–7
aggressive profiles 220

Analyst 83–4, 120–3, 148–56
Anderson, Bob 202, 222, 237
authenticity 22, 35
    nature of 22–4
awakening experiences 25–34
awareness
    developmental markers 45
    understanding of others' 210–11
'B-cognition values' 63, 64
Barrett, Richard 185
Being self 62, 63–4, 73–4, 196, 203–4, 217, 224–5, 237
beliefs 44
    'feeliefs' 53
belonging 52
belonging/relationship needs 46, 61, 63
    adolescent stage 58
    early childhood stage 53
    indicators 64
    late childhood stage 54
body self stage 45, 48–50, 132, 186
brain 11
    cerebral cortex 13

mammalian 12–13
primitive 12
structure and function 12–13
cerebral cortex 13
change methodologies 18–19
circles of influence 238–40
co-accountability 216
coaching and mentoring skills 35
co-creative approach 214–17
cognitive intelligence 188
commercial pressures 208–9
communication 36–7
communication skills 35
compassion, unconditional 211–13, 228
compliant profiles 221–2
concern for others 39–40
concrete operational thinking 57
consciousness 7
collective levels, raising 230–3
independent self stage 196, 202
mindfulness and 7–8
transpersonal stage 205, 206, 207, 211–15
unitive self stage 223–8
co-responsibility 216
cultural diversity 233
'D-cognition' values 63
Dalai Lama 224, 228, 230, 235, 240
deficit motivation 65–7
fear and 71–2
societal 72–4
success treadmills 69–71
Dreamer 83–4, 127–30, 157–69
early childhood stage 45, 50–3, 132, 186
effectiveness 22–3, 35
emotional de-programming 134, 135–6
emotional intelligence 188
emotional responses, 12
emotions 76–7

relationship map 77
empathy, unconditional 211–13
enculturation 47
engagement, power of 36–7
Entrepreneur 82–3, 109–12, 170–82
envisioning a new future 36
Executive 82–3, 105–8, 148–56
experiential learning 135–6
facilitators 18, 38, 238
'fair witness' state 191–2, 195
fear
Analyst 123
deficit motivation and 71–2
Dreamer 130
Entrepreneur 112
Executive 108
Idealist 127
Motivator 115
Observer 97
Optimist 90
Pragmatist 100
Rationalist 120
Realist 94
Supporter 105
'feeliefs' 53
five fundamental needs 46–7
freedom 194–5
genetics 24–5
Ghandi, Mahatma 224, 229, 230, 240
Hall, Dr Brian P 74, 185, 202, 239
hidden persona 58
higher consciousness 223–4
developing 184–5
honesty 40
horizontal change 133–4
I-thou, being to being relationships 206–7, 227
Idealist 83–4, 124–7, 137–47
identity 46, 189–90

subject-object relations 48
independent self stage 191–3, 194–6, 200, 201
transpersonal self stage 203, 204, 209–18
unitive self stage 223, 227, 228, 233, 236–7
imagination 36
inclusiveness 235–6
independence 55
independent intentionality 197–9
independent self stage 45, 132, 147, 186, 189, 191–202, 217, 237
    creation of identity, 194–6
    motivational factors 197
    socialisation and 192–4
    structure of consciousness 196
    transitioning to 225–6
inspiration, power of 36–7
integration of selves 218–22

intelligence 187–90
    types of 188
interdependence 213–14
internal and external behaviours 76–7
intimacy 204–5
Kegan, Dr Robert 184, 201, 202, 239
King Jnr, Dr Martin Luther 224, 228, 230–2, 235, 240
ladder of consciousness 6–9, 44–8, 185–7
language 46, 47
leader
    definition 22
    intentions and motivations 6, 23
leadership
    authentic 22–4, 35
    characteristics 8
    childhood opportunities 25
    cultural transformation and, 20–1
    development of, 8, 21

essential capabilities 36–41
    nature of 5, 10
    ordinary people, 10
    self-mastery and, 9–11
limbic system 13
listening skills 35
love
    romantic 60–1
    unconditional 46–7, 53, 228
Maharishi Mahesh Yogi 184, 224–5, 228, 230, 235
mammalian brain 12–13
managerial role 20–1
Mandela, Nelson 224, 228, 230, 236, 240
mapping 78–80
    strength in a quadrant 84
Maslov, Abraham 46, 58, 63–5, 72, 143, 155, 184–5, 197–9, 201
meditation 17, 224–5
mindfulness 7–8, 19, 40–1, 73–4, 194–5, 203, 226, 238–40
    consciousness and 7–8
    'fair witness' state 191–2
    meditation and 17
moral intelligence 188
motivational factors 46, 197
    transpersonal self stage 207–9
Motivator 82–3, 112–15, 137–47
nature/nurture debate 25
non-verbal cues 36–7
non-visible culture 19
Observer 81, 94–7, 157–69
openness
    tools for developing 18
Optimist 81, 87–90, 137–47
organisation
    definition 39–40
organisational culture 38, 40–1

changing 19–20, 38–41
   nature of 19
   networks 38
people skills 35
perception 69–71
personal development 6–9
   leadership and 5
   levels 238–40
   transformational change 16–17, 132–6
personality 43, 76
perspectives
   awareness and understanding of others' 210–11
   holistic 229–30
physical needs
   body self stage 49
political pressures 208–9
Pragmatist 81, 97–100, 170–82
primitive brain 12
projected persona 58–9
psychological needs
   body self stage 49
Q12 mapping 25, 40–1, 76–7
   stages 85
   strength in a quadrant 84
Q12 Profiling System 14, 40–1, 132–6, 194, 218
Rationalist 83–4, 117–20, 170–82
Realist 81, 90–4, 148–56
rejection, power of 52
relationship map 80–1, 86–100
   emotions and 77
relationships
   I-thou, Being to Being 206–7, 227
   intimacy 204–5
   self-actualisation drive and 199–202
resistance/absorption principle 52
respect 39
security needs 46, 63

body self stage 49–50
   indicators 64
self-acceptance 195
self-actualisation drive 197
   independent intentionality 197–9
   relationships 199–202
self-awareness 7
   methodologies 18
self-esteem needs 17, 46, 63
   adolescent stage 57–9
   indicators 64
   intrinsic 195
   late childhood stage 54, 56
self-knowledge 13–14, 40–1
self-limiting habits and patterns 18
self-mastery 21, 40–1, 87, 117, 194–5, 198, 222, 224
   developmental markers, 10–11
   growth towards 195
   ladder of consciousness 44–5
   leadership and, 9–11
   patterns and habits, 11
self-sufficiency 55
shared interpersonal reality 60
social culture, 6
socialisation process 47–8
   adolescent stage 59–61
   early childhood stage, 52–3
   injunctions 51–2, 53
   late childhood stage 55–7
socialised self see adult socialised self
societal deficit motivation 72–4
spiritual intelligence 188
strategic and tactical thinking 35, 208
success treadmills 67–9
   deficit driven 69–71
Supporter 82–3, 102–5, 157–69
survival needs 46, 63

body self stage 49–50
   indicators 64
thinking map 83–4, 116–30
   intellect and 78
tipping point 231–3
transformational change 16–17, 132–6
   cultural transformation 19
   emotional de-programming 134, 135–6
   experiential learning 135–6
   horizontal change 133–4
   leadership, role of, 20–1
   methodologies 18–19
   vertical change 134–5
transpersonal self stage 45, 132, 186, 203–22, 237
   I-thou, being to being relationships 206–7, 227
   identity 209–18
   influence, exerting 238–9
   integration of selves 218–22
   intimacy and 204–5
   lines and stages of development 189
   motivational values and behaviours 207–9
   transitioning to 226
treadmills 63–5, 195–6
   Analyst 123
   deficit motivation and 65–7
   definition 65
   Dreamer 130
   Entrepreneur 112
   Executive 108
   Idealist 126
   Motivator 115
   Observer 97
   Optimist 90
   Pragmatist 100
   Rationalist 120
   Realist 93

   success 67–9
   Supporter 105
trust 39
   tools for developing 18
unconditional love 46–7, 53, 228
unconscious mind 11–13
unitive self stage 45, 132, 186, 189, 223–37
   transitioning to 226–7
universal principles 234–5
verbal cues 36–7, 56
vertical change 134–5
visible culture 19
wholeness 195
Wilbur, Ken 184–5
   quadrant diagram 186–7, 231
workplace culture see organisational culture

ABOUT THE AUTHOR:

Walter Bellin pioneered and developed a wide range of methods to maximise the personal and professional potential of individuals, teams and organisations. He is an international consultant who consults with senior management teams of private and public sector organisations in the areas of corporate development, leading change (specialising in culture change), strategic business planning and leadership development. He runs personal and leadership development workshops in the USA, Australia and the UK. Walter's personal webesite is: **www.walterbellin.com**

Walter and a colleague developed the Q12 mapping system, based on Walter's personal development programmes. If you to wish to use the Q12 profiling system, there are two ways to do so:

- There is a simplified version of the Q12 profiling system (called Vitallyme) which does not show the actual mapping diagrams, but presents in narrative form, your personal profile. This simplified version can be printed directly off your computer. You can access this by logging onto the website at **www.vitallyme.com**

- The longer version, which includes more information and visual diagrams of your maps, is usually used on personal development workshops and on corporate workshops for leadership development or culture change programmes. However, you can do this as an individual as well, though you will need one of our qualified coaches to assist you in interpreting and applying the instrument as a personal development tool. If you wish to use this in a workplace setting — or just use it personally — you can begin by logging onto the Q12 website at **www.coredimensions.com.au**

Websites for further information

       www.corporatecrossroads.com.au

       www.walterbellin.com

       www.facebook.com/walter.bellin.79

Also available as an ebook

 Like us **www.facebook.com/JaneCurryPublishing**

 Follow us **@janecurrypub**